Conversations with John A. Williams

Literary Conversations Series
Monika Gehlawat
General Editor

Books by John A. Williams

Fiction

The Angry Ones aka *One for New York*. New York: Ace Books, 1960.
Night Song. New York: Farrar Strauss & Cudahy, 1961.
Sissie. New York: Farrar Strauss & Cudahy, 1963.
The Man Who Cried I Am. New York: Little, Brown, 1967.
Sons of Darkness, Sons of Light. New York: Little, Brown, 1969.
Captain Blackman. Garden City, NY: Doubleday, 1972.
Mothersill and the Foxes. Garden City, NY: Doubleday, 1975.
The Junior Bachelor Society. Garden City, NY: Doubleday, 1976.
!Click Song. Boston: Houghton Mifflin, 1982.
The Berhama Account. Far Hills, NJ: New Horizon Press, 1985.
Jacob's Ladder. New York: Thunder's Mouth Press, 1987.
Clifford's Blues. Minneapolis: Coffee House Press, 1999.

Nonfiction

Africa: Her History, Lands and People. New York: Cooper Square, 1963.
This Is My Country Too. New York: New American Library/World, 1965.
The Most Native of Sons: A Biography of Richard Wright. Garden City, NY: Doubleday, 1970.
The King God Didn't Save: Reflections on the Life and Death of Martin Luther King, Jr. New York: Coward-McCann, 1970.
Flashbacks: A Twenty-Year Diary of Article Writing. Garden City, NY: Anchor Press / Doubleday, 1973.
Minorities in the City. New York: Harper & Row, 1975.

With Harry J. Anslinger

(As J. Dennis Gregory) *The Protectors: Our Battle against the Crime Gangs*. New York: Farrar, Strauss, 1964.

With Dennis A. Williams

If I Stop I'll Die: The Comedy and Tragedy of Richard Pryor. New York: Thunder's Mouth Press, 1991.

With Michel Fabre

Way B(l)ack Then and Now: A Street Guide to African Americans in Paris. Paris: CEAA, 1992, 1996.

Drama

Last Flight from Ambo Ber. Pelham, NY: American Association for Ethiopian Jews, 1983.

Poetry

Safari West. Montreal: Hochelaga Press, 1998.

Edited Volumes

The Angry Black. New York: Lancer, 1962.
Beyond the Angry Black. New York: Cooper Square, 1966.

With Charles F. Harris

Amistad I. New York: Knopf, 1970.
Amistad II. New York: Knopf, 1971.

With Gilbert H. Muller

The McGraw-Hill Introduction to Literature. New York: McGraw-Hill, 1985.
Bridges: Literature across Cultures. New York: McGraw-Hill, 1994.
Ways In: Approaches to Reading and Writing about Literature. New York: McGraw-Hill, 1994.

With Lori Williams

Dear Chester, Dear John: Letters between Chester Himes and John A. Williams. Detroit: Wayne State UP, 2008.

Conversations with John A. Williams

Edited by Jeffrey Allen Tucker

University Press of Mississippi / *Jackson*

www.upress.state.ms.us

The University Press of Mississippi is a member of the
Association of American University Presses.

First printing 2018

Library of Congress Cataloging-in-Publication Data

Names: Williams, John A., 1925–2015. | Tucker, Jeffrey A., 1966– editor.
Title: Conversations with John A. Williams / edited by Jeffrey Allen Tucker. Description:
Jackson : University Press of Mississippi, [2018] |
Series: Literary conversations series | Includes index. |
Identifiers: LCCN 2017036853 (print) | LCCN 2017038471 (ebook) | ISBN 9781496815378
(epub single) | ISBN 9781496815385 (epub institutional) | ISBN 9781496815392 (pdf
single) | ISBN 9781496815408 (pdf institutional) | ISBN 9781496815361 (cloth : alk. paper)
Subjects: LCSH: Williams, John A., 1925–2015—Interviews. | African
American authors—Interviews. | Authors, American—20th century—
Interviews. | Influence (Literary, artistic, etc.) | Fiction—Authorship.
Classification: LCC PS3573.I4495 (ebook) | LCC PS3573.I4495 Z46 2018 (print)
DDC 813/.54 [B]—dc23
LC record available at https://lccn.loc.gov/2017036853

British Library Cataloging-in-Publication Data available

Contents

Introduction

As much as any writer featured in the University Press of Mississippi's Literary Conversations series, John A. Williams, whose works draw considerably from his own experiences as an African American writer, prompts a consideration of the significance of the author to how his writing is read. Granted, it has been decades since the New Criticism encouraged the close reading of a text's formal elements to the exclusion of historical factors or the author's biography, and seventy years since Wimsatt and Beardsley published "The Intentional Fallacy." Following Michel Foucault's analysis of "the author function" and Roland Barthes's "The Death of the Author," which asserted and even celebrated the proliferation of meanings produced by readers' engagements with a text, "the author" is certainly no longer the privileged locus of textual meaning; rather, it is one context among many, including the reader, other texts, and the historical milieu in which the text is created, as well as the text itself—and that is just for starters. Yet, all of this does not mean that "the author" should be abandoned; a writer's life and career, as well as their comments about their own work, taken with the occasional grain of salt, can still contribute to a reader's comprehension and appreciation of a literary text. Such is the premise of this series, and Williams provides numerous examples of meaningful connections between a writer's life and their art.

Described by James De Jongh in the *Dictionary of Literary Biography* as "arguably the finest Afro-American novelist of his generation . . . certainly among the most prolific" (280), John A. Williams was the author of twelve novels, seven volumes of nonfiction, a play, a book of poetry, and an opera libretto, and he was the editor of many other volumes. He is perhaps best-known for the novel *The Man Who Cried I Am*, a roman à clef about expatriate black writers in Europe who gain knowledge of a US government plan to counter urban unrest through the internment of African Americans. "A rite-of-passage kind of book for many black collegians" in subsequent years (Bates), the novel has been described by Richard Yarborough as "a big book. Very demanding . . . full of sophisticated ideas, subtly expressed" (qtd. Bates). *The Man* represents a commonality among Williams's works that makes them especially relevant to the Literary Conversations series: the representation of the life of a writer. Steven Hill, the protagonist of *One for New York*, originally published as *The Angry Ones*, works for a vanity press, as Williams himself did. Ralph Joplin, in *Sissie*, is the literary figure as prodigal son, confronting memories and the illness of his mother. *The Man* features African American writers abroad in Europe, parallel to Williams and his own stays in Spain and the Netherlands. Cato Caldwell Douglass is a writer frustrated by the mechanics of and the racism in the publishing industry in *!Click Song*, which Williams himself identifies as autobiographical. And Clifford Pepperidge is a diarist in addition to being an imprisoned jazz pianist in *Clifford's Blues*.

Although he may not be as well-known today as he was during the black liberation struggles of the 1960s and '70s, Williams represented the acme of literary achievement for many readers. Gabriel Motola described him as being "in the same class as Kurt Vonnegut, John Cheever and Arthur Miller, those who deal with the social issues and how they affect the individual" (qtd. Fraser). Despite his share and more of impediments, Williams is notable for his "endurance (which) comes not from compulsive careerism, but from the glowing fact that he is a writer of integrity, vision and commitment, as well as enormous technical skill," according to Arnold Rampersad. "His vision is the purified essence of that integrity at play in the social world" (2). The biographical essay that opens Williams's entry in *The Norton Anthology of African American Literature* describes his fiction as "always fast moving and psychologically gripping" (1833). Such effects are often produced by the compression and expansion of time as well as the deployment of multiple points of view in order to cover vast ranges of history with the high-resolution of subjective experience, techniques Williams frequently notes that he picked up from Malcolm Lowry's *Under the Volcano*. At the end of his interview with Earl A. Cash, Williams identifies himself as a "writer-historian," and as Gilbert H. Muller notes, Williams has a particular knack for "forgotten, neglected, or abandoned history." Dick Strout, at the beginning of his report on Williams, explains that *Captain Blackman*, in which an Army officer wounded in Vietnam envisions himself as a black soldier in major military operations throughout US history, was the product of ten years of research; it is this kind of deep investigation that prompts Ishmael Reed to contrast Williams to William Styron—whose *The Confessions of Nat Turner* was the topic of critical responses from *Ten Black Writers*, including Williams— when he states, "Nobody can accuse John A. Williams of not doing his homework." These qualities earned Williams numerous accolades—including the Richard Wright–Jacques Roumain Award, an NEA Fellowship, the Before Columbus Foundation's American Book Award, and many honorary degrees—as indicated in the chronology included in this volume.

Williams's career is further distinguished by his work as a journalist and educator. He wrote from Africa and Europe for magazines such as *Ebony*, *Jet*, *Newsweek*, and *Holiday*, which provided experiences that would inform novels like *The Man*, *Captain Blackman*, *Jacob's Ladder*, and *Clifford's Blues*, as well as *Africa: Her History, Lands and People*, a nonfiction book for young readers, and his collaboration with Michel Fabre on *A Street Guide to African Americans in Paris*. Williams also taught creative writing, journalism, and literature in a number of positions around the country; his longest tenure was at the Newark campus of Rutgers University, where he was Paul Robeson Professor of English. As with the above novels, the literature anthologies coedited with Gilbert H. Muller demonstrate how all three of these identities—literary author, journalist, and educator—intersected for Williams, forming a tripod on which his career was based.

Williams and his writings have been not only consequential, but also controversial. In 1962, following the publication of Williams's jazz novel *Night Song*, the American Academy of Arts and Letters awarded him the Prix de Rome, which included a year-long residence in Italy and a cash prize. However, after an in-person interview with the director of the Academy in Rome, the prize was rescinded, causing a scandal in the literary world and much consternation on Williams's part, which he channeled into the essay "We Regret to Inform You That." This controversy also appears in fictionalized form in *The Man* and is a frequent topic in this volume's interviews. The Prix de Rome affair, however, was nothing compared to what Williams endured following the publication of *The King God Didn't Save*, his critical analysis of the mainstream media's construction of Martin Luther King for popular consumption as a spokesperson and messiah for African Americans. According to Cash, "the reviews ran two to one against Williams," criticizing the book as "lacking in compassion, brash, [and] slanderous" (19). Readers of all races were upset by the attention Williams paid to King's marital infidelities, even though that was only one segment of a much larger argument. *The New York Review of Books* published a review entitled "Martin Luther King's Second Assassination," speculating that Williams was either "bitter about being rebuffed in his offer to help in organizing the 1963 March (on Washington)" or angling for street credibility (qtd. Cash 19). Williams responded to these criticisms in the 1971 interview with Fred Beauford included in this volume. Although subsequent writers would also contend that the FBI tried to leverage King's indiscretions against him and the movement that he led, it is clear from later interviews that Williams felt the sting from the criticisms of his book for many years thereafter.

As potent as they were in the 1960s and '70s, Williams's ideas are just as relevant for postmillennial audiences. It is hard not to think of the King Alfred Plan from *The Man* when confronted with President Donald Trump's language and actions against Mexican and Muslim immigrants. Indeed, the 2016 national election makes newly relevant Williams's comments on democracy, immigration, the media, and fascism in the 1995 *Forkroads* interview with his second son Dennis, as well as "Assess the Mess," the spoken-word piece by Williams that opens *Transform*, the 2003 album by the rock band Powerman 5000, on which his youngest son Adam played guitar. The application of lethal force by police to the bodies of unarmed black citizens, to which the recent Black Lives Matter movement responds, forms the premise of *Sons of Darkness, Sons of Light.* Composed during the "long hot summers" of the 1960s and set in the then-near-future of 1973, this "militant revolutionary fantasy" (Yarborough xii) opens after a white police officer shoots an unarmed sixteen-year-old black youth "five times in the chest" (11). Eugene Browning, an African American professor and member of a civil rights organization, arranges that officer's assassination, leading to near-apocalyptic racial conflict, the bombing of New York City's bridges and tunnels, and a police action called Operation Black Out; *Sons* is subtitled "A Novel of Some Probability." Throughout his interviews, Williams demonstrates an awareness that antiblack violence is a fundamental aspect of American history, making him a kind of Afropessimist *avant la lettre*, although he also claims to be an optimist in his interview with Dan Georgakas, tells Leigh Crutchley that violence doesn't have to be humanity's first option, and insists to John O'Brien that love is the true basis of any society worthy of the name.

The interviews gathered here make a diverse group in several ways. The historical scope comprises each of the previous five decades, from the 1960s to the early 2000s. A variety of types of print publications, academic journals as well as newspapers and other popular periodicals, are represented. Appropriately, given Williams's experience working in various forms of media and that his novels have been adapted for film and television, transcripts from television and radio interviews as well as the American Audio Prose Library are included. And the interviews with British, Dutch, and German interlocutors demonstrate a longstanding European interest in Williams's works.

As for what kind of portrait of the artist emerges from these conversations, a number of interviewers comment on Williams's comportment and appearance. Aside from Williams's trademark "Mephistophelean" beard, Cash sees nothing notable. John Albert Jansen finds him professorial, and Vincent F. A. Golphin is surprised that he is not taller. Georgakas characterizes Williams as "soft-spoken." Joseph T. Skerrett Jr. says that he is "rough of voice, casual of speech," and the tone of his statements about *The King God Didn't Save* to Beauford is "bitter." The Charlie Rose interview shows that as late as 1990, Williams was still being referred to as an "angry" writer, a label ascribed to him perhaps after Ace Books published his novel *One for New York* with the title *The Angry Ones*. That Williams found such an interpellation discomfiting at times is suggested by the fact that when the edited volume he originally published as *The Angry Black* was republished in 1966, the literature collection had the new title *Beyond the Angry Black*. But make no mistake; Williams is direct and earnest when expressing his thoughts and feelings in conversation. Cash describes him as "unequivocal without giving the impression of being foolhardy or pompous." In several interviews—particularly with Cash, Wolfgang Binder, and Jansen—he has much to say about "the function of the black writer"; however, he frequently turns such questions upon readers, and not only in response to the reception of his book on King. In conversation with Steven Corbin, Williams reverses a common formulation to assert that society has a responsibility to its artists. The identity of "writer" is most dear to Williams; it is both ontological and performative for him, both what he is and what he does. In interviews with O'Brien, Skerrett, Dennis Williams, and others, he describes an early identification with James Baldwin, who needed to write in order to affirm his own experience in an otherwise hostile world, and he matter-of-factly tells his son Dennis that writing had become both habit and practice, a near-involuntary part of a daily regimen: "like putting on my pants."

Each of these interviews was selected for what it contributes to a reader's understanding of Williams and his writing; several, however, deserve special notice. Cash conducted the first major in-depth interview with Williams, a two-parter that was published as the Appendix to Cash's book *John A. Williams: The Evolution of a Black Writer*. The Georgakas interview provides some insight on *Amistad*, the black studies publication that Williams coedited with Charles Harris. Williams's interview with James V. Hatch for *Artist & Influence*, a publication of the Hatch-Billops Collection, Inc., is distinguished by the camaraderie between the writer and the renowned scholar and dramatist. For most of his career, Williams was based in New York City; however, this interview features his remembrances of growing up in the 15th Ward of Syracuse, New York. Williams comments on the racial and ethnic diversity of his neighborhood as well as a solidarity among African Americans, which manifested itself in the guidance he received from men like Herbert "Hoppie" Johnson—the inspiration for Chappie, the coach whose former pupils return to honor him in the *The Junior Bachelor Society*—as well as the local youth activity building known as the Dunbar Center, and families generally looking out for one another and each other's children. Williams also acknowledges those who supported his writerly aspirations as a youth, at Syracuse University, and early in his professional career. There are similar reflections on Syracuse in Williams's interview with his son Dennis for *Forkroads*, which, with its setting at the family's vacation home in Worcester, New York, makes the reader feel like they are eavesdropping on a father-son talk. The American Audio Prose Library interview features Kay Bonetti Carlson demonstrating her skill and experience as an interviewer of professional writers, maximizing breadth of scope without sacrificing depth of inquiry. Just as insightful, though it focuses on a single work, is the 2000 interview conducted by Gilbert H. Muller, Michael Blaine, and Raymond C. Bowen. This discussion of *Clifford's Blues*—Williams's last and finest published novel, about a gay, black, jazz pianist in Dachau—addresses its premise and source material as well as formal elements such as characterization, narrative, point-of-view, and thematic content.

Certain topics make multiple appearances throughout the interviews, such as interracial relations, including the resistance, from blacks as well as whites, to mixed couples. A lasting memory of racial trauma from his naval service in the Pacific during World War II, which was also when he started writing poetry, is mentioned several times. The most persistent interview topic is racism in the literary scene and publishing industry. Starting with the 1963 essay "The Literary Ghetto," Williams consistently criticized the practice of comparing black writers only to other black writers instead of their white contemporaries, a racial silo effect that also resulted in books by white writers never being reviewed by black writers and critics. Just as frustrating was the habit of publishers and critics to promote one African American writer at a time, as if the world was too small for a diversity of black thought and art. On a more positive note, several interviews highlight productive collaborations throughout Williams's career, such as the National Public Radio interview with Tavis Smiley, occasioned by the Leslie Burrs–composed opera *Vanqui*, for which Williams wrote the libretto. And Joe Hunter interviews Dennis Williams alongside John about co-writing *If I Stop I'll Die: The Comedy and Tragedy of Richard Pryor*; the first part of this interview was selected for this collection from among the many featured on the locally-produced WPVI television programs *Changes* and *Perspectives* in Philadelphia that were conducted with Williams, whom Hunter consistently and earnestly introduced as "America's finest living writer."

One surprising aspect of these interviews is that, other than a few brief mentions, they feature little about the author Chester Himes. In the American Audio Prose Library interview, Williams notes that his friend was the basis for Max Reddick in *The Man*. He mentions to Hatch the "falling out" that he and Himes had, but for more on the friendship between Williams and Himes, readers will have to turn to *Dear Chester, Dear John*, a collection of letters edited by Williams and his wife, Lori, and *Conversations with Chester Himes*, edited by Michel Fabre and Kenneth Kinnamon. Both books feature "My Man Himes," an interview with Himes conducted by Williams.

For all of his knowledge and insight, Williams occasionally makes statements that deserve to be challenged. For example, he dismisses *Sons* as a mere "pot-boiler," although the fact that it earned him more money than *The Man* may indeed prove his point about how backwards the publishing and literary worlds can be. His evaluations of other writers' works, such as those of Toni Morrison in the Binder interview and of James Baldwin's *Another Country* in the Skerrett interview, do not match my own. Other comments, in part because they are not fully developed, are baffling. Just how was Baldwin's success, as he tells Cash, due to his homosexuality? How are black women writers, as he tells Ron Netsky, less threatening than black male writers? And contrary to another comment to Netsky, did not Ralph Ellison write other things besides *Invisible Man* and *Shadow and Act*? Everyone is entitled to their opinion, of course, and a few headscratchers, in a collection of commentary from an artist as candid as Williams, are perhaps inevitable.

In hindsight, my own interviews with Williams seem somehow both surprising and inevitable. The Department of Rare Books Special Collections and Preservation (RBSCP) at the University of Rochester's Rush Rhees Library has been the home of the collection of Williams's papers and memorabilia since 1987. I started teaching at the university in 1999, the year that *Clifford's Blues* was published. This novel's representation of the intersections of race and sexuality as well as of a black experience excluded from official historical narratives spoke directly to my teaching and research interests, and I wanted to study Williams even further following the enthusiasm that the students in my Introduction to African American Literature course showed for *Captain Blackman*. In 2003, the University of Rochester awarded Williams an Honorary Doctorate of Letters. It was that weekend, the same during which Golphin interviewed Williams, that I first met John and Lori. About a year later, Richard Peek, a close friend of the Williamses and then the director of RBSCP, told me that Williams had been diagnosed with Alzheimer's disease. Richard was of the opinion that recording John's thoughts about his life and work was a matter of utmost urgency. I agreed, but who would we get to interview him? Richard suggested that I do it. We discussed the matter with John and Lori, who agreed to periodic in-person interviews starting in early 2005 at their home in Teaneck, New Jersey. We did a total of eleven interviews, each between two and four hours in length, and each focused on one of John's books. In general, John was good-humored, generous with his time, open to my interpretations, and forthright in his agreements and disagreements; he was less a guru than an earnest and eager discussant. His long-term memory was fine, remarkable even; his short-term memory was on occasion noticeably compromised. He would tell a richly detailed story about something that happened over fifty years ago and then tell it again, and then again at our next meeting. Richard attended some of the early interviews, and Lori was a near-constant and vital presence; she assisted John with the recall of names, places, and fine details and provided her own perspective on his career and writing. Golphin gets it right when he says that John and Lori were "a team." My visits often would conclude with a drink, a home-cooked meal, and a bit of the PBS *NewsHour* or *The Daily Show*. I always left the Williamses' home with feelings of warmth, and I will always cherish the opportunity I had to spend time face-to-face with a literary figure whose works have meant so much to me.

For this collection, I have selected a transcript of the interview we did on *Safari West*, a collection of poetry, the genre that Williams called his first love. This was one of the last meetings we had, and by that time, we were going about interviews in a somewhat informal, conversational way. I do not present it as a model for how to conduct such an interview; my newness to this mode of discourse, even at that late stage in the sequence, is very much on display. However, I am glad that it highlights one of my favorite books by Williams, the one that is probably his least-known. We covered a lot of territory in this interview and in others; however, there were some questions that I just never got around to, which now, unfortunately, will have to remain unasked.

When Williams died at age eighty-nine in July 2015, a friend of mine, a New York City–area writer and educator like Williams, sent me the following message: "Sad. He never got his due." It was a recurring theme among the many remembrances that followed. The *New York Times* described Williams as "chronically underrated" (Grimes), and NPR noted how he "never reached the level of fame of writers like [Richard] Wright, Toni Morrison and Alice Walker" (Bates). Many of the more recent interviews in this collection make similar assertions, and some attempt to explain this lack of notoriety, given the quality and quantity of Williams's writing. Netsky, for example, suggests that Williams was simply too "radical." One wonders about the possibility of lingering resentment toward Williams following *The King God Didn't Save*, or if it is all another symptom of the one-black-writer-at-a-time syndrome. Perhaps being a link between the Black Arts Movement and an earlier era of black writing left Williams in a kind of no-man's land, "this odd, in-between position," as Yarborough says, "younger than Wright and Baldwin, older than Toni Morrison, Alice Walker and Ishmael Reed" (qtd. Bates). Whatever the reason, Richard Peek tells Netsky to prepare for a new wave of interest in John A. Williams. This volume follows a panel on Williams at the 2016 meeting of the American Literature Association in San Francisco—which was held, in a bit of synchronicity, the same weekend as a memorial service for him in New Jersey—and is intended as an example of that new interest and as a practical tool to further the teaching of and research on Williams's writing in the twenty-first century.

Upon Williams's passing, I recalled one of his poems. Composed in 1992 for a deceased friend, "A Stone for Marty Scheiner" acknowledges loss and absence; however, it also recognizes all that was made possible—including life, light, and kindness—by those who have left us: "The stone was cast into the sea / Only the Ancient beheld the hole it made / Silt and slugs embraced it * Sun caressed it * Life arose / Around it" (64). The life of John A. Williams had an impact similar to that captured in these lines, which demonstrate the craft and insight of his writings more generally.

Many individuals and organizations provided support, assistance, and advice during this volume's completion. My sincerest thanks to the John A. Williams family, including John and Lori Williams, Dennis A. Williams, Gregory Williams, and Adam Williams. River Campus Libraries' Department of Rare Books Special Collections and Preservation (RBSCP) at the University of Rochester, has been immensely helpful with its friendly and knowledgeable staff; many thanks to RBSCP's Director Jessica Lacher-Feldman and former directors James Kuhn, Richard Peek, and Peter Dzwonkoski; extra special thanks to Special Collections Librarian Phyllis Andrews and Archivist and Librarian Melissa Mead. This book is very much the product of Richard Peek's instigation and vision; I thank him for his insight and encouragement. Thanks also to the Special Collections Research

Center at Syracuse University's E. S. Bird Library and to Polly Thistlethwaite and Alycia Sellie at CUNY–Graduate Center's Mina Rees Library. Audio interviews were transcribed by Heidi E. Bollinger, David Ewans, and Landmark Associates, Inc. Masani McGee helped proofread, and Naaja Rogers performed valuable early research assistance. Eric Likness provided timely and helpful IT advice. Permissions were obtained with the help of Karin M. Tucker, who is not only an expert at copyright clearance, but also a wonderful sister. John Michael and Bruce Simon are valued friends and colleagues who provided excellent feedback when this project was starting to take off. Thanks also to Jonathan Binstock, Morris Eaves, Duncan Faherty, Dorothy Gilliam, Alexandra Kuzmich, Robert Reid-Pharr, Ezra Tawil, and Alfred Vitale. This volume was made possible through the generosity of the University of Rochester College of Arts Sciences and Engineering and Dean Gloria Culver, as well as the support of the Department of English and its chair, Rosemary Kegl. As always, thanks and love to my wife, Belinda Redden; our daughter, Elizabeth Sophia Redden Tucker; and my mother, Gwen Tucker.

JAT

Works Cited

Baker, Houston A. "John Alfred Williams." *The Norton Anthology of African American Literature.* Ed. Henry Louis Gates, Jr., Nellie Y. McKay, et al. New York: Norton, 1997. 1833–34.

Bates, Karen Grigsby. "A Tribute to John Williams, the Man Who Wrote 'I Am.'" *NPR,* 13 July 2015,www.npr.org/sections/codeswitch/2015/07/13/422545643/a-tribute-to-john-williams-the-man-who-wrote-i-am. Accessed 18 Dec. 2016.

Cash, Earl A. *John A. Williams: The Evolution of a Black Writer.* New York: The Third Press, 1975.

DeJongh, James L. "John A. Williams." *Dictionary of Literary Biography* Vol. 33. Ed. Thadious M. Davis and Trudier Harris-Lopez. Detroit: Gale, 1984. 279–88.

Fraser, Gerald. "Neglected Black Writer Overcomes a Stricture." *The New York Times* 27 Sept. 1981, www.nytimes.com. Accessed 1 Jan. 2017.

Rampersad, Arnold. "Introduction: John A. Williams." *John A. Williams: An Exhibition.* The University of Rochester, 8 Nov. 1987. 2–3.

Reed, Ishmael. "The Man Who Defied the Formula." *Writings of Consequence: The Art of John A. Williams.* University of Rochester River Campus Libraries, Department of Rare Books Special Collections and Preservation. 6 Apr. 2003. http://rbscp.lib.rochester.edu/2974. Accessed 1 Jan. 2017.

Williams, John A. *Sons of Darkness, Sons of Light*. 1969. Boston: Northeastern UP, 1999.

————. "A Stone for Marty Scheiner." *Safari West*. Montreal: Hochelaga Press, 1998. 64.

Yarborough, Richard. Foreword to *Sons of Darkness, Sons of Light* by John A. Williams. Boston: Northeastern UP, 1999. vii–xvi.

Chronology

1925	John Alfred Williams is born on December 5 in Jackson, Mississippi, to Ola May Jones Williams [Page] and John Henry Williams, the first of four children.
1926–1943	From six months of age, Williams is raised in Syracuse, New York, in the 15th Ward. He attends Washington Irving Elementary, Madison Junior High, and Central High School.
1943	Enlists in the United States Navy, pharmacist's mate 3/C, and, during World War II, serves in the South Pacific from 1943 to 1946, when Williams receives an honorable discharge.
1946	Finishes high school and enrolls at Syracuse University. Begins doing general reporting and features, which continues until 1955, for publications such as the *Progressive Herald*, *Post-Standard*, and *Herald-Journal*, Syracuse, New York; the *Chicago Defender*, *Pittsburgh Courier*, *Los Angeles Tribune*, and the *Village Voice*. Writes book reviews in sources cited above as well as the *Los Angeles Times*, *Chicago Tribune*, *Washington Post*, *New York Times*, *Essence*, *American Visions*, *Fiction International*, *Quarterly Black Review*, *Multicultural Review*, and *Small Press Review* from 1946 to 1993.
1947	Marries Carolyn Clopton in Syracuse, New York.
1948	First son, Gregory D. Williams, is born.
1950	Receives Bachelor of Arts degree in English and Journalism from Syracuse University and begins graduate school.
1951	Second son, Dennis A. Williams, is born. Williams holds positions in foundry and supermarket.
1952	Begins work as caseworker at the Onondaga County Welfare Department.
1953	Self-publishes *Poems* in Syracuse, New York.
1954	Williams and Carolyn Clopton separate. Moves to California, where Williams works at the life insurance company Gold

State Mutual, as well as for CBS and NBC-TV publicity special events.* Moves to New York City.

1955 Works for Columbia Broadcasting System for special events programs. Becomes publicity director for Comet Press Books. Completes first and second drafts of *The Angry Ones*.*

1956 Edits and publishes the *Negro Market Newsletter* until 1957.

1957 Divorces Carolyn Clopton. Becomes assistant to the publisher at Abelard-Schuman until 1958. Becomes director of information for the American Committee on Africa, where he writes press releases and arranges press conferences for Kwame Nkrumah, Joost de Blank, Eduardo Mondlane, Tom Mboya, and Nmadi Azikwe.

1958 Based in Barcelona, reports on touring black entertainers and events of interest to African American readers for *Jet Magazine, Ebony*, and the Associated Negro Press.

1959 Covers special events and personalities in studio and via remote for WOV Radio, New York.

1960 *One for New York* (also known as *The Angry Ones*) is published by Ace Books. Organizes rally in Madison Square Garden for the National Committee for a Sane Nuclear Policy.

1961 *Night Song* is published by Farrar, Straus & Giroux.

1962 Prix de Rome controversy, in which Williams's nomination for the Fellowship was rejected by the American Academy in Rome, documented by Williams in his essay "We Regret to Inform You That." Receives grant from the National Institute of Arts and Letters. Edits *The Angry Black*, published by Lancer Books.

1963 *Sissie* is published by Farrar, Straus & Giroux. *Africa: Her History, Lands and People* is published by Cooper Square Press. Writes pieces on politics and race in the United States and Europe for *Holiday Magazine* until 1966. Acts as contributing editor at *Herald-Tribune Book Week* until 1965.

1964 *The Protectors*, ghostwritten by Williams for Harry Anslinger, is published by Farrar, Straus & Giroux. On special assignment in Israel, Egypt, Sudan, Nigeria, Cameroon, Ethiopia, and Zaire for *Newsweek*.

1965 Marries Lorrain Isaac on October 5. *This Is My Country Too* is published by New American Library/World. Writes and narrates WNET's *Omowale: The Child Returns Home* on location in Nigeria.

1966 Co-producer/writer/narrator of WNET's *The Creative Person: Henry Roth*, on location in Spain. Edits *Beyond the Angry Black*, published by Cooper Square Press.

1967 Third son, Adam J. Williams, is born. *The Man Who Cried I Am* is published by Little, Brown & Co. *Sweet Love, Bitter*, adapted from *Night Song*, is made into a film by Film 2 Associates.

1968 Publishes "The Manipulation of History and of Fact: An Ex-Southerner's Apologist Tract for Slavery and the Life of Nat Turner; or, William Styron's Faked Confessions" in *William Styron's Nat Turner: Ten Black Writers Respond*, ed. John Henrik Clarke.** Lecturer in Creative/Article Writing at the City College of New York, City University of New York, and Lecturer in Literature at the College of the Virgin Islands. Weekly interviewer of newsmakers on "Newsfront," including Erskine Caldwell, Muhammad Ali, and Eldridge Cleaver, for WNET Television (PBS).

1969 *Sons of Darkness, Sons of Light* is published by Little, Brown & Co.

1970 *The King God Didn't Save: Martin Luther King, Jr.* is published by Coward-McCann. *The Most Native of Sons: Richard Wright* is published by Doubleday. Coedits *Amistad 1*, with Charles Harris, published by Random House. Awarded the Centennial Medal for Outstanding Achievement from Syracuse University. Visiting professor at Macalester College. Serves on the editorial board of *Audience Magazine*.

1971 Coedits *Amistad 2*, with Charles Harris, published by Random House. Visits Grenada, West Indies, for the first time.*

1972 *Captain Blackman* is published by Doubleday. Regents' Lecturer at the University of California at Santa Barbara and guest writer at Sarah Lawrence College during the 1972–1973 academic year. Works as contributing editor at *American Journal* until 1974.

1973 *Flashbacks: A 20-Year Diary of Article Writing* is published by Doubleday. Receives the Richard Wright–Jacques Roumain Award. Distinguished Professor at LaGuardia Community College, City University of New York, until 1979.

1974	Distinguished visiting professor at Cooper Union during the 1974–1975 academic year. Visiting professor at the University of Hawaii during the summer semester.
1975	*Mothersill and the Foxes* is published by Doubleday. *Minorities in the City* is published by Harper & Row.
1976	*The Junior Bachelor Society* is published by Doubleday.
1977	Works as contributing editor at *Politicks*. Awarded Creative Writing Fellowship from the National Endowment for the Arts.
1978	Awarded Honorary Doctor of Literature degree from Southeastern Massachusetts University. Visiting professor at Boston University during the 1978–1979 academic year. Contributing editor for *Y'bird #2*, an Ishmael Reed/Al Young publication.
1979	Accepts position as professor at Rutgers University–Newark.
1980	Works as contributing editor at the *Journal of African Civilizations* until 1988. Visits Grenada under new government and takes first trip to Kenya.*
1981	*Last Flight from Ambo Ber* is produced by Peoples Theater in Boston. *The Sophisticated Gents* miniseries, adapted from *The Junior Bachelor Society*, airs on NBC-TV.
1982	*!Click Song* is published by Houghton Mifflin. Writes weekly column on all topics, including local, national, and international, for the *National Leader*. Receives Lindback Award for Distinguished Teaching from Rutgers University.
1983	*Last Flight from Ambo Ber* is published by the American Association for Ethiopian Jews. Receives an American Book Award from the Before Columbus Foundation for *!Click Song*. Becomes United States Observer at the 23rd Premio Casa Awards in Santiago, Cuba.
1985	*The Berhama Account* is published by New Horizon Press, and *Introduction to Literature*, first edition, coedited with Gilbert Muller, is published by McGraw-Hill. Receives the New Jersey State Council on the Arts Award.
1986	Exxon Visiting Professor at New York University during the 1986–1987 academic year.
1987	*Jacob's Ladder* is published by Thunder's Mouth Press. Frequently writes opinion pieces on all topics for the *Los Angeles Times* until 1989. Receives Distinguished Writer Award from the Middle Atlantic Writers Association and the Michael Award from the New Jersey Literary Hall of Fame. John A.

Williams Archive established at the University of Rochester, and John A. Williams: An Exhibition held at UR from November 1987 to April 1988. Williams's mother, Ola Page, dies.

1988   February 2 proclaimed John Williams Day in the City of Syracuse, New York. Receives citation from the City of Philadelphia. John A. Williams Archive Exhibit held at Syracuse University.

1989   Receives Carter G. Woodson Award from Mercy College. John A. Williams Archive Exhibit held at Rutgers University.

1990   Becomes Paul Robeson Professor of English at Rutgers University. Williams's father, John Henry Williams, dies.

1991   *If I Stop I'll Die: The Comedy and Tragedy of Richard Pryor*, coauthored by Dennis A. Williams, is published by Thunder's Mouth Press. *August Forty-five* is produced by Rutgers University.

1992   *Way B(l)ack Then and Now: A Street Guide to African Americans in Paris*, first edition, coedited with Michel Fabre, is published by CEAA in Paris.

1994   Retires from Rutgers University. *Bridges: Literature across Cultures* and *Ways In: Approaches to Literature*, both coedited with Gilbert Muller, and *Introduction to Literature*, second edition, coedited with Gilbert Muller, are published by McGraw-Hill. Visiting professor at Bard College during 1994–1995 academic year. Visiting professor at the University of Houston.

1995   Receives honorary Doctor of Letters from Syracuse University.

1996   *A Street Guide to African Americans in Paris*, second edition, coedited with Michel Fabre, is published by Cercle D'etudes Afro-Americaines in Paris.

1998   *Safari West* is published by Hochelaga Press. Inducted into the National Literary Hall of Fame. Receives American Book Award from the Before Columbus Foundation for *Safari West*.

1999   *Clifford's Blues* is published by Coffee House Press. *Vanqui* libretto, commissioned by Opera Columbus and composed by Leslie Burrs, is performed in Columbus, Ohio, on October 15. Honored as the namesake of the John A. Williams Lecture Series at Rutgers University.

2001   Awarded Honorary Doctor of Letters degree from the State University of New York at Old Westbury.

2002   Diagnosed with dementia, later diagnosed with Alzheimer's disease.**

2003   John A. Williams Archive Exhibit held at the University of

	Rochester. Awarded Honorary Doctor of Letters degree from the University of Rochester.
2008	*Dear Chester, Dear John: Letters between Chester Himes and John A. Williams*, coedited by Lori Williams, is published by Wayne State University Press.**
2011	Receives American Book Award from the Before Columbus Foundation for Lifetime Achievement.
2015	John A. Williams died Friday, July 3, in Paramus, New Jersey at age eighty-nine.

Chronology courtesy of the Department of Rare Books, Special Collections and Preservation, University of Rochester River Campus Libraries: http://rbscp.lib.rochester.edu/2959#2.

* Portion adapted from Gilbert Muller's *John A. Williams* Chronology.

** Editor's additions.

Conversations with John A. Williams

On *Sons of Darkness, Sons of Light*

Leigh Crutchley / 1969

Recorded at the BBC-London (November 12, 1969). © Eyre & Spottiswoode, Ltd. Courtesy of the Department of Rare Books, Special Collections and Preservation, University of Rochester River Campus Libraries.

Leigh Crutchley: John Williams, your book *Sons of Darkness, Sons of Light* has just been published. It's your fifth novel and is, as I think you describe it, about selective violence. What is selective violence?

John A. Williams: Well, selective violence is pretty old, I think. It's political violence. If you want to deal in contemporary history the assassinations of both the Kennedys, if you want to go to World War I the Arch Duke Ferdinand, violence that is calculated to change the course of history.

LC: Why did you use this as your theme?

JAW: Because I don't really believe given the makeup of humankind in the world that anything else really works but violence, to some degree.

LC: To what are you applying it in your book?

JAW: In this particular book, of course, I'm applying it to the racial situation in the United States. The leading character is a black professor of history. He's having some family problems, but he's also largely concerned with what's going on in the country in this year of 1973 that the book is set in. And it's his contention that education, nonviolence doesn't work, so he himself initiates a course whereby the end result is the assassination of a police officer who killed a young black boy.

LC: Why have you come to the conclusion that nonviolence doesn't work?

JAW: Because I'm pretty much a student of history. I do a lot of historical reading and because I'm very much alive and aware of the situation in America today. I've lived through the period of Martin Luther King. I know the period of the abolitionists like Garrison, the Quakers. We've had very, very many nonviolent movements in the States that just haven't worked.

LC: On the other hand, nonviolence was a great help to your particular cause, wasn't it? As King proved.

JAW: Well, we now have reservations about that. On the surface, I think, this appeared to be true, but in reality we now have very, very severe reservations. We did get several civil rights acts out of the period of Martin Luther King. But the problem with all new acts or laws is that they can be written on the books, but they must, of course, be enforced. Where there is no enforcement, in effect, you have no law.

LC: Whatever we may think about violence as far as a protest is concerned against any political act, it works as particularly well inside a novel. A novel with violence is an exciting novel and yours is an exciting novel, but you have a message. What is the message you're writing about?

JAW: Well, the message is that in America we will have nothing left but violence, unless we can settle our problems without violence. For me this is a very important message. Because it affects not only America, but the entire Western Hemisphere. We know that most of us are basically violent people. That appears to be our nature according to the studies that have been coming out lately. I think that people who claim to have a great deal of intelligence need not necessarily have recourse to violence.

LC: As a novelist you are believing in your subject?

JAW: Yes, I am.

LC: We're sometimes frightened by books that have a message. I wasn't frightened by yours because I think the story stands well on its own, doesn't it? Fair and square on its own.

JAW: Well, I hope it does. It has been called a melodrama. I'm not sure that it is, but basically, what is life but a melodrama? Dickens, your Charles Dickens proved this. Even with the melodrama there was this great slice of life, which is truth; it's ugly, it's sentimental, and everything works out right in the end. In this particular book I'm not saying that everything works out at the end. What happens is that there's a return to individual considerations, a man patching up a bad marriage with his wife. We must all start from this point.

LC: Have you been accused of incitement through your writing at all?

JAW: Not yet, but I wish I had. I say that with some pride because I would like to feel that my writings were important enough to in many ways influence the course of not only my country's history, my people's history, but the world. I suppose every writer would like to be a Dostoyevsky, a Dickens, a Balzac, a Herman Melville, and to this end I feel that I failed.

LC: You've named a number of white writers.

JAW: Yes.

LC: Have there been any colored writers accused of incitement and excluded because of their writings?

JAW: Well, I think something of this happened to Richard Wright to a small degree. Of course he had Marxist affiliations, and at that particular time he was writing in the States. I think he left the party in 1940. But he was considered to be pretty much a troublemaker, not only in America, but when he got to France. I think this is all to his credit. I've been rereading his work, and I find that it's stands up even here in 1969–1970. It'll always stand up.

LC: Publishers aren't afraid of you because of color?

JAW: I like to think that they were courageous publishers, but that's a writer's ego speaking. I think black writers in the main, up until perhaps three years ago, were dealt with rather harshly if at all by publishers in America, but there has been this explosive awareness and consideration of what black writers are saying. Now this means that black writers are getting a greater opportunity in America than ever before.

LC: In *Sons of Darkness, Sons of Light* you use a kind of Jewish parallel, don't you, with the colored situation?

JAW: Yes. I'm taking black situations in America in the 1960s and perhaps continuing into the '70s and relating that situation to the Jews in Palestine in 1948 at the end of World War II. And the reasons I think are fairly obvious. That the Jews gained Palestine, what is now known as Israel, through the employment of selective acts of violence against the British government and army and succeeded in getting the partitioning of Palestine. Now twenty some odd years have passed. I think the parallel to some degree is still valid between their situation and ours.

LC: You subtitle the book *A Novel of Some Probability*.

JAW: Well, yes, as I said it's set in 1973. The conditions for what is going on in the States right now will probably exist far beyond 1973. For a people who have tried every avenue there always remains one and, perhaps but one person, to trigger that action. I say it's still to come. This is why I've subtitled it *A Novel of Some Probability*.

LC: John Williams, what are you going to do next?

JAW: I'm finishing a book on the late Reverend Doctor Martin Luther King, which I like to feel is a critical study of his life and times. Then I'm doing a novel on the Negro soldier in America, a character who is part mythical and part real, who fights in every war from the Revolution through Vietnam. I'm also coeditor of a new magazine called *Amistad*, a semiannual publication of paperback format, paperback size, two hundred pages.

LC: You feel that through the novel form and through literature you can help the cause of the colored people?

JAW: Not only the colored people, I think—and not many of us will say this or admit it—but basically we must have at the core of our actions, considerations for all humanity. Now I'm not saying it's because I'm Johnny Niceguy. I'm saying it because simply nothing else works.

An Interview with John A. Williams

The Harvard Crimson / 1971

John A. Williams, author of *The King God Didn't Save*, was born near Jackson, Mississippi, and like fellow black novelist, John O. Killens, began writing while he was a soldier in a Jim Crow regiment in the Pacific. Williams, along with Killens, Ellison, and others, was strongly influenced by Richard Wright, who was also from Mississippi, and like Wright, Williams has traveled and lived in Africa and Europe. Perhaps it is because of this common background and experience that he has obtained a particular understanding of Wright and is the author of a perceptive biography of him, *The Most Native of Sons*.

The King God Didn't Save, a controversial biography of Martin Luther King Jr. is Williams's tenth book. The others include five novels, *The Angry Ones, Night Song, Sissie, The Man Who Cried I Am*, and *Sons of Darkness, Sons of Light*. His last two novels have dealt particularly with the increasing level of violence and irrationality in the attitudes and actions of white America and the effect of this on black people everywhere.

This interview took place at the Boston University Afro-American Studies Department in Brookline where Williams delivered a guest lecture.

Harvard Crimson: You once said, "Writing is a craft or profession or rite of stupidity that can bring oblivion swifter than anything else I know." In light of the reaction to *The King God Didn't Save* which definition seems the most accurate?

John A. Williams: Well, I don't know. It's—some people have called it stupid, and some people have predicted that I was headed for oblivion. What was the other thing?

HC: Craft or profession.

JAW: Well, it wasn't a profession either. It was something that I felt compelled to do because I see certain things I don't wish to see in the black movement that people are involved in, and that is to deal with things in the same superficial manner that white people deal with things, to never probe beneath the surface to get at the gear, the mechanisms of things. So I did the book, and it may well be that all of these things will fall upon my head. But I'm only sorry I did it in terms of the unease that it's caused my family and, I suppose, me too. These are things that pass. It wasn't as though what has happened is totally unexpected. I expected it to be something about what's it's been like.

HC: Could one say that your book is also about the God King didn't save?

JAW: The God King didn't save—that's fair enough. In that section that involved Protestants, Catholics, and Jews, our three major religious organizations, the feeling I tried to set down is that, in spite of all the professions of religiosity, these groups are more politically involved than in any other consideration. I think I did say that this man came along talking about religion, dealing with religion, and he was met with violence. As far as I'm concerned, religion had its last opportunity to flourish or reflourish . . . when Martin Luther King was alive.

HC: Had King lived, what directions might he have followed?

JAW: I think his last year or so pointed him in the direction of less reliance upon the aid and assistance of the federal government, but more on his own charisma. The Poor People's March of course is a primary example, and he had been, as James Forman said it, in the armpit of the federal government. Jim had been trying to get him out from under that so he could do his own thing without being monitored and advised. I think he, King, was getting into that. Unfortunately, he was monitored in other ways. And King was not the only one. Since the book has come out, I don't suppose not a month goes by when somebody doesn't tell me about some other pictures or some people in pictures that I hadn't even heard about before. So, apparently the surveillance of King was infinite, let's say. But I think . . . well, try to put yourself in the situation. Here you are, a charismatic leader, and perhaps more than that. Perhaps the bona fide leader by virtue of having received the Nobel Prize, by virtue of commanding audiences wherever you go. Here you've been doing what any other man does given the opportunity–human response to human invitation, if you will. Suddenly these people come up and say: well, we've been bugging you and wiretapping you; we've been photographing you, and you better stop it. At that point, the man has to make a choice whether he is going to be concerned about himself, his family, his children—that's five people—or millions of black people, not only millions of black people in 1967, but millions of black people for all the rest of time. I think he probably made a choice to go with the masses.

HC: Do you see anyone filling his gap today?
JAW: Well, I don't see anybody. I think I sort of predicted in the book that Jesse Jackson would be groomed next, and last fall or winter *Time* magazine did a cover story on Jesse. I don't think we are ever going to have a leader who comes down—I'm using this advisedly because it is totally impossible for black people to have one leader—King was assigned to us by the white power structure, and we took him. We took Malcolm. And they got rid of Malcolm and we were left with King and several other lesser deities. But I don't think we'll ever see a leader assigned to us again from that route of publicity . . . because we've learned that when leaders are bred in the fashion of King and Malcolm X that something very terrible happens to them ultimately. They can be assassinated in the press or assassinated for real.

HC: In the book you deal with the power of the media . . . How are we to deal with it?
JAW: I have to agree with you that the media can make or break or cripple or assassinate anybody it chooses to, not only black but white as well, polka-dot. I don't foresee in the immediate future any high-level black editors on powerful American newspapers or magazines. By that I mean decision-making levels. I don't see black people getting into that in my lifetime. The system's so tied up that we almost have to forget it for now. Guys your age and my little boy Dennis's age may ultimately arrive at those levels, but you have to ask yourselves, what is it going to cost you? What kind of compromise are you going to make? Yet, if we throw television in with newspapers, you see that we're in a totally untenable position. The black press is nothing, and it's very difficult to speak to a brother or sister through the white press.

HC: Even with the magazines we have now, we lack a national publishing force.
JAW: That's really what we need, a national publication—maybe more than one.

HC: What about *Muhammad Speaks*?

JAW: That's a treacherous paper in many ways. I've known a few guys who worked for them. They've never been critical since they left, but I guess I was turned off because of what they did with the King book. I'm not sure that the guy who wrote the piece had ever read the book. I suspect that he hadn't. When *The Man Who Cried I Am* came out, I was a saint. I could do no wrong. Now this book—not only do I work for the CIA, but I'm probably just coming back from an all-expense, CIA-paid tour of Europe and sitting down at a gold-plated typewriter. I would hope that the readers would find that a bit ridiculous, but those are the extents that publications of this kind go to when the readers allow them to. *Muhammad Speaks* and the Panther paper are not the answer to the kind of publications we need.

HC: Towards the end of the book you said, "To what Constitutional, to what moral authority do the black, the poor, and the young now appeal? This book is basically addressed to that point . . ." Then a few lines later you said, "There is no reliable authority." Do you think there are any useful values that can be derived from the African experience and applied to this moral void?

JAW: Yes, I think that there are values that can come out of Africa, and very positive ones. I would, on the other hand, be reluctant to accept these as the overall cure because I feel we've been on this toboggan and you have to get off where the damn thing stops. You know, if it's fifty thousand miles from Africa then that's where you have to get off and do your thing. If you can reach back and bring some good from Africa to where this thing has stopped—beautiful.

The authority that people must appeal to, as far as I'm concerned, is totally lacking from contemporary society. It seems to me that we are in a time when before much longer the people must protest. I'm not only talking about black people, but white people who are getting tired of these damn taxes. I'm talking about white people who are getting tired of shaky business ventures because of this silly war we're in. I'm talking about all kinds of people that are tired of the direction we seem to be moving in. Well, if this means revolution in the streets like the French Revolution, and I'm talking about a real revolution with all of the attendant gore . . . then it will have to come. What we've been trying to do unsuccessfully since before the Civil War . . . is to create this relationship with the white underclasses, but they've been duped away from it. I think that there will probably be some kind of revolution—fractured, with whites doing their thing and blacks doing their things, but all directed toward government, toward change. The terrible thing about that is that when that is done, then you're going to have the blacks and whites at each other's throats again because they didn't unite in the first place. Once more, I think the outlook is very pessimistic.

HC: In an article in the December '70 issue of *Black World* you said that the tradition of black communications needed to be molded anew. What forms would you like to see it take?

JAW: I think I'd like to see more rapport between older black writers and younger black writers. I think the publishing industry has had us in such a bag—you know, we're going to give you this as an advance, but you don't tell Iob how much you got because we didn't give him this much. The critics like Jimmy Baldwin, but they hate Ernie Gaines. It'd be a disaster if them two cats got together and all the rest of that, which is nonsense. I mean, you view the white literary establishment— Styron, Roth, [unintelligible], Updike, all of those cats—well, maybe they get together and maybe they don't, but the fact is they got their signals all so together, that it's not necessary. But we don't. We need to clean up some of this garbage and verbiage that has been built up between the black generations. We need to explain to ourselves our own writers. Explain that Ishmael Reed is a fantastic satirist as well as brilliantly knowledgeable of all facets of black people. That Bill Kelley has finally come around. . . . The publicity made it appear to be so impossible that young guys like Kelley and Reed could ever get together because Kelley went to Fieldston School and Harvard or wherever the hell he went. But that's crap. Kelley is in the same bag with Ishmael Reed, with me, with Baldwin, with Ellison, because we're black. Our problems deal with our approaches to our experiences, the way we can command or demand advances so we can support our families, and these are way out of line with the advances white writers get. Things of this nature.

HC: There seems to be a movement towards the past afoot, particularly among whites. A return to Jeffersonian concepts of necrophilia. In the past, these periods when America seemed to be doing an intellectual about-face have always coincided with a loss of black people's rights, a breaking of what seemed to be a progressive trust. Do you see any way of counteracting this trend?

JAW: I really don't know or foresee any hopeful trends. This is not basically our fault. I think that black people in terms of political clout and education are doing as much as they possibly can because most of these things are dependent upon public money—whether it be state or federal. As always the burden is on white America, and even today white America as a mass is not terribly interested in what happens to us. The business with pollution and environment and so on and so forth—I think white youth veered to this business much too quickly for there to have been any real sincerity in what they seemed to have been involved in with us in the early sixties. And this is where you have to go, to the white youth, because the older people are cliché-set in their ways. All they want to do is just hold the dam until they die and let it become somebody else's problem. But if they can begin manipulating their children to perhaps necessary, but in terms of the immediate needs of this country, ethereal goals, then when the kids reach their ages, it's going to be the same thing all over again. I'm just not that hopeful on the white side that anything good is going to come.

HC: In an interview in the *Paris Review*, Ralph Ellison said the search for identity is, "THE American theme. The nature of our society is such that we are prevented from knowing who we are." Do you agree with that, and do you see any particular reflection of it in the situation of black Americans?
JAW: This is most true of black people, and maybe only true of black people. You know, we've had a great deal of recent political awareness of ethnic political potential, and I'd say the Jews are a foremost example of awareness of the ethnic limitations and the exercise of that ethnic power. Ellison's statement is mostly true of black people, and I would disagree with his seeming contention that it's a problem for all Americans. It's not. I think that even Indians or Spanish-speaking Americans are more positive of their identity than are we because they have languages to fall back on. We are saddled with this old American English, and that's all there is to it.

John A. Williams: Agent Provocateur

Fred Beauford / 1971

From *Black Creation* (Summer 1971), 4–6. Reprinted with permission of Fred Beauford.

John A. Williams is a short, well-built man in his middle forties. He moved easily in his neat book-lined West Side apartment as he excused himself from me to go into the kitchen to check on his lima beans. His wife and young son had left him with the cooking for the afternoon.

"She can't cook lima beans," he explained.

He spoke in a soft, agreeable voice. For a minute, as he strolled out of the room, it became hard to connect this quiet-looking man with the violent storm that was swirling around his latest book, *The King God Didn't Save*.

In fact, he had come on a bit defensively when I first asked him about the response to the book.

"Most people who are talking about the book haven't read it," he answered straight out, with a slight touch of bitterness.

The King God Didn't Save deals with, among other things, the fact that Dr. Martin L. King was a midnight creeper and that J. Edgar Hoover, the stone-faced "Emperor of the F.B.I.," had found out about it and had used the information to whitemail him.

"Look," Williams explained, "there's nothing wrong with what a guy does in his private life. But these were the items that compromised King and compromised the movement."

How could that be? I responded.

He took a few seconds to answer and began to look remarkably like the Williams on the back cover of his book that I had at home: thoughtful and a little distant.

It has become a modern cliché to blame the media for every evil of society from bad breath to neighborhood rebellions. Unlike most critics of the media, however, Williams is in a much better position to see the truth. He has written for national magazines and major newspapers, worked in television, and has traveled to more than twenty-six countries, including stints as a *Newsweek* African correspondent and *Ebony/Jet*'s man in Europe.

In addition, he has written ten books and many short stories since leaving Syracuse University in 1950 with his BA. His last novel, *The Man Who Cried I Am*, was highly acclaimed by both black and white critics.

He returned from his beans with two cans of beer and passed me one. We talked a little about his two grown sons from another marriage. One was working as a school teacher upstate. Williams said "the kid" was beginning to see how the system was "killing our children."

He had said in his book that King was the creation of the white media. This was one of the points that his critics most objected to. I asked him about it to get back to the interview.

The thoughtful face appeared again. "I think I said in the book that King received a lot of attention because he had the best show in town. I think I said that to a large degree. But he had all the properties white folks like to see our leaders have. He was the old-time classic black leader. He was a minister. So that made him all the more ready for the production that the establishment went into. To the extent that he used the white media, as some said, that really doesn't hold water. If so, then why are we in the situation we are in today?"

The question was rhetorical, of course. He had already said in the book that "King got under my skin" because of his political philosophy. But he explained further: "The Civil Rights Act was only passed for a five-year period. Now it seems to me that there is an innate agreement which says that all rights that belong to black people are to be viable for only five years. Now we know damn well that these are inherently our rights. So when a man bargains for five years on something that should be ours for life, then I think there is something wrong with the situation."

This disagreement with King's philosophy, he agreed, was only a minor point in *The King God Didn't Save*. But Williams has trouble agreeing with many who say that he dwelled unduly upon King's sex life.

"Well, I think that for anyone who has read the book," he said, the barely detectable edge creeping back into his voice, "there is no such thing as dwelling on. I think that if you put together all the passages in the book that deal with King's private life it would amount to one-and-a-half pages out of the 221-page book . . ."

The major point of the book as far as Williams is concerned was the fact that after J. Edgar called King into his office and told him to cool it or face the badmouth, King began to hold his fire. This caution, Williams noted, cost the movement valuable momentum. Williams also believes that when King did speak loudly again against the War and started planning for the Poor People's March on Washington, that his days became numbered.

"It's old enough to be almost cliché now," he said, "but as soon as a black leader starts expanding his area of operation outside of just black people, when he starts to deal with all kinds of disadvantaged people—Indians, whites, browns—then his whole operation becomes shaky. Establishments don't make black leaders so that they can go out and mess with Indians and poor whites and Puerto Ricans.

"Now this was something Malcolm was into with his trips to Africa. We can trace this back to Trotter's (Monroe Trotter, black leader who opposed Booker T. Washington) activities in Europe about World War I; we can trace it to Richard Wright; we can trace it to a lot of people. These things happen, and there are a growing number of people who are no longer willing to believe that these things are coincidences."

A number of people have indeed pointed out that the only people killed in this country (by the same type of lone mental retard), are always those men who have been most capable of organizing a broadly based coalition of the have-nots. I wondered if he thought that there was a vast conspiracy in the land.

"Everybody is into this conspiracy thing," he answered, "and these killings may or may not have been conspiracies in the correct sense of the word. A conspiracy means a band of people get together to commit some evil deed. Now it may just be the historical momentum of this country that draws people together, and they don't have to say one damn word to each other. They all know why they are in the same room; and they all know why they want to do certain things, and how to do them.

"I've been in touch with some people who see patterns in the deaths of John Kennedy and Martin, but I can't connect the deaths of all four (the Kennedy brothers and Malcolm and King) any more than anyone else can. But that doesn't mean that the four deaths were not staged by the same people."

I noted that it would have been ironic indeed since the Kennedy brothers were the ones who had authorized the wiretaps on King.

"They were looking for Communists," he answered.

Williams said that he wrote *The King God Didn't Save* because he wanted black people to understand just what happens to black leaders in this country when they show signs of stepping out of a given role or what happens if they get too powerful and try to forget their maker as King was trying to do. What enraged him most about the reception to his book is that most people seem to have missed the major message.

"People in this country don't read very well. They come out of a Mickey Spillane school, and they read what's on the surface. There's little examination of what lies under the words. And that's disheartening."

Most of his disheartenment, however, is directly at black people, whom he feels "are particularly" missing the point of the book. "We are still the only ones left in the dark," he said.

Why?

"We really don't want to face up to the situation," he answered quickly. Then his voice compromised a little. "That's basically hard to do. Living. Earning money. Supporting your family. Trying to make your family comfortable. Send your kids to school. And after all, you have been raised in America, and you are taught things that are not so easily dissolved as you grow older. You keep hoping for better things. That it is not going to be the way you don't want it. But it is the way we all think it isn't."

He had one final point to make about King's influence on making blacks in this country "face up." "King's most important value," he said, "was that he gave the lie to all this Christian ethic. Once we realize that the country is not into all this brotherhood, then it's a whole new ball game."

What kind of ball game—race war, Third World revolution, the new youth culture takeover?

"I think that the involvement of the white youth culture in drugs and communes and campus movements and ecology is directed away from the black movement. . . . Show me a hippy commune, and I will show you people who are copping out. And it is not only because society is so damn bad, but it is because they don't want to cope with the real issues. I am not being faked out by none of this junk. Take that *Gimme Shelter* thing (California rock concert). I didn't discern any outcry when the Hell's Angels stabbed that black cat. I mean, nobody was running through Berkeley. There were no parades. You know, just back to the same old thing."[1]

What about black politics, I observed; we do have a few black mayors . . .

"I have less and less faith in the political machinery in this country. It's no big thing that there are black mayors. We always get things that no longer have any value. The cities have been cleaned out. The Mafia has cleaned them out. And the white people left who are not involved in the Mafia are so beaten down that they are ready to give anyone a chance. If Felix the Cat wanted to run for mayor, he would pick up a good following. That's how bad things have gotten," he answered.

Did he have a plan for action?

"No," Williams answered, "But a plan there must be."

Note

1. Williams refers to the death of eighteen-year-old Meredith Hunter during the Rolling Stones' performance at the 1969 Altamont Speedway Free Festival. (JAT)

Interview—October 25, 1971 and Interview—June 9, 1972

Earl A. Cash / 1971

From *John A. Williams: Evolution of a Black Writer* by Earl A. Cash. New York: The Third Press, 1975. Reprinted with permission of Earl A. Cash, author.

Interview 1

My first meeting with novelist John A. Williams was on October 25, 1971, when he came to give a reading at the University of New Mexico. We had corresponded previously and had planned to have further discussions on his arrival. A small man with thin, receding hair and with what he calls a Mephistophelean beard, Williams exhibited an infectious warmth and affableness which immediately helped one feel comfortable in his presence. Still under the impression that writers tend to have quirks, I became more amazed as I discerned that Mr. Williams appeared to have no obvious eccentricities. In fact, there was little, externally, to distinguish him as a writer.

For approximately three hours, we talked—mostly, he answered my questions on his writings, his political opinions, and his concerns and expectations for American blacks. Williams's candor which permeates his nonfiction can be found as well in the following transcript of my interview with him. Where some authors might have hedged, he was unequivocal without giving the impression of being foolhardy or pompous.

The interviews (there would be a second in the summer of 1972) may appear slightly dated, but they confirm ideas and beliefs which have been presented in the works of the writer. Moreover, the reader will get a picture of a man calling attention to history and all its lessons. If a desperation emerges, it is precisely because Williams feels that man is generally too indifferent to past and present events and their effect on what is to come.

Cash: You seemed to be fascinated with the black musician's world. What influenced that?

Williams: Well, I think if we hadn't been poor, I would have been a musician. When I was a kid, I was in a drum and bugle corps, and I was a good bugler. I wanted to study trumpet, but as cheap as it was to study trumpet at that time and to rent one—my folks didn't have the money, so I just stayed a good bugler. And that was it. The strange thing is that my boy did study trumpet, and he is a good trumpeter.

Cash: So, you didn't have any humanitarian purposes in *Night Song* like recording for posterity or for the readers a more in-depth insight into the black musician and perhaps the role played or what his role was all about?

Williams: I don't think I set out to do that consciously. God knows I know enough musicians to know what they were going through, what they do go through.

There's something else that struck me lately. In *The Angry Ones* and in *Night Song*, you've got this tandem pair of black guys Keel and Eagle and Obie and Steve. You've got the same thing in *The Man Who Cried I Am*. Now early I was very aware that this was the only way to deal with black dialogue; that is, to have another confidant. Or as in the case of *The Man Who Cried I Am*, Harry is not always a confidant. He is an antagonist. But at least they can have a dialogue. And to a larger extent having two characters function like this, you're really dealing with one character, but using two parts.

Cash: I see what you mean. I suppose that's why Obie complements Steve Hill by giving his commentary every so often. Speaking about dialogue, I note that in many of the novels the characters are black and educated. If you have a black educated man, he is likely not to speak the slang or use the terminology of the masses. Do you find that dialogue easier to deal with than if you were to work with a less educated group? Is there any expediency in one as opposed to the other?

Williams: Again, I have to deal out of my own experiences. As a matter of fact, one of the novels I'm working on now, the one that encompasses the guys from all classes, several of the characters are skilled workers. They've not gone to school or anything. The peculiar thing about a place like Syracuse is whether you've gone to college or not, everybody's language is approximately the same. We notice differences, say, in people who come up from the South. Because their language is different doesn't mean they're lower class. Even before they came there we had lower-class people who spoke as well as any preacher who got up on the pulpit. Maybe it's just the difference of location, New York State vs. Mississippi or whatever, and the kinds of education that people got. It's something I really hadn't thought about until you just brought it up, but it's really remarkable.

Cash: I think whether we like it or not, language is one of the means of stereotype. So if you're speaking what might be called the black dialogue, people associate you immediately with the low class. And if you speak standard English, they associate you immediately with the middle class, which is ridiculous and can really throw people off-base. It's like anything else. You have a suit on, you're well-shaved, and some Whites are prone to give you nice comments. On the other hand, if you are looking grubby, they'll hardly acknowledge your existence.

Williams: In this new book, there's a guy who's a pusher. Two or three guys work in the foundry. Yet, the language really isn't that different from the guys who grew up, went to college, and moved away and who are now coming back. I mean, to talk to my father—who lives in Syracuse and has remarried, as has my mother—man-to-man without any concern for certain fine points of grammar, he talks just like me. There are certain things he does once in a while with his verbs and pronouns, but, hell, I heard even Robert Graves does that.

Cash: This brings me to another question which arises because you do deal with blacks who have a college education and many who have gone beyond that in their own readings and experiences. Let's take Eugene Browning in *Sons of Darkness, Sons of Light.* There are perhaps many reasons why his revolutionary idea, his salvific act, doesn't work. History in itself would have shown him it wasn't going to. But, he was a professor, a teacher, who decides to get into the action. So, he joins the IRJ; I suppose an advanced type of NAACP. Yet, he's out of touch. I thought if Browning had come to the man-in-the-street, black or white, and had said to him, "Here is my plan; what do you think?" the guy probably would've said that it's not going to work. I think, perhaps, one reason Browning felt his plan would work was because he was wrapped up in his own world which was not only the world of books but a world in which he was the middle-classer going around collecting money for his organization.

Williams: But there are two things. First Browning's plan did work. All he wanted to do was have the cop killed. He's not really responsible for the other things that happened. Second, the older we grow, the more cautious we tend to become about many things. He was very concerned about having this act done but not being punished for initiating it himself–which also worked. When the other things started breaking up these were not at all related to Browning except that his original act sort of sparked everything else that happened.

Now, one of the reasons why, I suppose, I did that Browning thing was to somehow tell people that it doesn't matter how much education you've got if you're black. There's no such thing as removing one's self from it. You're always to some degree involved. And as Sartre, a Johnny-come-lately, has just said recently, the intellectual has got to put his body on the line as well as his mind. Now he says that knowing full well that many people are not about to do so. But, if you're talking about young intellectuals who are probably not that well known in France, that's a different story. They can be hurt. They can be killed. So, the question of putting one's body on the line with one's mind becomes something you might want to equivocate about. And that's exactly Browning's position.

Cash: You have the Don in *Sons of Darkness, Sons of Light* tell Browning that the mistake many people make is that they feel that being an intellectual, or being educated, and indulging in violence are mutually exclusive. I see reflected in the story with Browning and with some of the other characters the questions about the black student as a whole; that is, the student who would get a college education or more. His problem, a problem he's got to resolve, is how he's going to relate to his people, be they uneducated or educated, and get out of just sitting in on meetings with his peers.

Williams: I think that's a real big problem. There has been a lot of cry about the validity of the education in the American system and that black people should not become part of it. My point is I believe in education; not merely in formal education. All you can get through formal education is some desire to go further than you already are. And to that extent, I think it would be a beautiful thing for a lot of kids who have doubts about going. Another thing, I've spoken to a number of these black kids on the campuses in their dashikies and Afros, who are on the arm, so to speak, in Upward Bound programs and equal education. They have gun drills in the basements of their homes and all the rest. They sort of overreact to finding themselves on this great highway to becoming middle class. But I call them middle class because one of the first routes to becoming middle class is to go to college. They called me an old Uncle Tom and so on. I can't help that. So we have a real problem with these kids—and there are more and more black kids going to colleges right now than ever before in American history—as to whether they're going to take this information and education that they're going to be exposed to and return to the people and apply it in some meaningful way or just be one of these guys who walks out of school and gets a job as vice president of IBM. I think there're a lot of kids who aren't really thinking of this. They're saying one thing but very readily accepting something else. That's the problem.

Cash: You have Browning wonder, at one point in *Sons of Darkness, Sons of Light*, why black groups had to go the African route. Do you question this also?
Williams: I just feel that the African route is very deceptive. While I understand and approve of the new reaching back for roots, I think it only really works when there is a reciprocal action going on. Now the Africans by and large do not know and couldn't care less about what's going on in America. The elite give lots of lip service to our Brothers in America. They could have made it possible for black Americans with engineering, medical, teaching, and social work skills to pass back and forth using their skills in Africa becoming really acquainted with the groups. But, they don't want that. I know because I've been there twice, and I know people who have been social workers and scientists. I knew a guy who worked for the space station in Kano, Nigeria, who quit the US government to go help the Nigerians. And they wouldn't have him. Last thing I heard he was selling chickens in a supermarket. So I think to be aware of Africa, I mean this in one basic sense, we've got to realize that we've been living all this time under the shame of having been slaves or having been brought from Africa—as the books tell us not really fighting too well to stay in Africa. My parents, their parents before them have all been trying to deal with this. And now we are dealing with it. It may be we're through dealing with the Afros and dashikies and can deal realistically with Africa. I think we've got to say, yes, this is our homeland; this is where we came from; this is how we came. Now we're here, and we're doing our thing. Maybe I'd like to go back over and take a tour. I would recommend it to every black American to go to Africa, if possible, and look around. But it's all been so damn superficial for me because I'm sick and tired of hearing about the ancient African empires of Kush and so on because many more meaningful things took place there a long time ago. Our black scholars seem to stop at the eighteenth dynasty and so forth; instead of getting into, as the white archaeologists are, that diffusion of people all over the world, to the new world thousands of years before Columbus. There are all kinds of evidence that there were black people among them. We don't

have any scholars, African or black American, that I know of who are getting into this thing, which in many ways is a hell of a lot more meaningful that dealing with Kush. This is why I feel a lot of it is superficial.

Cash: Maybe one reason the black Americans change their names and outfits is that it gives them a certain solidarity and emphasizes a heritage that they feel they do have. For many, too, I think, it's become a symbol of something more valiant, an external show of their defiance. Oh, I thought it significant that in *The Man Who Cried I Am*, you have the story of the King Alfred plan coming via an African.

Williams: Well, that was as good a place as any for it. By the way, I wear dashikies, too, occasionally. They're very comfortable.

Cash: To move to another facet of the novels, in *The Man Who Cried I Am* you have a betrayal. You have a betrayal in *Night Song* which is across racial lines. But, you have the slick blacks in *The Man Who Cried I Am* who turned against Max and Harry. You have a similar thing happening in *Sons of Darkness*: Greene simply did not trust his friend, Trotman. What have you to say about all this lack of trust?

Williams: I think that's a basically human reason for falling out. When I was getting married for the second time and somebody asked me if I had known the girl long, I said quite long. And, he said the most valuable thing in the world is to be with someone that you can really trust. I thought about that a long time, and I think he's actually right. I've been involved in many things with the Brothers and without the Brothers. There have always been areas of betrayal, kind of more vicious with the Brothers than with other people. Just incredibly vicious. I don't know what it is except that as far as I can see it's one of those human frailties that Shakespeare dealt with all the time. It's like when I was growing up in Syracuse and I felt some racial slight, I'd get salty and the teachers would say you got a chip on your shoulder, which means I either had been betrayed or wary that I was about to be betrayed or something.

Cash: Another statement made by Browning is that he will return to teaching, but he will teach down the system. This is his new resolve as the novel concludes. What do you feel about this?

Williams: I think this is pretty much what I am trying to do. When I go around lecturing, somebody might ask me about improvements in the country. I tell them about Albuquerque, for example, and ask why in the hell must I wait fifteen years so I can sleep in the Holiday Inn of all places. And this is what I like to think I am doing. I'm very pleased that I have three sons, which is not to belittle women, but I think that males tend to be prime movers. So, they're sort of like three new cables; I try to teach them, without being obvious about it, what's going down, what they should expect from themselves and so on. That's really what I mean.

Cash: About this idea of stereotype, many black writers rebelled against the white stereotype of blacks by building an opposite stereotype. And so you get in some books and movies blacks who would be super . . .
Williams: Super spade?

Cash: Yes. So, in trying to avoid one stereotype, one falls into another. Isn't the black author, like the black man in America, on the dodge from falling into stereotypes?
Williams: Actually, I don't think there's been much reaction on the part of black writers to the white stereotype of black people. Sam Greenlee, of course, has a super spade in his book. I don't know that John Killens has ever dealt with a super spade, or Chester Himes, and I don't think that I did. I know I would like to. Maybe the guy who comes closest to it is Ishmael Reed. But, his characters are so satirical until you don't think of them as being super spades. That's an interesting point. I don't think there's been that much reaction, as you say, except maybe in comic books. My oldest son does a lot of work with comic books in terms of teaching his kids. He has been collecting all these books that now have super Charlie and super Spade, and they're fighting the crooks together. That's the area where you find it.

Cash: Well, maybe if you went to the area of the movies, you'd find this more prevalent.
Williams: I think it more viable in movies at this point than in novels. *Sons of Darkness, Sons of Light* in many ways was a pot boiler for me anyhow. I sat down and wrote it comparatively quickly compared to the other books. This was a reaction to my continued poverty after *The Man Who Cried I Am* came along. It looked as if, finally, I'd be able to make a little money and help both the boys who were in college at that time. The critical acclaim was good, but I was just as poor as I had always been. As a matter of fact that book in paperback is all over the place, but the paperback publisher tells me it hasn't made a dime. The whole thing is so damn crazy it's better not to go into it. So, I sat down and wrote this book. I think it's one of my worse

novels. It brought in more money than *The Man Who Cried I Am*. And it's just the way things happen in America. The things that are crap or tend to be crap or are not as good as other things, always for some reason do better.

Cash: Do you have a pessimistic outlook for militant organizations mobilizing?

Williams: Yes, I do. In the first place—it may be a black thing, I don't know—we seem to abhor secrecy. You can't have a militant black group in this country unless it's infiltrated. It's just impossible. The only groups you can have that're valid and functioning and haven't done anything yet are those that operate in total secrecy. We just don't seem to be able to pull that off. I think that's what's totally necessary in this society that is shot through with surveillance systems, peoples, codes, and so forth.

Cash: In your novels, you've shown us characters who try one way which mightn't be as effective as they want so they will go another way. As you say in the last line of *Sons of Darkness*, this is the way with things, the rhythms of trial and error, of going from one plan to another. What would you then propose for blacks struggling for equality? What idea might you have that would be more workable?

Williams: I don't know if it would be more workable, but I guess one gets a little desperate. As I said before, it's kind of a far out plan. But, it is that of employing, utilizing black people who look like whites. The number, I think, is about twenty or thirty million, which is pretty close to the whole population of Spain or Great Britain. That's a lot of people. Utilizing some of these people to infiltrate into the technological systems of the armed forces over a period of years, several years, maybe half a century or so. And at some point just everyone in concert pushing a button that dismantles the whole goddamn thing. And there you have it, a technological collapse, which means an economic collapse. In terms of relationships with other world powers, they would no longer exist.

Cash: In *The Man Who Cried I Am*, you have Max and Harry running into some static because they had flirted with communism. What are your feelings particularly about the Marxist doctrine as it tried to encompass blacks?

Williams: I think it's pretty obviously failed, mainly because black people were never its initial thrust. When Marx, Lenin, Trotsky, and others spoke about exploited people, they were thinking mostly of the exploited peoples of Europe. It really wasn't until the end of the Second World War that the communists started to leave the Asian-European mainland and go to Africa or the Caribbean. And again that's an example, particularly with Asians, of what I was saying with the plan in this new novel [*Captain Blackman*]. Guys like Chou En-lai and Mao and the big man [Ho Chi Minh] who died in Hanoi recently—all those guys were involved in Marxism at a very early period and really only came to be powerful people, let's say, in the late thirties, shortly before World War II. They got their own following during World War II. That's a long time. And it's that kind of patience that I think is going to be required of any change in this system, if the damn thing holds together long enough. But as you said about going back to the Bahamas [the interviewer's birthplace], after this prolonged study there may be nothing to go back to. That's always a big problem.

The basic thrust of the Marxist is history. And black American history was something they, just like black Americans themselves, knew very little of, and what they knew they did not bother to utilize. For example, they did a lot of work in the South, or they thought they were going to do a lot of work in the South, but they didn't reckon on the kinds of opposition they were going to have from the crackers. Just tremendous opposition. Then they started in the urban centers: New York, Chicago, San Francisco, and Los Angeles. But as Chester Himes points out even among the communists, say, who were highly placed in the arts, the black communist was still a black man. He'd have to eat in the kitchen if he came to pick up something from those people.

Cash: In *The Man Who Cried I Am* as Max attempts to elude his assassins, he says to himself that he had really come to realize that America had pushed blacks to a choice. It was either going to be destruction or otherwise peaceful coexistence. In *Sons of Darkness, Sons of Light*, the same thought is echoed. One character says that it was silly to try to revamp a system that had insanity at its very core. These are dark, gloomy pronouncements. Yet, I can't help but note that the novels still end with some hope. Is that an ambivalence that you share personally?

Williams: I don't think it's a personal ambivalence. I think it's a human ambivalence. You want things to go on. You have to hope for two reasons: first, if not you have to jump off a bridge like Hart Crane or somebody, and I don't think I'm anywhere near doing that. Number two is that as long as you have the hope, there are things that you can do to bring about those things that you hope will happen for the better, either physically or by writing or what have you. I think this is the only thing that's made it work as awkwardly as it has—there have been a lot of people who have hoped that Armageddon wouldn't come. Maybe just by virtue of saying hello to a nigger with a smile one morning that sort of puts it off for another day. So you operate on that premise.

Cash: Well, let's leave this topic for a while and go to another area in which the black has been slighted by the media and sociological study: that of the black woman and mother, her role in the family throughout the years and how, perhaps, this led you to write *Sissie.*

Williams: You mentioned earlier that in reaction to the white stereotype of the happy-go-lucky darkie that there might come about a super spade. I think this kind of reaction has really happened in terms of black mothers—not in novels so much, but maybe articles. I read something not too long ago, one of a continuing number of pieces, which deals with the great, good and golden strength of black mothers in raising their children. I think that's a reaction because the fact of the matter is that black mothers are no worse or no better than any other kind of mother. But we get into this thing because somebody said black mothers are no damned good and what we do is create a black Mary Magdalene. As for black women in general, the same thing is going on. A friend of mine did a piece last summer in the *New York Times* on why black women are not interested in women's lib. She said a lot of foolish things to be a very intelligent woman which was that black women had more sensuality and a basic sex thing than white women and that black men really ain't shit and are totally in awe of the system. I had lunch with her and asked why she wrote all that bullshit. She couldn't really backtrack, but she was hemming and hawing for about twenty minutes giving me her explanations. I think she realized that it was kind of silly—particularly since publications like the *New York Times* and many others in this country will only publish pieces by black writers if they say pretty much what the editors of those publications think or want them to say. For her to have done a piece regaling the sensuality of black women and the worthlessness of black men is like playing right into their hands. It's one of the things black writers have to be aware of these days. Other writers have not had to be bothered with those kinds of political overtones in their work.

Cash: It seems to me a real irony that Sissie says at one point she never had a dream of her own because she just wanted her children to be able to dream. Yet, this is not sufficient to convince her daughter Iris to love her. And even the son would not bring his family to his mother's death because he didn't want to be contaminated in any way. The way the novel works appeals to me most. I don't think it can really be compared because it's a whole different type of novel to *The Man Who Cried I Am*.

Williams: The structures are the only things that are similar. I like *Sissie*. As a matter of fact, Ralph Joplin is coming back in one of the new novels I'm working on. He's one of these guys who comes for this reunion. You know, I think there has been, ironically, at least for people in my generation, this great emphasis on education. Your children have got to do better than we did. That's human nature. That's how evolution expands and expounds. But I see that it's a very costly process with great numbers of people I know. In the circle in which I grew up three of the guys turned out to be homosexuals. Lots of pressures. Lots of very strange things going on. And now all for what? I still maintain that education is to be valued as a starting point. Now my parents, for example, can sit back and say they did all this for what. I've got the same problems of racism that they had, maybe more subtle, maybe not so immediate, maybe not so harsh, but the end result is all the same. So, I find out now that both my parents who have always been acutely aware of racism and disgusted made us aware of it. They went through a period when things weren't so bad, but right now you talk about those "militant" kids. I don't think there's anybody more militant than people my parents' age. They're in their late sixties, and time is running out. They can look back over the lifetimes of their parents and see that only inches have been gained. They've got to be salty.

The whole business with black families, again, is a reaction to so much of the white sociological documentation on how poorly off the black family was or is without understanding that however a family is composed, it has to function. It must function or go under. Very often it doesn't matter whether there are two parents there or one parent or no parent. Things have to go on. There's been enough experimentation and documentation in other societies—the Israeli society, for example, where they proved it's not necessary to have parents around. They raise the kids in kibbutz nursery. What the hell is a parent? It's just a vehicle and a lot of us, like myself, of course, are on great ego trips when we think we're that important to our children. I imagine to a certain extent we are, but physiologically it's also been established that when parents, say, of monkeys aren't around or even of people, baby monkeys or baby children will find something else to love.

Cash: I was thinking back to the problem of education and this idea of pushing which you deal with in *Sissie*. It seems very realistic that the child who is pushed to the extent of feeling that he's not loved but simply being used as an instrument for parents' aims—that child will grow up with some remorse and antipathy toward the very field that he's become adept in and to the parents who pushed him into it. There is also a possibility of such a reaction on the part of the child even when the parents mean well. Doesn't this make getting one's children educated a risky business?

Williams: I think as long as education is still socially accepted by the majority, there'll be no problem with kids wanting to be educated. I never even really had to discuss it with my two older boys. They were just determined that they were going to college. Determined is even the wrong word. They just felt it was their goddamn duty to go to college, maybe because I had gone. One even went to my school which he didn't necessarily have to do. The other one didn't. I tried to dissuade my oldest boy from taking divinity studies, but I did that rather subtly, I think. As a result, he found his own direction. That's really been the extent of my involvement in their educational processes. I've tried to dissuade my other son from being a writer because he can write at any time. I thought he would have more value to the revolution by becoming a constitutional lawyer, for example. He said he would think about it.

Cash: What about education and blacks? After all, if education is the way of introducing you to the system, when you do become educated, it has been "successful." Doesn't it make you then much more apathetic, systematized, or more prone to accept things without complaint? Isn't education, then, a way of quelling militancy?

Williams: Well, it's always seemed to me that I was like a spy in the educational system going in to see how Charlie works. Then I could bring this back and tell my sons, friends, and relatives what's really going down. I think it's more important to become involved in this kind of educational system than a lot of people realize simply because you cannot stand outside and think about conducting any kind of revolution if you don't know what the enemy is doing. It's sort of like a patrol. You have to know what the other guy is doing, so you send your patrol out always to keep in contact with them so that you know when he's going to launch an attack over this bridge or over this plain. Unless you're in contact with him, you won't know.

I keep running into lots of black kids who claim that they will not read white writers. That is suicide—again for the same reasons. In order to know how the system works you have to study it, know it. Otherwise, how can you get out here and talk about revolution? Against what? Just because the guy is white (which obviously is very often reason enough)? But you have to know how he's working within that whiteness in order to successfully subvert what he's doing or overcome it or whatever. So I really have no patience for people who say they don't want to be involved in that system. What they're really saying is "If I do baby, I'm long gone because Charlie's got me" instead of going in there and getting what's to be derived and coming out and bringing it back to the people. That is my view of participating in the educational system.

Cash: Another idea that comes to mind is that starting with *The Angry Ones*, you portray Steve Hill's boss as a homosexual. You have a homosexual patron in *The Man Who Cried I Am*, where you also have numerous scenes of the cobalt treatment for Max's cancer of the anus. I saw all this as saying that if blacks are to get anywhere they've got to kiss asses or surrender their masculinity, their very backbones. If Steve had pandered to his boss's seduction efforts, he would have been on the way to getting a raise and more. Max could have had more popularity than he did, if he would have played up to Granville.
Williams: Let me begin that answer with a quote from Ishmael Reed. "In America," he says, but I think it's true everywhere, "art is cock." I think this is pretty true. I don't know about that cobalt machine. And I wasn't, not consciously, dealing with the kinds of things a black man would have to do in order to enter the system. But, obviously, as you point out with Rollie and Granville things could have been a lot different had Steve and Max pandered to them. I guess I was dealing from my experiences in this business in terms of how one can become a success or not. Very often the avenues to success are blocked by people who are homosexual or, at the most, bisexual. There's no gainsaying the fact that Jimmy Baldwin's tremendous success lay in great part in his being homosexual—no doubt whatsoever in the black literary community or the white literary community. I make this judgment on the basis of Hernton's article (Calvin Hernton, "Blood of the Lamb" in *Amistad* 1, ed. Williams and Charles Harris, New York: Random House, 1970). I've not been directly approached. Everybody knows I'm straight, so that's that. If people know that, then it's pretty well all right. But what they look for is some sign of weakness. For example, I was twelve years between marriages. I don't know how they viewed me, but I had a great time. I mean, I had twelve years of just fun from one end of the world to the next. But the single status may have triggered something in their own minds about how I was.

These two instances with Granville and Rollie—these two characters are drawn on characters who are very obvious and prevalent in the black and white literary community. They're very real obstacles. One of the reasons why LeRoi Jones is always talking about faggot white men is that he's gone through the same thing. I know so many black artists in Europe who are ostensibly straight people but who basically are not. We have Black Power and Jewish Power and all those other Powers; there is also the presence of Gay Power, and it is not to be dismissed in the arts and elsewhere.

Cash: In *Night Song*, Keel suffers impotency because of Della. This reinforces the idea of the black being sort of castrated or his very potency being affected in relation to the white.

Williams: I think that's a little bit obtuse. As I recall, he became impotent because of rage. It was a question of hurting this woman through the sexual act, which he didn't want to do. So, he short-circuited himself, and he became impotent. I guess the effect is really the same, though, isn't it?

Cash: Yes. I would like to get your comment on interracial marriage.

Williams: I get a lot of questions from young black female students and sometimes not so young and often not students. The vogue right now is that this black man–white woman thing has got to go. That's really becoming a terrible thing to handle in New York. Although the evidence is that no matter how much people complain about it, that's exactly what's happening. Interracial marriages are increasing. A lot of black women have basically idiotic reasons for being opposed to this. And sometimes the reasons are not so idiotic because here in 1971 any woman is open to competition; I don't care if she's got polka dots. Black women realize this, and they appear to be reluctant to enter into combat for black men. So, they will very often sit back and talk rather than act. It's, as far as I can determine, not a question of preference as much as happenstance, one of the things I dealt with in *The Man Who Cried I Am*. Cecil Brown, on the other hand, who wrote *Life and Loves of Mr. Jiveass Nigger*—his whole thesis is that white women treat black men better. But, it all gets down to individuals. They must make the decisions, and nobody can make them for them.

Interracial couples appear in my novels because that's pretty much the life I've lived. I grew up in a community that was well mixed in Syracuse at that time. It was not a ghetto as black ghettos now go. We had all kinds of people. I played house with all kinds of girls. That was the way I grew up. My first wife was black. At the end of that marriage, girlfriends have been just about anything that was there and willing, and we had a thing together. My second wife is white. We know a lot of mixed couples. I can't say any of them are having problems as a result of this new thing that's going around. I think it's something that will pass. It's again a part of the revolutionary rhetoric. How for example can a black man be less faithful to his race by virtue of having a white wife? And you would still praise Frederick Douglass, for example: we get out and do this for Fred Douglass; we get out and do that for whoever else was great and had a white wife. These are things we don't take into consideration. This is what makes me think it's a passing thing with the revolution, which is not to say that the gals aren't sincere when they're bitching. But, we've got to deal with some of these things not always on a purely emotional level, and it's not always a way out to say that we are an emotional people. Of course, we are. But we have to use something of the intellectual process to mitigate pure, destructive, if it's always going to be that way, emotionalism. I know what they're talking about, and I don't know what they expect me to do. Run and hide or what? I have to go on doing my thing. As it's happened, some of the most vociferous people like Nikki Giovanni, who obviously with a name like that comes out of some kind of white background, was death on this two or three years ago. But she's not now. So, I think things pass.

I've been to some places like the Caribbean, for example, where black people wouldn't look at me twice until my wife came up beside me, probably saying, "Oh, that cat's got a white wife. He must be something special." Then they'll start relating to me. The whole thing is really so screwed up and sick that I just can't be involved. I'm forty-six or forty-seven and I've got a lot of things to do. I just can't be bothered with all that silly bullshitting. As far as I'm concerned, that's really what it is. Suppose I took my wife out, shot her, and I said, "Okay, I'm free. Now one of you babes marry me." Maybe I'll get a lot of offers now 'cause I'm what they call a successful writer. But the times I went through with my first wife when I was sitting down there writing–Oh Lord!–and even after that with the girlfriends I had who were black and a number of white girlfriends: "You're a writer! How are we going to live?" And that just sort of took care of that. There you are on interracial marriages. That's my view.

Cash: One friend of mine disliked *The Man Who Cried I Am* mainly because of the mixture of realism, particularly your using characters who were such close parallels to actual people.
Williams: I really don't know what he was complaining about. It seems more and more fiction is written this way in any case, the roman à clef. I'd have to ask him if he raised the same objections to William Styron's *Nat*

Turner, which is quite baldly and incorrectly based on a black hero. I find truth is more real than fiction. But you can't always present the truth as the truth, so you have no choice but to present it as fiction.

Cash: Yes, Alain Robbe-Grillet makes that same point. You mentioned in your books some of the difficulties the black writer faces. Is it the black writer's duty to write black? That is, to write about his race and try to contribute some way through that writing?

Williams: I think the black writer has two functions of equal importance. One is that given this time and its processes, he really has to deal with and for his people. He has to become an educator, a teacher, a storyteller, a satirist, any vehicle that will help make his people aware of their positions. At the same time, he's also bound to become an expert in his craft: writing a novel, writing poetry, what have you. The most important thing is the message. I would like to feel that the better the craft, the smoother the message comes out. A clumsy vehicle delivers a clumsy message. That's what black writing should be about. Also, to the extent that the American novel form has thus far served us so poorly in terms of how we appear in them, as they're written by whites, we really ought to try to experiment with the novel form. Turn it around. Find something else that we can do either to advance it so that a novel written by Norman Mailer will be so outdated that he'll have to sit down and write like us.

Cash: Is there a distinguishing element about black fiction? I was once asked is there such a thing as black literature, as a genre. When one reads a novel by say Alan Paton, what's to make that distinguishable from, say, a novel by Richard Wright? Can one not get the same aesthetic appreciation from John Howard Griffin's experiment as from another by a black author?

Williams: Well, I think that's a little complicated to answer. There is a black literature simply because white critics have demanded that black literature exist—not only the critics, the college systems have done this. An instructor will teach a course in the black novel while he really should be dealing with a course in the American novel with black authors. Hell, Chester Himes and Richard Wright were contemporaries of Hemingway. John O. Killens is a contemporary of Norman Mailer, so is Jimmy Baldwin, so am I. But the insistence is on teaching these writers in isolation. This may turn out to be a pretty big boomerang: a boomerang in the sense that if maybe you've got five or six black authors, or maybe you go back like Saunders Redding did and you get a whole spectrum, what happens is that the kids who know nothing about black writers say, "My God, I haven't even heard of some of these guys." Out of a course like that somebody might ask about other black writers. You name ten or twelve and after a while they're going to start believing some of the things that we say about censorship and how difficult it is or was for black writers to get published. Then you have to really start to worry about why this is so. The student may think, "Last year I couldn't believe there was one single black writer in all of American history. This year I'm assigned to read an eight hundred page book that's filled with nothing but niggers. What's going on?" It's crazy.

To the extent that you're dealing with Alan Paton's writings or John Howard Griffin's—and as much as I despise the man, I suppose some people would want to put William Faulkner in the same group—the presence of works like theirs sort of makes it truthful what we used to say years ago before we were deeply involved in the revolution and dealing really only with black people; that is, we're dealing with a universality. And it may be black but it's still universal. When a guy like Paton sets out to write or Griffin or Bernard Malamud in his new book in which the black character is very badly done, aren't those guys saying once they attack a subject like that that there must be some humanity in it, some validity in it which makes what we've been saying all along to be quite truthful? So, if black literature exists, there's going to be a boomerang, and it's more than black literature.

Cash: Do you think we'll also have a backlash in or against black studies?
Williams: There is today a gathering effort on the part of some of the establishment to curtail, contain, and perhaps, eliminate black studies. That's the backlash, but I do believe that black studies will improve and last, perhaps, in better forms than those now in existence. Then, there are rumors now in New York that black writing is finished. I don't know. It's probably true since more writing is handled in New York as a commodity in any case. It may be true that people have had it with this package. I know that book salesmen say one thing in New York, but when they're out on the road, they do something else altogether. I've always felt that the time would come when the doors would swing closed on this great surge of black literature. I still think it might, but I don't think it's going to close as tightly as it did against the so-called Harlem Renaissance. There're many more people involved now. There are more white editors who are trying to perceive this literature as being more than just a commodity. There are a few black editors, none of whom are really top notch, but maybe they'll get there. The presence of some black editors offers a little bit of insurance—not much, but more so than ten years

ago. Some of it will be cut back. Quite frankly, if I can speak as a man who has some degree of pride in his craft or skill, I think some of it should be cut back. Because they're so busy hustling black writers as a commodity, they're really publishing a lot of shit. Black people are not fools, you know. They say, well Jesus Christ, the time is here now. I'm going to write me forty-five poems, and the first one will be called "White Cunt." I've seen poems like this. The next will be called "Off the Pig." And the third one will be called "Charlie I'm Going to Kick Your Ass." They send them in, and they're published. It's really laughable but in the long run detrimental not only to the masses of black people who are just as conservative as the masses of white people and don't want to read that stuff—it's detrimental to the black writer who's done this because he thinks he's produced a work of art, a skillful work, when in reality he's done no such thing. He's invested very little time or energy in studying his craft. When I say studying his craft, the only way you can study writing is to read, read, read. A lot of these kids don't want to read, and they wind up short all the time.

Cash: Commercialism. I wonder about this, and I'll just muse a while then you can give me your comments. Your paperback novels have a black man and a white woman on the cover as if that's going to be the crux of the novel, but it's a commercial technique. I wonder what this commercialism does to the whole movement of black interests. Then, too, I was watching television the other day and saw some Chicanos wearing large sombreros and decked out in Mexican garb. It was quite commercialized. There are people who sell these things and make profit out of this desire to maintain one's heritage. What do you make of all this?

Williams: One of the things I noticed with some sadness while walking around Albuquerque this morning was that everybody's making money off the Indians and the old Spanish thing except the Indians and Mexicans.

Let's start first with the soft cover jackets. You don't have any control over that. You hope that they will be tasteful. They never are. I wrote to Pocket Books when they brought out three books with a black guy and white woman on the cover. I wrote to the editor. I said, this is really bullshitty because I think what you're doing is turning off buyers. This is what went in 1950. It's not going now. I never heard from them. It shows the kind of racist nature that editors are still involved with. This is what's going to sell books. We'll put this darkie up here with this blond. I don't think that a hell of a lot of black people are buying books with jackets like that anymore. What this also means is that they don't give a damn about black readers. That kind of commercialism would be bad if it were only a question of money. As I say, it's racism as well, which is worse. I bought an Afro pick. I thought it was wood. It was made of plastic. Macy's now sells dashikis. And I'll bet you ten to one, the biggest company putting out Afro wigs is white. But what do you do? You stop wearing dashikis? You stop wearing wigs, or you stop wearing Afros? Then who's going to manufacture the combs?

Cash: Or the shirts?

Williams: If there's one thing black people need to understand about this man, and most black people don't, it's that anything that comes down the pike is saleable. If you're involved with a man who will sell other people, you know goddamn well he'll sell anything. Maybe black people know this in some small distant part of their souls, but they sure act like they never heard of it before.

I came out here for an inclusive fee of six hundred bucks. I thought there would be a real black group here. Well, I find that it's very small, but I'll get a chance to see whoever is in it tomorrow. By the time I get through with all this, I'll probably clear about $150. But we've got guys who won't leave Newark or Chicago for less than $700, $800, or $1,000 clear to talk about the black revolution to a lot of white folks. We were talking earlier about being so depressed with the things that are going on. Those guys are just as repetitious and greedy as the man is. So it makes very little point for them to stand up and talk about how bad this man is when they are probably worse than he is or, at least, just as bad.

Cash: I would like to know something about your early life.

Williams: I was the oldest of four living children. I've got a brother and two sisters. I went to public schools in Syracuse: Washington Irving grade school, Madison Junior High. I went to both Central High School, where I played football, basketball, ran track, and Vocational High School. I didn't graduate from high school before going into the service. I was in the Navy for three years, and I came out and I finished.

Cash: What year was it that you went in?

Williams: That was 1943. I came out of the Navy in '46, January, I think. I was in for just about three years. Finished high school that year and went to college that year. It was a very curious thing. I got married that year too. I did a lot of things that year. Years later I had a discussion with my ex-wife about . . . I don't know how it came up, but I wanted to tell the boys that I hadn't finished high school before I was twenty-one. But for some reason, she was pretty shocked at this. I said, what's wrong with that? I don't know if she had implanted some kind of groovy image about how smooth things were. So anyhow I told them. They said, okay, fine. I wanted them to know so they wouldn't have any misconceptions about the kind of life I had as a young man, as a teenager. It was rough sometimes, and sometimes it wasn't. I went to work sometimes; I went to school sometimes—had a lot of friends, many of whom I still have.

Anyhow, my wife and I were married. I was going to school and raising a family. Greg was born in the next year, '47 or '48. I was going to school, working part-time, and we were living mainly on the GI bill and my part-time work which carried me into the foundries sometimes. Worked as a hospital orderly. A lot of jobs. Things you do to keep body and soul together. We broke up in '53 or '54 and divorced a couple of years later. I lived in California for a while. I worked for a black insurance company, which was an experience. I came back to New York City so I could be close to the kids, got a job in a vanity publishing house. This was the setting for *The Angry Ones*. I worked there for about a year and was writing *The Angry Ones* at that time. I asked for a raise the next year, and the man said, you're fired.

I published a weekly newspaper, an 8½ x 11 newsletter called the *Negro Market Newsletter*. I'd also done some publicity and public relations in Syracuse on a part-time basis and in California for NBC and CBS. So I thought I was knowledgeable enough to start a paper that would be for white advertising and public relations agencies dealing with the Negro market, which everybody was talking about at that time. I would gather the news, write it, lay it out, take it to the printer, pick it up, fold it, and mail it every week. My big allies at that time were the black guys who were Negro market specialists within those agencies. I thought this, but as it happened, they turned out to be the very people who killed it because they thought it was too good. After all, they were doing what I was doing. If this newspaper kept going around, they wouldn't have any jobs. So they didn't take the subscriptions they promised to and a few other things like that. Then I was really on my ass for a while because this thing really hadn't made any money, and I was living on unemployment which at that time was $36 a week; my room rent was $20. I made out, I mean, I lived. I survived. There were times I got odd jobs that brought in a little money. I stayed with friends on two occasions. I just sort of fell into things: an advertising agency job, an assistant to a book publisher who was a psychopath; then I had managed to save a little money so I went to Spain for a while. Came back and was involved in doing a lot of radio work for a station in New York. The year I came home from Europe *The Angry Ones* was published. Then I did *Night Song* and *Sissie*. I worked on these together. *Night Song* was finished first, and I got the contract with Farrar, Straus and Giroux plus I'd done another book that came out when *Sissie* came out in '63, a book on Africa for children. So, I had a little money. It wasn't a lot, but people would call on me to do reviews. I was also limping along doing magazine articles. Then in 1963 *Holiday Magazine* asked me to do what John Steinbeck had done in his book *Travels with Charley*, which resulted from his driving around the country. He did that in '60, I think. Now they wanted a black man to do it and I did. *Holiday* was the best magazine in the country at that time. It was like a real shot for whatever career I thought I was into. I did that and it was a pretty big success. That's really been the difference. And like they say, here I am.

Cash: Between '63 and '67, did you do further European travelling?
Williams: Yes. I went on a very long jaunt in early '64 right after I finished the *Holiday* piece. I worked on the second draft while I was travelling through Europe, Israel, and Africa. As a matter of fact, I sent the second draft back from Addis Ababa. I guess I was away for six or seven months that time, most of it in Africa. I got back to the US in '64 and went back to Africa in '65 to do a television show. Later in '65 I married again. We spent a year in Europe, mostly in Spain and Amsterdam. I think I've been back three times since then.

Cash: Seems like the experiences of Max and Harry in *The Man Who Cried I Am* parallel your own.
Williams: Actually I could see the times when Max was like myself because I had done some work for *Newsweek* in Africa with a specific job in mind to look for a desk in West Africa. I had been down to the Congo and a few other places. I had covered part of the Ethiopian-Somali war for *Newsweek*. But in the main, Chester Himes was my Max. His was the figure I held up pretty much.

Cash: Many critiques of *The Man Who Cried I Am* focus on the King Alfred plan. I think a fascination with that conclusion alone really cheats the rest of the novel and its art.
Williams: I agree with you completely. Whenever I go someplace, that's the only thing people ask me about. It's getting awful.

Cash: I have run out of questions. Is there anything else you'd like to mention?

Williams: I want you to read these last two chapters of this new novel [*Captain Blackman*]. This is structured kind of strange, and it uses a lot of documentary material. Before each section there is a quote which is for real or a documentary sentence. It tells you what the next part is going to be about. This section is about the murder of two hundred black soldiers during World War II by the American army.

I seem to be publishing a number of books with angry in the title. Today I wouldn't have to take that kind of crap from publishers. *My* title for *The Angry Ones* was *One for New York.* As you know, this was published as a soft cover original. If it hadn't been published at that time I probably would have tried to forget about writing all together. It had been written five years earlier, and I was really close to hanging up the whole business. So when they said they wanted to make the title something that's going to grab people, I was powerless to stop it. I did a paperback anthology that was called *The Angry Black.* Now again this was after I published *Night Song* and *Sissie.* In this field, power is relative, you see. Even at that point I didn't have the power to say, no, you aren't going to use that because I'm not dealing with anger here; I'm dealing with something else. But the publisher felt he could sell books if he had anger in the title. So that particular edition went into a hard cover edition with another publisher who felt that there should be some consistency between editions. Then New American Library republished an edition in soft cover of the same damn book with very few additions and *angry* was in the title again. I never believe in tipping my hand that way. That's one thing if you're black you learn. If you're angry, control it until you're in a situation where you can really do something about it.

We were talking about black musicians and about Eagle before. Eagle, as you may not know, is really based on Charlie Parker, who was one of the most electric images in modern jazz. I had previously published an article on Charlie Parker and had planned to do a nonfictional book on him. I had a lot of information at my disposal. Eagle was, as I say, based on the Charlie Parker figure.

Returning to *Captain Blackman* I wanted originally to do it as a nonfictional book, but I kept running into stone walls. I couldn't raise the magazine money to travel to places where I wanted to go to get the material. I'm talking about contemporary material. The historical material I had. Wherever I went, I did go to two or three army bases in America, I had those captains and lieutenants hanging on my shoulders. Magazines were not interested in a black man's view of black people in the army. They only wanted the story told by a white guy. A few years ago everybody was talking about this new democracy in the army. This was a white man's interpretation of what was going on. It turns out to have been false. If I had been able to raise the money to do those pieces, the first places I would have gone to would have been the stockades. That's where the truth always is—in the jails. Maybe my reputation preceded me. Not only was I not able to raise the money, but I had difficulty in getting clearance from the Pentagon to make the trip to Vietnam, Thailand, and places like that. So, I decided to do it as a novel just to show that what I wanted to say, I wanted to say badly enough to do it in one form or another.

Interview 2

In mid-May 1972, John A. Williams and I met in New York. On my way to Syracuse University to study his manuscripts, I stopped off in New York City for an informal chat and a copy of *Captain Blackman*, then just released. Almost a month later I returned to the City and on Friday, June 9, 1972, Mr. Williams, his son Dennis, Mrs. Gloria Dickinson—a New Jersey teacher interested in the author's political thoughts—and myself spent most of the day discussing Williams's writings. My questions centered on *Captain Blackman* since it was the most recent work.

Cash: *Captain Blackman* brought to mind Arna Bontemps's *Black Thunder* (1936), an account of Gabriel's revolt in 1880. I wonder if you were inspired by that work.
Williams: No, I don't think so. I read it about three years before, at the time of the Styron controversy [a reference to several black critics' reaction to William Styron's *The Confessions of Nat Turner*], and I was struck by what happened when a white man did an account of a slave revolt and the attendant publicity and what happened when Bontemps's book was reissued. It was reissued to almost a complete silence. It didn't influence me in any way.

Cash: Another comment relating to *Black Thunder*, you wrote in John Henrik Clarke's *William Styron's Nat Turner*, and I quote, "If, however, *Black Thunder* were to be published tomorrow, it would not have the slightest chance of making critics and readers reconsider their thoughts on history as it involved slaves." What, then, do you expect *Captain Blackman* will do as it involved black history?

Williams: I don't know what it's going to do. I know what I wanted to do and that was again to give black readers some of the history they haven't had. The reaction of my publisher to that book was very strange. A lot of the white editors, male white editors, really liked it. But almost to a man, and I've heard this outside that particular circle, what they talk about is that touching—I'm quoting now—scene between Abraham and the Indian. They don't talk about the slaughter of black troops in Italy or anything else. And as I haven't read any reviews, I don't know what the reviewers are saying or what sections they're dealing with. But it's like they really don't want to deal with the basic premise of the book, which I hope will come through with the young black readers.

Cash: I suppose the point I was trying to make is if you felt that should *Black Thunder* be re-released today it might have very little chance of affecting the readers' views on the position of slaves in history, why should you be more optimistic with your book and its affecting the black soldiers' place in history?

Williams: But, there's a difference. There's a confluence of events here. One is that as long as Bontemps has been around, he hasn't gained, whichever way you want to look at it, the notoriety or the publicity that I've got. So I think there'd be a greater tendency on the part of younger people to read a book that I had done than to read something that Bontemps had done. I don't mean to belittle Bontemps at all. He's a prolific writer who possesses an amazing depth that some young black writers will never be able to match. He deserves far, far more than he's received at the hands of readers and critics alike. And if he's bitter about his treatment or lack of it, he certainly doesn't show it. Probably more due to my book on King than to *The Man Who Cried I Am*, I think a few more people read me, for perhaps the wrong reasons. I don't know. Furthermore, although still small given the population ratio, the black reading public is infinitely larger today than it was in 1936 or '37 when *Black Thunder* was originally published. When it was re-released at the time Styron's book came out, one could feel that it was to shoot Styron down or at least to make critics draw comparisons. But the critics having done their hoopdedoos over Nat Turner as drawn by Styron, weren't about to take back what they said. In other words, they bent over backwards to ignore it—*Black Thunder*—and did it very well. I had no such experience.

Cash: In returning to Henrik Clarke's book of criticism on *Nat Turner,* in your essay there you criticize Styron for not being "both a novelist and a historian." Did you set out to show him how it should be done?

Williams: No, I didn't set out to teach anybody lessons. I'd set something for myself, and that is—I don't know if we've talked about this, but I don't like to write the same book over and over again. For me writing novels is sort of like playing jazz, you improvise, and you try to do new things, extend yourself more than you have with the previous book. That's all I was trying to do. If he happens to learn anything from it, so much the better.

Cash: But you would say you've capitalized on the mistakes you thought Styron made?

Williams: I don't know. I think his basic fault was to take what was historically accurate and ignore it. All I've done is to take what is historically accurate and put it on a fictional basis. I happen to think that if you're going to write historical fiction, that's the only way to do it.

Cash: Well, going specifically to *Captain Blackman,* you have characters in there with special or particular names like Abraham and Gideon and Little David, all biblical names from the Old Testament. Did you have some significance behind that selection?

Williams: The Abraham and Ishmael thing is self-explanatory. Little David in one of the earlier drafts was to be a regimental bugler. I think in the later drafts I just forgot that. But, I think also I was working sort of subconsciously along the lines of what would have been a guy's name given that time and place in history.

Cash: That brings me to Mimosa. What about that name?

Williams: In an earlier draft there was an explanatory note. Mimosa is a flower that when you touch it, it closes up.

Cash: A touch-me-not.

Williams: Right. And in a later draft that just got lost, but I wanted some essence of that for people who know flowers to sort of carry on.

Cash: That's the association I made.

Williams: Well, you know flowers. I'm sure a lot of people might wonder. But then I do things with that name in different times, like Osa and Mims. As you also noticed, perhaps, a lot of the names carry throughout history.

The same guys who serve in the Vietnam company serve in other companies and so on.

Cash: Mimosa is illiterate, a slave, and she is raped by white soldiers the first time she appears. The second time she is a student at Drake, and the last time she is in the foreign service in Saigon and has lots of power and influence. So, from the first time you meet Mimosa to the last, she progresses both career-wise and, of course, in physique. She's described in the beginning as being small, but the last time you see her the word you use is *Amazonian.* And one soldier reflects that Mimosa and Blackman go together as they're both big in stature. What did you intend the reader to make of this progression of Mimosa through time, through history? Was this some commentary, maybe, on the black woman?

Williams: Yes, that was pretty subconscious. All I was trying to do was fit her as a viable black woman into each situation in which she appears: the World War I thing, the World War II thing, and the Vietnam thing. I don't think any more than that, but when you were asking the question I said to myself, wow, maybe on a subconscious level, I was doing all those things.

Cash: Woodcock, a medic, is called Newblack because of his light skin. One character notes that he would not be recognizable as black if it weren't for his Afro.

Williams: I don't think I meant that simply to mean because he was fair. Mostly it's been my observation that the most militant black folks—and maybe this is a contradiction in terms of what I have to say—tend to be fair, and I find that they have the biggest Afros and so on. But I think I must have been thinking of that with Woodcock. And also by Newblack I meant not only the physical arrangement of things but people who seem to have just recently become conscious of the fact that they are black.

Cash: Woodcock is the same person who in the end pulls off the coup. As Alain Locke pronounced the New Negro in the twenties, are you pronouncing the lighter-skinned blacks like Woodcock as New Blacks, a possible strategic weapon in the struggle?

Williams: I think that really is the indication of what I was trying to do with Woodcock. That's why I set up that arrangement whereby Blackman says if you didn't have such nappy hair, you'd be white. That was the precise arrangement. Instead of these people getting one of these big, bushy Afros, they ought to go back and get conks and be like the man and plant some bombs and things.

Cash: You suggested Africa as a possible place for blacks to prepare themselves for guerilla warfare. Would not your suggestion, if taken seriously by blacks, also be a warning for whites, who may be in a position to repress black people?

Williams: Okay. But my feeling is that we tend to underestimate the ability of the white man to know what's going on. I think he knows exactly what's going on. The other thing is that in spite of the rhetoric about Africa and the possibility about moving to Africa and so on, I really can't see that happening immediately for two reasons: I think black Americans are still too much American. The other reason is that in order for this really to work black African leaders have to take the initiative and say we need, for example, five hundred teachers, and set up contractural deals so that five hundred black teachers can go to Africa and teach. I know of no such deal that's going on. That's only an example. There's a need for engineers, communications experts, and what have you. These things have not been dealt with in terms that could be considered beneficial to us. So the failure on the part of African leaders and the failure—not the failure but the sort of tacit acknowledgment that no matter how bad the situation is in America, black Americans are still Americans—I think that's what's holding us up.

Cash: There is a confrontation between the blacks and the Indians in which the Indians chide the black man for joining the white soldiers against the Indians while blacks would not fight the white man. No doubt you see this as another one of those ironies of history?

Williams: Yes, it is essentially correct. But there must somewhere be— they're starting to come out now—records of the number of blacks who fought with the Seminoles, when Jackson finally went in there and tried to massacre everybody. It is, I suppose, one of the more pathetic moments in our history. Black folks were used. You want a job; you want to get in off the street. We'll put you out here in the plains, and you can kill Indians or they can kill you. And, it worked out fairly well.

Cash: I was fascinated by the way you combined the fact and the fiction and how the novel seems to have an aura of the surreal. What do you think about the conclusion? Some reviewers called it a horrifying and shocking ending. Do you think that ending might detract from the book on the one hand or it might increase the sales of the book?

Williams: I hadn't thought about it. I believe in books that have solid endings, that say something, you know. I suffer from criticism of being melodramatic because of that. The end of the novel is the end of the novel, not on page twenty-five or whatever. My editor had some pressure from the publishers for me to either drop the last section or set it apart because it was tied in to the chapter before. I said, "That's ridiculous. I'm not dropping it. If you want me to put in another section or chapter, I'll do that." And we both agreed that it'd make the book stronger just by standing alone, and people who raised protest obviously hadn't anticipated that at all. But there it is, all by itself, instead of merging. Additionally, I don't know how you could handle it any other way in a book like that. I'd not, certainly, try anything so trite as to have an uprising in Vietnam. You just fly over and napalm everybody—either that or the kinds of things that are going on at these army bases. No, I just felt it had to be big and involving the whole military political situation, and you get into that if you start talking about missile sites and sub-sea floor sites and crap like that. They don't think niggers know anything about that—really don't.

Cash: To get to a point that's a little off from the book but still relevant, I think; you often mention that you don't review the reviews. Do you find yourself, then, paying any more or less attention to critiques, probably verbal, that might come from your immediate family, like your wife and sons?
Williams: I can't help but pay attention. The ones that come from the family are usually favorable, so I just take my little pat on the back and that's that. But people will call and say, "Gee, that was a great review" and things like that so that by osmosis, pretty much, you get some ideas of what these reviews are all about without reading them specifically yourself. And, perhaps, you can pick up nuances yourself which other people haven't. Then it depends on whether you know the reviewer. Like, take the first review that came in which Lori [his wife] read; that critic is always calling me paranoid so that the turn of his review, judging from Lori's response, was more or less expected. And what sort of supports my idea of not reading these damned things is that these people are so damned consistent. There're no surprises in any of them.

Cash: Would you object, therefore, to my getting Dennis's [his second son] reaction to *Captain Blackman*?
Williams: No. I wanted the book to be very important to him because he's got a very low draft number, and if he wasn't in school his ass would have been gone.

Cash: [Taking Dennis aside (he's now a senior at Cornell), I asked him the following question.] What do you think of *Captain Blackman*?

Dennis: I liked it. I think it came off pretty well. It's not a safe book by any standards. Whereas *The Man Who Cried I Am* was politically unsafe, of course, literarily it was on better ground. But *Captain Blackman* is politically even more unsafe because it deals with the whole course of history. It's even, in a sense, more radical. And literarily it's also radical because of the techniques used and everything. It's very touchy the way it's going to work out, and the whole dream thing—the going back into the past—I stopped trying to make it make sense and just let it go because the dream thing is plausible, I guess. But it really is sort of not necessary; I know he was telling me once how he was trying to work out the technique. What he was going to do was use ghosts. Characters that go through time were going to be treated as ghosts. That seems pretty good too. It's sort of like once Blackman's consciousness first goes back and these alter egos are created, they sort of have a life of their own, for they seem to exist for long periods of time in the past. I think there are about six or seven different Blackmans. Another thing I was thinking about the other day, the dialogue is really good, like in the Cadences sections. For example, you have men sitting around the conference tables in the war rooms making the plans. Some of the dialogue was based, I suppose, on records, and documents and transcripts. I don't know how actual all the dialogue is supposed to be. It's the kind of thing that some unbelievers might consider just pure fantasy or fiction. Then the idea of this dialogue of American and European generals sitting around and talking about what to do with the blacks—you know, I'm just sure it's going to blow a lot of people's minds. And this kind of thing is not funny. As I've said, books of this type might be satirical, expected to be tongue-in-cheek or something like that, but it's absolutely serious. It's not meant to be taken as fantasy or as a joke. And whether people believe the dialogue to be fact or fiction really does not make that much difference to the overall effect of the story. The ending, by the way, adds a little extra punch, summarizes everything, and gives a little hope too.

There are times when it seems that he wanted certain facts put in there, and you can see he's going to get them in one way or another. You can see how things are manipulated—battles, periods of war—to get to certain instances. I guess the whole World War II thing is concentrated on Tombolo where the white soldiers wipe out the black soldiers in the swamps. Again by that point, you've had enough of battles that you really don't care if the whole history of the war focuses on that specific. The flow of the book, though—it comes off.

Cash: [Returning to Williams] In *This Is My Country Too*, you referred to—in an interview with Arthur Schlesinger Jr.—you referred to him as a "writer-historian," and you call yourself a "writer," merely. Don't you think that now you deserve the twin title also?
Williams: Damn right! [laughs]

The Art of John A. Williams

John O'Brien / 1971

Reprinted from *The American Scholar*, Volume 42, No. 3, Summer 1973. Copyright © 1973 by the Phi Beta Kappa Society.

John A. Williams was born in Jackson, Mississippi, in 1925 and spent his youth in Syracuse, New York. Although he did not publish his first novel until he was thirty-five, his last twelve years have been prolific: he has written five more novels, a biography of Richard Wright, a journal of his travels through America in 1963, and a controversial book on Martin Luther King, and has edited several other books.

Williams's critical reception, although wide, has been an imbalanced one. His reviewers point to his concern with racial, social, and political themes in his work while they overlook the philosophical and psychological structures that give meaning to those themes. For instance, the situation of blacks in America supplied Williams with the perfect metaphor for studying the nature and influence of history and for testing whether man, either as an individual or as a race, can transcend the nightmarish role that history has fashioned for him. But his critics have not granted him this kind of concern nor have they looked at his attempts to explain the unique psychological insights he has gained in studying the effects of racism nor have they investigated the existential framework in which he writes. As Williams points out, these matters are discussed only in relation to white writers.

The interview was conducted on a bright, chilly day in early November 1971. We talked without interruption for almost two hours. As his remarks in the interview make clear, Williams approaches critics with caution. He speaks in a low, subdued voice and lets his words carry the weight of his meaning. I began the interview by asking him about his article, "The Literary Ghetto," in which he attacked critics and publishers for their continued, although more subtle, racist treatment of black writers.

John O'Brien: You said in an article that appeared in the *Saturday Review* that you wished for once that you could read a review of a novel by a black writer in which it wasn't compared only to novels by other black writers. Does such treatment of black writers have its roots in racism?
John A. Williams: I think it's racism and I think it's something that black writers have dealt with, with accommodating behavior for several years, and we still do. The fact is that when you can point out the elements of racism in the business as I did in that article, it doesn't make a goddamn bit of difference. They still do it. On the soft cover of *The Man Who Cried I Am* it says, "The best novel about blacks since Ralph Ellison." That is defining the territory where black writers are allowed to roam. But you know, I'm a contemporary of Styron, Mailer, and Bruce J. Friedman. Chester Himes and Richard Wright were contemporaries of Hemingway, toward his later years. And Ellison. But we never somehow get into the area where we're compared with white contemporaries. It's always with black contemporaries. What else can you say, but that it is racism?

O'Brien: The point of the article then was that comparisons should be made along literary rather than racial lines?
Williams: Well, yes, sure . . . I'd like for somebody to begin stacking up *Native Son* with some of Frank Norris's stuff, and I'd like to see Chester Himes stacked up to some of these detective-story writers and some of the fiction writers who are still writing fiction from his generation. I'd like to see how I'd stack up against Styron and others who are my contemporaries. Now this doesn't mean that I'm seeking to divest myself of my identity, but I think that one of the reasons why these comparisons are not made in many cases is that black writers would come out better. It's sort of like with Jack Johnson, the heavyweight champion. You can't have those black guys winning at everything, or even looking as though they could possibly win. That's bad business. Things begin to happen to the economic structure of the literary world.

O'Brien: Do you think that black writers are doing things to the form of the American novel that simply are not understood by readers and critics?
Williams: In terms of form itself, the novel is changing. I think that black writers are initiating, if not forcing, a kind of change from the "straight ahead" American novel, vis-à-vis Hemingway and Fitzgerald. There's an inclination to do to the novel what Charlie Parker did to jazz. I don't know

whether you remember this period in jazz music that is called "bop" where the method was to take . . . well, you could take any tune that was standard, say "Stardust," for example. They would go through it once and then would come through again with all their improvisations so that it was only recognizable in part. You knew where the players were at certain points in the music, and only by virtue of touching on those old standard parts in the second passage through did you realize that it was really "Stardust." That's the way it works. And I think that's what's happening to the novel. You see it in William Melvin Kelley's last book, *Dunford's Travels Everywheres,* which is not only an exercise in form but also an exercise in language. Ishmael Reed's books. George Lamming has a book which just came out called *Natives of My Person,* which is an allegory about the seventeenth-century English slave trade. I read novels like these and it's incredible. You're reading English, but it comes through in such a way that it doesn't seem like English; it comes through like Spanish, French . . . anything except what you're familiar with.

O'Brien: Is the difference between what these writers are doing and what white writers are doing mainly a literary one, or is there something else too?
Williams: I think that there is a difference in approach to "consciousness" between black and white writers. I don't think white writers have ever had to consciously or subconsciously concern themselves about real problems of life and survival. You can take Salinger's Holden Caulfield. The mentality that issues forth from books like that is that the evil is not within us. It's an outside thing, which perhaps has to be combated. But it's going to be combated on white horses by white knights in white suits of armor. There's no question about it. There's no concern expressed for the world that's not white. The difference with black writers is that their concern has been made extremely conscious, not only by their position in the literary world, by the editors and critics, but also by virtue of their awareness of what the situation is.

O'Brien: Then the black writer has been forced to be more concerned with social and political issues just because of his position in society?
Williams: I think *forced* is the right word. There are many, many black writers today, and in the Harlem Renaissance and even prior to that, who would have been happy to have had acceptance on the terms of being a writer. I think it's the critics who have made the decision for us, by boxing us into an area where our books have been labeled "protest." A very narrow pigeonhole. And I think it sort of deprived us of the ability to mirror through our

work all of humanity. So *forced* is a good word—forced in terms of our area being well defined, well drawn for us.

O'Brien: Do you think of yourself as belonging to a realistic tradition in fiction? Have you purposely avoided experimentation?

Williams: I suppose I am a realistic writer. I've been called a melodramatic writer, but I think that's only because I think the end of a novel should be at the ending of the book. Not on page sixty-two or page twenty-five. In terms of experimenting, I think that I've done some very radical things with form in *The Man Who Cried I Am* and in *Captain Blackman*, which had to be an experimental novel in order to hold the theme of the novel. What I try to do with novels is to deal in forms that are not standard, to improvise as jazz musicians do with their music so that a standard theme comes out looking brand new. This is all I try to do with a novel and, like those musicians, I am trying to do things with form that are not always immediately perceptible to most people.

O'Brien: Do you recall your first attempts at serious writing? How old were you? What kind of things were you writing?

Williams: I started writing when I was overseas in the Navy during the war, and it wasn't very good. It was mostly what one would call "free verse" poetry. I always had a feeling that I was capable of being a writer. I never felt that I was deluding myself by trying to be a writer. The problem with writing for me personally lay outside writing itself. It was considered an illness to be involved in the arts since in the black community there were no artists to speak of. One did not earn his keep by writing poetry or novels. That was out there in never-never-never land. What I really wanted to do was get a good job, work from nine-to-five or ten-to-four, and live in that fashion. But it became clear to me after several years that even so simple a thing as that was subject to stresses because of discrimination. It was only then that I turned to writing full time. Pretty much for the same reason James Baldwin did, to remain sane, to feel that one was really in touch with oneself, that you were not a ghost, but a functioning person capable of thinking and perceiving and feeling.

O'Brien: Have you gone through periods where you felt that you had said everything there was to say or periods where you felt that your writing was not accomplishing what you wanted it to?

Williams: I don't go through periods now when I think that I won't be able to write again because of some mental block. I do feel occasionally that I've said just about all I wanted to say, but after a few days that passes. I've also had the feeling that writing has not moved things as much as I wanted things to be moved, and perhaps there might be something else I could do that would get things done. To this extent I've considered quitting writing simply because it hasn't, for myself, produced the things I want to see produced, the things I feel must be produced within my lifetime. But you get past that feeling with the passage of time.

O'Brien: Have you observed any pattern in how ideas for novels come to you? Must you experience most of the things you write about?
Williams: No, I haven't observed any pattern. I've had some ideas for novels for several years without putting down a line and every time I think of these ideas I add something more. I don't believe in outlines; at least they've never worked for me. When I finally sit down to write, I'm off and running because I've had the material stored up for so long. I would prefer to experience certain things myself, but I know that's not absolutely necessary. I can project on the basis of my own experiences, the experiences of others, and the testimony of still other people.

O'Brien: Is any one part of a novel more difficult to write than another? Do you hit any lags, perhaps after you get the basic action down? Is there a kind of crisis point which, if you get past, you know that everything else will fall into place?
Williams: For me the first fifty pages of a novel is the hardest. This may be a psychological thing. After I hit fifty pages I know that I've got a novel. It's not that the conception of the novel is difficult for me. But by the end of the first fifty pages I've smoothed out the form and I've got the structure licked. Then I'm off from that point.

O'Brien: Could you describe your work habits? Where do you write? How much each day?
Williams: I work every day. The time can vary from three to five hours, with many, many breaks in between. If it's going well I'll work at night as well, up to maybe nine o'clock or so. I no longer feel that I have to have a certain kind of atmosphere. In fact I never felt that way. I've always prided myself on being able to write anywhere. And I guess I still can. I have no ritual to go through in order to prepare myself for writing. I sit down and I write,

although I have had periods when I have the urge to sharpen about two dozen pencils or polish shoes. It's not a ritual so much as it is giving myself time to think without being consciously aware of thinking of what I am going to deal with that morning, where I have to go back over the work I had done the day before, what it is I am going to repair or change or heighten.

O'Brien: Can you recall the circumstances in which you began working on *The Angry Ones*? Did you have any difficulty in finding a publisher for your first novel?

Williams: It was in some ways a very autobiographical novel. I felt very intensely about that book and about things that were happening to me at the time. I once rewrote the whole damn book in a day and a half at one sitting because there seemed to be the possibility of its being published by New American Library. The preliminary reports had been good, but after that day and a half of rewriting that book, it was turned down. It had been turned down by a number of publishers. What made me sit down and write the book in the first place was that I didn't have anything else to do. It was a question of holding on to my sanity, a question of writing down some of the things that had happened to me. Seeing those situations in print made me rather determined never to forget them. That gave me a new grip on life, feeling that there was a lot out there that I had to do.

O'Brien: Are you conscious of having been influenced by other writers?

Williams: Nobody has really influenced me. This is because I read without discrimination when I was a great deal younger. In terms of form, my single influence has been Malcolm Lowry in *Under the Volcano*. I tried to emulate him in *Sissie* and improve on what he did with the telescoping of time. But I think I did it much better in *The Man Who Cried I Am*.

O'Brien: What nonliterary influences have there been on your work?

Williams: I don't really know. I've read an awful lot of history. A great deal of it preancient history. I sometimes get very depressed because I know that all of this business is quite temporary. We become too self-important about our society, our crafts and skills, our families, and so on. I believe with some other people that human life on this planet goes in cycles. We're here for maybe ten, twenty, thirty thousand years. And then something happens, a cataclysm and the poles start sliding around, and it's all gone. Then you start evolving again. I suppose I'm one of the rare guys you'll talk to who believes this. Nonetheless, I'm here, and I'm sort of constrained to act in patterns that are normal for the time I live in. I suppose that happens so that you'll have some assurance of life existing even after a cataclysm. I don't know what you would call all this. I'm pessimistic about the progress that humans are going to make with each other within the time span that we have, how many hundreds or thousands of years that may be.

O'Brien: Do you think that music has influenced you?
Williams: I've always liked jazz and some classical music. If I had been from a well-to-do family when I was a child, I would have been a trumpeter. But when the time came to move on to a trumpet, we simply could not afford it. I haven't been too much for music lately. I don't know why, whether or not it has to do with work. You're too busy playing the baby's records. But I like music, and I always say, "We ought to play a stack of records on Saturday or Sunday." But we never do. Somehow I wind up watching football games, just like any other piece of stone on Sunday afternoon.

O'Brien: Have you felt the influence of Albert Camus?
Williams: Maybe. I don't really know. I just don't know. These are things I think about. I can't say I consciously move about as a devotee of any particular philosophy.

O'Brien: Which of your novels are you most pleased with?
Williams: Well, I guess that I keep changing novels because I do different things with each one. Out of two previously published novels my preference was for *Sissie*. That was before I wrote *The Man Who Cried I Am*. I felt that in that novel I said things better and with a vehicle that had infinitely more horsepower. In *Captain Blackman*, I think something different is taking place and I think that I brought that off well. So, I liked that too. Maybe when I am sixty or seventy years old I can look back and really see the differences and see which one I like. But now, things keep changing. I like *Sons of Darkness, Sons of Light*, least of all.

O'Brien: Why is that?
Williams: It's a potboiler. I just feel that it came too easily. It was one of those novels that I don't like very much, that I call a "straight ahead" novel. You start at A and wind up at Z and then you get off the train.

O'Brien: Has *The Man Who Cried I Am* had the most critical acclaim?
Williams: That is what I keep hearing. But I think I hear it for the wrong reasons. People keep talking about King Alfred. There were many other things

in that novel besides King Alfred, but all they talk about is King Alfred. I can't say that that pleases me too much, although I believe there exists such a plan as this. The acclaim has been political. I wouldn't mind so much if it was both political and literary. But the literary acclaim has been missing.

O'Brien: It's been suggested that some of the characters in *The Man Who Cried I Am* are paralleled by real-life figures, that Richard Wright is represented by one of the characters and yourself by another.
Williams: I think that there are elements that could be taken as the character of Richard Wright. Actually the character that everyone thinks is me, is only me partially. I had Chester Himes in mind.

O'Brien: Max and Harry in that novel are two authors who are forced into becoming politically conscious and active.
Williams: I think *political* is a big word, but I think I know what you mean. And you're right. They have been forced into this kind of political role. And when I say political role, what I'm talking about is a larger humanistic role. It's outside the scope of just putting books together. The thrust may be political, per se, involving what your government is doing, but it is also an involvement in what other people are doing. It's being concerned about people, somehow relating to them, even with all their personal problems. I like to think that important writers are without flaws in terms of how they deal with other people. I feel this and sometimes say to myself that this is very childish. I think that a man who is a writer, who is good with words, should have an obligation to be a good man in his day-to-day life. It would be nice if the writer did have the responsibility to be more humane with people. Unfortunately, we know that this isn't true. You can talk of Faulkner, or you can talk about Dostoevsky—bigots both.

O'Brien: Do you see certain similarities between the heroes in all your novels? Is it, essentially, the same hero?
Williams: Some people say that it's the same character in each book—that he goes through all the books. I think to a large extent they're different characters. If you wanted to be strict about it, you could say that literally they're the same character. If you wanted to be more strict about it, you could say that they are the same two characters. Steve's confidant is Obie. In *Night Song* the characters would be Keel and Eagle. In *Sissie* it's Ralph and his sister. In *The Man Who Cried I Am* it's Max and Harry. In *Sons of Darkness* the two actually are Hod and his girl. In *Captain Blackman* the protagonist runs throughout the story. He's one man. He is the person around whom

the whole story revolves, but there are other people who are pulled into the story as the story progresses. And they flush it out from a point of view that Captain Blackman could not possibly see it from. With two characters you can more fully develop a situation than you could with only one who would have to be babbling off at the mouth all of the time, or thinking all of the time, for the reader to get the complete story. I've always felt that I need two people to handle the dialogue, to move it, two people who know each other well. I find that too much narrative becomes a pain in the ass. You get on a roller coaster and start breaking out the flags. Dialogue is always better.

O'Brien: Do you see a progression in your heroes? In your first novel the hero is in search of a good job; in your most recent novel the hero starts a revolution.
Williams: Wait till you read the next one. [laughs]

O'Brien: Is there a difference between what Steve thinks is necessary to be human and what Eugene does?
Williams: I think so. Browning thinks in revolutionary terms out of the boredom and frustration of middle-class existence. And Steve, who hasn't had that, is thinking of getting where Browning is. He's not thinking about a revolution; he's thinking about three squares and a nine-to-five routine.

O'Brien: Most of your characters have a need for and are in search of love. If they find it, they are saved.
Williams: I believe in love, which means that I live in a society. I also believe that all things, revolutions included, begin with individuals and individual choices.

O'Brien: Then love is looked to as a kind of ultimate solution?
Williams: I don't see that anything else has worked. Not even money. And I think that love grows out of some kind of respect. Most people just don't understand it or the processes of it. It's the only thing that can work.

O'Brien: There seems to be a progression from the first novel, where money is thought to be a final solution, to the second novel, where love seems to take that place.
Williams: Well, yes, but that's in the realm of books. I think economically things were better in the second novel. Not much, but better. When you get to *Sissie*, of course, ostensibly, things are even better. You've got Ralph running around Europe . . . and, it's not necessarily true, but it seems that

anybody running around Europe must have the money to get back. He has some kind of economic status, however small. And as my own economic condition has improved, I think this has been matched by the conditions of the characters in my books. One of the books I'm working on now deals with a guy who has worked in a foundry for twenty-five years, but even so he owns a house in a fairly exclusive neighborhood. He's probably the only guy on the block who works with his hands. I spend a great deal of time in the opening chapter describing his kitchen and the car that he loves (a big four-hundred-horsepower job). You've got a black man who appears to be economically solvent, and perhaps he is. But he's still black, and what that really means is that he's never really secure.

O'Brien: The theme of racial assimilation was important in your first novel and perhaps not so important in some of the later ones. Did your views change?

Williams: I tell everybody that regardless of whatever "revolutionary move-ment" is now current, I think we've got assimilation and there is probably more of it, in spite of a necessary period of separatism. There's got to be integration. People are deluding themselves by saying that we won't have it. This particular neighborhood is sort of a post-Village neighborhood, and the interracial couples are fairly frequent. If you had time to walk around on a nicer day you'd see it. It's pretty incredible. And there's more of it now than there was ten or fifteen years ago. I think that there is a lot of talk going on about how little there is and how many people are opposed to it. I'm sure that certain so-called militants really mean it when they say they're opposed to it. But I've seen changes in the philosophy of Nikki Giovanni, who lives two blocks away from here. I've been over to her place a few times, and, you know, she was vigorously opposed to any kind of interracial marriage. I don't know what brought about the change, certainly not us [Williams and his wife] because we're not that close. But I see changes taking place. I had a run-in with Don Lee over this situation. In his review of *The Man Who Cried I Am*, he brought in my marriage on the tail end of it. . . . I told him I thought it was out of order. We almost came to pretty good blows there. We've since made peace.

O'Brien: Are you conscious of your usual treatment of white liberals in your novels? Without exception, I think, they wind up exploiting blacks.

Williams: I guess I'm pretty conscious of it, and I think that's pretty much the way things are. I can say this with some assurance since I do a lot of work in the white world. My editors are all very white; my agents have all been white. There are only a couple of black agents around, but I've never felt that I could go to an agent just because he was black. I'm not that crazy. An agent is an agent, just like a publisher is a publisher. It's a moneymaking proposition. But I've been, over a period of years, depressed about some of my white friends. I know white liberals very well. I've known white liberals, friends, who showed me the guns they brought in from Colorado or New Mexico. And I say, "What do you want that for?" "Well, just in case." "In case of what?" "Well, you know . . ." Everybody's worried about black people getting guns, but if they ever had a shakedown in some of the middle-class apartments around this city, it would be incredible. Absolutely. I don't want to be misleading here. I have many white friends whom I don't categorize as being liberal, conservative, or anything else. I try to deal with them as people, and I feel that they deal with me as a person. I don't think there is more that can be asked of a relationship across the races except mutual respect.

O'Brien: Racial guilt, which you discuss in your introduction to *Sissie*, is a recurring theme in your novels. Do you consider this one of your major themes?

Williams: It could very well be, and I have personally felt some of this, though to a lesser degree now. When you are the first one in your family in seven or eight generations to go to college at a great sacrifice to yourself and your family, there has to be some degree of guilt. But my older kid is now in graduate school and he's teaching and he's married. Number two is a junior at Cornell, so the pattern is started. Nobody is going to have to feel guilty about going to college, as silly as that was.

O'Brien: How can your characters escape from the enormous guilt they feel?

Williams: Well, I suppose if they are going to be my characters in my books, they relate to the idea that, with time, one feels less and less. I would imagine that . . . well, for example, the book I'm working on now. The foundry worker has a son who is at Columbia, and there's no sense of guilt there. All the guys his age have kids away at school. That's the thing to do now. I would suppose that the longer I live and the more I write, the less I feel personally. And this will be reflected in my characters.

O'Brien: Must your characters (I think here especially of the characters in *Sissie*) come to some understanding of themselves and their situation before they can be relieved of the guilt?

Williams: Yes, I think coming to an understanding of what happened gives the release, and understanding often comes with time. If you're dealing with a novel, you're restricted by time and space. So, you've got to set up certain things to make this happen.

O'Brien: You suggest in the preface to *Sissie* that the matriarchal system in America is a myth. Who invented the myth?
Williams: I think I say there that the white man did.

O'Brien: As a way of releasing himself from responsibility?
Williams: Well, I don't know whether it would be that, or that it would be something more simple. That is, it put the black male outside the activity in the scheme of things.

O'Brien: In *Sons of Darkness*, Dr. Jessup represented a certain kind of radicalism in the novel. Is the thrust of the novel away from Jessup's ideas for social change and toward Eugene Browning's?
Williams: Yes, because he's the kind of guy who's around today. It's sort of like Marcus Garvey whose back-to-Africa movement was very much applauded by southerners, the KKK guys. He could send his scouts to the South in cities where a strange black guy usually disappeared overnight, but Garvey didn't lose anybody. That's because he was working hand-in-hand with the KKK—not hand-in-hand, but at least they knew what he was doing and approved of it. Now Jessup is one of these guys who believes that he can make deals with the devil and come away unscorched. Browning just never had that spirit. Browning is the kind of activist-nonactivist that all of us would like to be, so that we can press a button and set things in motion without paying the consequences. In this sense, his thing is really a big daydream.

O'Brien: Browning thinks he can do this without incurring any guilt?
Williams: He would like to.

O'Brien: Is he becoming aware at the end of the novel of those consequences?
Williams: Of course. Yes.

O'Brien: Has your thinking or ideas changed since you first began writing fifteen years ago? Are you surprised when you look back to see that you were thinking one thing or another?

Williams: No, I'm not. I didn't know how things would change, but I always expect things to change. What I was writing about then was what I wanted to write about. What I write about now is what I want to write about now. I think that there have been moments when, perhaps with *Sons of Darkness, Sons of Light*, I gave in to the pressures around me and did a book on revolution. But I'm not sorry I did it. In the process of working it out I came to see pretty much the kind of things that would have to happen for any revolution to become a success and also the things that couldn't happen. In that book I was dealing with nine tunnels and bridges leading into Manhattan. Well, hell, since last spring when the bridge and tunnel workers had a strike, I discovered that there were something like thirty-four bridge-tunnel approaches to Manhattan. A hell of a revolutionary I'd make . . . if I thought I could seal off Manhattan at nine points, leaving twenty-five more wide open!

O'Brien: What have been some of the reactions to your book on Martin Luther King? Do you think that the book was misunderstood?
Williams: I don't read reviews of a book until they're out for a year. Once in a while my wife will insist that I read a particularly good or bad one. With the King book I was glad that I had made that rule. I read some of the reviews just recently. They were pretty bad. I think that the misunderstanding was willful. A lot of people wanted to misunderstand, wanted to accuse me of being a traitor, a panderer for the FBI. A lot of people jumped on me, a lot of people in the black community. I got beat pretty badly. I think that over the past fourteen months or so there's been a better reaction to the book than when it first came out. Again, time, you know. But I really took a beating on that. It wasn't that I didn't expect to. I just didn't anticipate the degree of ferocity. . . . There were a lot of people running around saying, "Well, he's finished as a writer. He'll never write again." You start asking yourself, "Is that really true? Am I finished as a writer?"

O'Brien: Why did you write the book?
Williams: I thought that it would be a good thing for the black community to understand how much we're at the mercy of the system. And, of course, nobody wanted to believe that we were that badly off or that we could be that easily used. That's really the answer to it. Not this year.

John A. Williams:
On *Captain Blackman*

Dick Strout / 1972

© Garrison Systems Radio Network. Courtesy of the Department of Rare Books, Special Collections and Preservation, University of Rochester River Campus Libraries.

Dick Strout: Now this is Dick Strout reporting from Hollywood. *Captain Blackman* is a controversial new novel from Doubleday by John A. Williams. The result of ten years' research, it outlines the role of the black man in every American conflict from the Revolutionary War to our present situation in Vietnam. Through the fictional character of Captain Blackman, a compilation of all black men who ever fought in an American war, we see the full scope of brutality and inhumanity that followed the black man throughout his wartime service and military life.

Prior to writing *Captain Blackman*, John Williams penned several other highly acclaimed works and was coeditor of the Afro-American journal *Amistad*. In a recent conversation with John Williams we discussed *Captain Blackman*. Generally, the book maintains a historic fictional framework rather than just tracing the black problems in times of war. The protagonist, Captain Blackman, is placed in various time periods that involved American conflict. Mr. Williams described his method of shifting his character from point to point.

John A. Williams: I just simply used a dream sequence, a hallucinatory sequence where the book opens in Vietnam. Captain Blackman is wounded, and he has been teaching in his company black military history. As he's transferred from the battle site back to where he's in hospital, he hallucinates about these wars that he has taught and in which he finds himself taking an active part with the men in his company. In these past wars, he and his men suffer the same wounds that they suffered actually in Vietnam.

DS: The research Mr. Williams conducted for *Captain Blackman* is truly astounding. He related how and where it began.

JAW: It started with some vague interest over a dozen years ago in the black soldiers in the plains wars following the Civil War. More and more information accrued to me in light of interests. I grew up in a town where there were a sizeable number of black veterans of World War I from the 369th Division. People who discovered I had this interest passed along various clippings to me, and by and large I accumulated a lot of material. I also had done some work myself in Italy, and when I was not in Italy I'd hired a researcher from Milan who did some work for me. I went to the war museum in Paris and dug up a great deal of information from there, the National Archives in Washington, and a lot of it on my own.

DS: Having noticed the extreme realism of the novel, we asked John if he had personally served in the military.

JAW: During World War II, I was in the Navy as a hospital corpsman. I was in the Pacific for two years. The army information—I'm sure a lot of people are going to ask me about army service. I had no army service whatsoever.

DS: In his research in government archives, Williams discovered several startling facts about the servicemen returning home after World War II.

JAW: The army apparently wanted to find out what was going to happen to its newly returned service population at the end of World War II. They wanted some information on the attitudes of its soldiers. They discovered that most of the soldiers felt that Hitler was right to have done what he did to the Jews, that he had a right to be the big man in Europe because he had brought the Germans so far. Most of the soldiers felt that after World War II the big problems were going to come from Negroes, Jews, and labor unions in that order. As it turns out, I suppose the problem is now consigned only to blacks. Labor unions and the Jewish population seem to have been not as much a thorn in anyone's side as most people thought. The idea of soldiers taking over the government was explored. A lot of the soldiers didn't think it was a good idea, but they were not sure. A minority of soldiers felt that they should take over the government. It was very strange, the research that was done and eventually produced but which never was publicized in this country. Yet, the books are available.

DS: In *Captain Blackman*, John shatters the myths centering on many of our past military heroes. He shows that their reputations where sound military decisions and fairness did not extend to the blacks under their command.

JAW: I think the lack of fairness stems from the way society itself dealt with black people, so that was merely carried over into the military. As to debunking the myths, it's always been my condition that when you have a mythological figure, when you go around behind him, he's in half cast. He's not completely dimensioned. This country is pretty much like Germany in that it insists on keeping records. In other places, let's take the Ancient Egyptians for example, if a succeeding pharaoh didn't like what the pharaoh before him had done, he chiseled them off the face of the mountain. We don't do that; we keep the records. If anybody's interested in this and a subject and is willing to do research, you can always find the material in some dusty, moldy corner. It's always there.

DS: And Williams contrasted the feelings of the black veterans of Vietnam with those of the black GIs returning from other American wars.
JAW: I think the difference is the changes that have taken place again within American society. It's very difficult to find yourself involved in a war ten thousand miles away while your relatives are in the war in Newark or Detroit or whatever. I remember reactions that I had as a kid during World War II—I guess I had only been in a couple of months or so—at the Detroit race riot. We were forever reading about the riots involving black soldiers and sailors out south. One was not—could not be—one hundred percent behind any war effort, no matter where they sent you.

I remember once traveling to several islands in search of a ship that I was assigned to. For some reason, which I later discovered, I never found the ship because I was a black corpsman. Black corpsmen were, even within the Navy, completely unheard of by most sailors. I was sent on little details with white outfits and very often shipped back to the OGU, Outgoing Unit center. Finally, I went in to the man in charge of this one day, and I said, "I don't want to serve with white troops." That was my reaction to the kinds of things that were going on then, and I'd imagine that it's intensified five thousand percent for young black guys who found themselves in Vietnam in a situation like it is back here.

DS: The conclusion of *Captain Blackman* is a kind of a reversed *Dr. Strangelove*, in which there is a complete takeover of the military structure.
JAW: Simply an ending in which certain people dismantle the military establishment, it being Captain Blackman's philosophy that if this is dismantled then the ability of people to turn the government around and all it means at this moment would be easy to do. The people who do this are black people, but they are black people who are fair enough to pass for white

and who do so as military men in key positions around the world in various nuclear-powered craft, sea and air, and missile silos, and things of this sort.

DS: Ladies and gentlemen, John A. Williams with an interesting insight into his most recent novel called *Captain Blackman*. This Doubleday publication is not only very informative but extremely entertaining as well, dealing as it does with the plight of the black American fighting man in novel form. This has been Dick Strout reporting from Hollywood.

Novelist in Motion: Interview with John A. Williams

Joseph T. Skerrett Jr. / 1973

From *Black World* 25.3 (January 1976), 58–67, 93–97. Reprinted by permission.

The interview took place on the afternoon of March 5, 1973, in the living room of Mr. Williams's Manhattan apartment. After introducing me to his wife, Mr. Williams settled us both comfortably in the Danish modern living room, while Mrs. Williams busied herself in the kitchen.

John Alfred Williams is a slight, wiry, dark-skinned man, rough of voice, casual of speech. We spoke briefly before beginning the interview. He was relaxed, but not disinterested, and was quite animated in some of his replies.

Interviewer: Mr. Williams, I'd like you to describe briefly your early years of education.
Williams: Early years of education. Well, I went to grade school—Washington Irving School in Syracuse, started kindergarten there. I went to Madison Junior High School and both Central High School and Blodgett Vocational High School. Took the same things that everybody else took because they only offered one course, an academic course. I didn't graduate high school until after World War II. I came back and I finished in a semester because I spent a lot of time working during those high school years. That pretty much was it. I was interested in art, but I couldn't paint worth a damn. I was terrible in math. I guess I did best in history, geography, and English, spelling . . . and I liked to read.

Interviewer: Did you conceive of writing as an activity in high school, or did that come later?

Williams: I think it came a little later, but a lot of the stuff I read sort of turned me on, I guess, subconsciously to the fact that it was something I probably could do.

Interviewer: Do you remember who they were? The writers you liked best at that time?

Williams: No, I just read without discrimination. I read everything I could get my hands on, and—because I read fairly fast—I could take more books out of the library than other kids in my class groups. I just read everything, had no taste whatsoever.

Interviewer: Was it fiction or poetry or drama?

Williams: Well, it was mostly fiction, some poetry, very little drama.

Interviewer: Was it limited to American stuff?

Williams: No, just whatever we had around the house, which wasn't much; whatever was in the school library that was recommended by the people in charge of the children's lit.

Interviewer: After you completed high school in Syracuse, you attended the university?

Williams: Yes.

Interviewer: What did you study there?

Williams: Well, I was in English and journalism. My folks thought that by virtue of having been a medic in the Navy I should become a doctor. They didn't realize the difference between just carrying a medical kit and some morphine syrettes and actually investing all that time doing medical study. And because we had no one in our family who had gone to college or had, in fact, finished high school, the kind of high school that was in existence when I went, nobody knew just what in the hell I *should* take. There was very little advice at home in terms of guidance *through* college or *into* college, so I just sort of found my own way, wasting a little time but not too much, and wound up mainly in English and journalism with an emphasis on radio journalism.

Interviewer: Was there a breaking point in terms of education where you changed from one to the other?

Williams: Not really, because, as you know, in most liberal arts the first two years are designed so you can fuck around until you find your own thing without having to . . . being put in a position of losing those hours of credits.

Interviewer: Did you take a degree?
Williams: Yes.

Interviewer: And after that?
Williams: After that I went into a master's program, up to six or nine hours before my GI Bill ran out.

Interviewer: Was this in Radio/TV or in English?
Williams: The graduate work was all in English. At that time they had instituted a television department to go with the radio department. The university—everybody—was going into TV, and all I can say is that the department was not happy to have black applicants in the TV department at that time.

Interviewer: Is that why you didn't do work in that area?
Williams: Yes.

Interviewer: Would you say that any of this academic study influenced your work, positively or negatively?
Williams: Yes, I think a great deal of it did positively. It turned me off with a lot of teachers because I thought the material that they handled could have been better presented, but when I did the work on my own, I became very much involved and read, of course, a lot of things I would ordinarily not have read. I became interested in listening to analyses . . . and I found it quite valuable.

Interviewer: What year was it when you finished this graduate work?
Williams: That was 1951; then I went back to the foundry. I had worked there some of the summers, and that was my first job out of graduate school. [Later] I was a vegetable clerk, and then I became a case worker with the Onondaga County Welfare Department. I did public relations work part-time.

Interviewer: Were you writing at all during this period?
Williams: Yes, as a matter of fact I got, I suppose, my first real encouragement in writing as a freshman at Syracuse. You know, we had to write compositions and things of that sort, so I'd done a lot of pieces on the war, which was not unusual because, remember, at the time I entered college in the fall of '46, I was . . . with everybody coming back and all that, we tended to be older, and I think more experienced than some of the kids who were seventeen- or eighteen-year-old freshmen. I got a lot of encouragement there

and wrote for some publications and published some poetry in publications outside the school.

Interviewer: Have you continued to write poetry?
Williams: I've just gotten back to it in the past couple years . . . yes, but not to any large extent.

Interviewer: Did you find any influences on this poetry?
Williams: Influences in poetry . . . yes. I think music, jazz music. I found myself doing a lot of, I suppose you would want to call it, experimental poetry at that time. That is, taking certain standard and traditional meters and alternating them with other standard meters when they were not supposed to follow one another. Very much influenced at that time by bop and what those guys were trying to do.

Interviewer: When did you start work on your first novel?
Williams: About 1955, '56.

Interviewer: Was there any political, social, or personal impetus?
Williams: Well, I had left Syracuse to go to California and stayed for about a year in California. I came back East to New York City and worked for a publisher in publicity, for a year, and got fired when I asked for a raise. I didn't have anything else to do; you know, it's pretty much like Baldwin's statement that he found himself in that position. . . . I sat down to write in order to prove that I was of some value to myself. And that's when I started the first book.

Interviewer: Did it really follow on losing the job in advertising?
Williams: It started while I had the job, but I really was able to devote more time to it when I didn't have a job to go to. I found myself living off $36.00 a week—which went a hell of a lot farther than it would go today.

Interviewer: This was the book [*The Angry Ones*] published in 1960?
Williams: Right.

Interviewer: When did you finish it?
Williams: I finished it, I guess, about the end of 1956.

Interviewer: Did it immediately start the rounds in search of a publisher?
Williams: Yes.

Interviewer: It took four years to find a publisher? You smile as if you remember some of this with . . .
Williams: Yes. As a matter of fact, Earl Cash, who did the doctorate paper, had been up to the manuscript collection at Syracuse where I do have some papers, and he found one particular rejection letter that dealt with this novel. I—and it came as quite a surprise—had wondered what had happened to it, but there it was.¹ He reprinted the whole thing. It was a very bad time.

Interviewer: Was *The Angry Ones* your title?
Williams: No. How did you come to ask that question?

Interviewer: It's something that most authors have difficulty with, getting their titles accepted.
Williams: I think that is truer when you're just breaking in. My title was *One for New York*, but this was about the period when everybody was milking the combination of anger and black.

Interviewer: Like your anthology's title?
Williams: Yes, *The Angry Black* came because of that same thing, and while people who did a hard cover in another edition of that were perfectly willing to change the title, they did feel that since the title had some commercial appeal in softcover that we would all lose if we just changed the title completely. So we changed that to *Beyond the Angry Black*.

Interviewer: During the period while *The Angry Ones* or *One for New York* was seeking a publisher, did you begin another novel?
Williams: No, I was pretty demoralized. I was doing cute magazine pieces, humor pieces, for *Dude* and *Gent* and places like that. I called them "bop fables"—simply taking, oh, old Greek legends and making the characters sharp and using the terminology that was current at the time. I did one or two originals that I still like, "Ruby Doesback Goes to Mars," and so on. I did a "Bopper's *Romeo and Juliet*" and a "Bopper's *Hamlet*"—a little here and a little there. I worked part-time in an advertising agency, started with the American Committee on Africa as a fund-raising and public relations man, worked for a very psychotic publisher, and managed to accumulate enough money to go to Europe for the first time. Also, *The Angry Ones* had been optioned to a hard-cover house. I had great hopes for that, but while I was in Europe the option dropped. It was sort of like missed-meal cramps and bean feasts for quite a while until I got back home.

Interviewer: What was the impetus for *Night Song*?

Williams: Well, I had started to do a book on Charlie Parker—a nonfiction book—with another guy who wrote a jazz column for the *Village Voice*, but we came to a parting of the ways. On the basis of *The Angry Ones*, the soft-cover editor asked me if I would do a novel for her, and I said, "Yes." At this point I was sort of resigned to the fact that I'd be producing soft-cover books, which is really a different kind of life. Not that the writers aren't good, but the books—original soft-cover books—do not get reviewed. More important is that there is very little chance at resale, as there is in hard-cover-into-reprint. Anyhow, I started to do the book for her. In the meantime I had been working on *Sissie*. I had a short story which I took to a magazine that had been absorbed by a hard-cover publisher. They liked the story but said they were now looking for novels, so I took them a part of *Sissie*—which they liked. They wanted to know what else I had done, and by this time I had finished writing *Night Song*, so what they did was buy *Night Song* from the soft-cover house and publish it. Then they sold the reprint rights back to the original soft-cover house. And then *Sissie* was published.

Interviewer: So, in fact, you began *Sissie* at the same time or before beginning *Night Song*?

Williams: Yes. I forget which came first. It was about the same time.

Interviewer: Do you recall working on two at the same time?

Williams: Oh, yes; I usually work on two things at the same time.

Interviewer: On two novels?

Williams: Generally it's nonfiction and a novel. At that time, actually, I was working on three things because I had to put together a kid's book on Africa, which is now in its fourth edition. I was working on these three things at once. It's a pattern I've developed, probably strictly from hunger, but it hasn't . . . well, it has worked OK for me.

Interviewer: Was there any special quality or special awareness on your part of the fact these two books you were working on at the same time had as an important consciousness in one [*Night Song*] David Hillary, a white, and in *Sissie*, the black family which is the divided consciousness of the narration? Were you thinking about that, or was it just circumstantial?

Williams: I think it was circumstantial, but then there may have been some unconscious thing going on. I don't know. The longer I'm in this business the more I conclude that you can never be completely aware of what you put in a book. That's what I tell the kids I teach at Sarah Lawrence.[2] I'm not consciously aware of many things that people later discuss with me. This isn't to say, of course, that I'm conscious mostly of what I'm about, in terms of characters and so on. I also recognize that one's choice of words and choice of setting down certain words could possibly mean something else. If not something else, something *in addition* to what I thought I was meaning in the first place.

Interviewer: Did you know Charlie Parker personally?
Williams: No.

Interviewer: There is no model other than Charlie Parker for the character Eagle?
Williams: No.

Interviewer: Were there other models for other characters?
Williams: No real models, but lots of types like that in the Village where I was living. You saw them every day.

Interviewer: Has your thinking about novels, from the beginning, always involved broken-time sequence and flash-back techniques?
Williams: Not *The Angry Ones* so much, and not *Night Song* so much. I think, really, mostly in *Sissie* and *The Man Who Cried I Am* and *Captain Blackman*. I'm working on something now which is, I like to think, terribly convoluted with flashbacks within flashbacks within flashbacks. I have to stop working sometimes just so I don't lose myself. But it has always seemed to me that the novel, the traditional novel, is sort of like a house with four corners. It's not always the best vehicle for doing lots of things that I think novelists should be obliged to do now. I think, oddly enough, that black novelists and some younger southern white novelists are most about the business of destroying the form, the traditional form of the novel. And it's about time they did.

Interviewer: Would you be able to say anything about writers using broken-time sequence that you think affected you or that you thought worked very well?
Williams: You mean which writers or . . . ?

Interviewer: Were there any literary models that helped you come to an understanding of this technique?

Williams: Well, I think when I was at Syracuse, one novel that I read and liked and saw that I might be able to emulate and perhaps even best was *Under the Volcano*, Malcolm Lowry's thing. It's pretty much a new approach to the novel—at the time one of the newest approaches I'd ever seen. I've read (John) Hawkes, and (William) Gaddis's *The Recognitions*—which is a massive book, all kinds of fractures there—but you see I'm not dealing with the basic materials that either Gaddis or Hawkes are dealing with; that is, the people and the ideas, the historical complications that they find themselves in. So I think my approach has to be a little different. I think the other black writers who are involved in this—Clarence Major has a new book in which he's getting into this, I think; Bill Kelley also . . . These are things we have to explore because of what we are. We can get ideas from Lowry and Gaddis and Hawkes, but that's about it.

Interviewer: Would you be willing to align yourself with a group? For example, if one said that you followed the naturalist tradition of writing, would you agree?

Williams: Yes, I suppose I'd agree. I think that's perhaps one level. Sure, I think the combinations of naturalistic writing and surrealistic writing are things that lots of black writers do with particular ease. There seems to be a certain reluctance to accept the ability of black writers to deal in the surreal—not only on the part of white critics, but black critics as well. Take a guy like Middleton here with his kind of things; I don't know how well he would go over—well, *now* O.K.[3] But I think ten years ago, perhaps not so well in the States. In Europe, in Amsterdam where he lives, where everybody is involved in this kind of thing, it doesn't make any difference that he's black. Black writers have always been either naturalists or realists, and somebody like Bill Kelley can put a foot down wherever he wants, and it doesn't break his books down at all—like the original triple threat.

Interviewer: I gather you liked *Dunsfords Travels Everywheres*?
Williams: Yes.

Interviewer: Do you like Ishmael Reed's stuff?
Williams: Oh, yes.

Interviewer: The inevitable question about Richard Wright: where did you read or first come into contact with his work?

Williams: My folks had a copy of *Native Son* in the house; it came out in 1940 so that means I was about fifteen years old. I think that was the only work I read of his until I was a freshman at Syracuse.

Interviewer: Do you remember what sort of response you had to *Native Son*?

Williams: I was pretty fascinated by it . . . maybe that's the wrong word. I could understand it easily enough. At that particular time I could understand the motivations of Bigger Thomas. If there were Communists hanging around our neighborhood trying to proselytize black people, I never knew about it. But my mother worked as a domestic in a white household, and I knew that kind of patronizing thing went on. She would always tell me, "If you are coming to visit me at work, you come in the back door." And, of course, I'd always forget and go up to the front door. So I was completely into the book. I did not know at the time that much of it was based on a real case—nor did it matter to me.

Interviewer: When you were in school then—later, in college—did you read other works of Wright?

Williams: Just one, at that time. In the freshman anthology, something called, "How I Came to Write *Native Son*" ["How Bigger Was Born"]. I think that's the piece in which Wright—I now have the feeling, jokingly—said something about going out and getting his bottle occasionally and drinking and so on. Pretty much the same kind of piece that white publishers would run on black writers. In other words, they were not dealing genuinely with the creative process, and maybe Wright knew they never would. Maybe that's exactly why he did that particular piece.

Interviewer: Have you since read other of his works? And at what point? Or was the reading distributed over a long period of time?

Williams: Distributed over a long period of time, quite a bit of time.

Interviewer: Many critics have been struck by the similarity between the character Harry Ames in your big novel, *The Man Who Cried I Am*, and the public image of Richard Wright. Any comment?

Williams: I don't think anybody knows the real public image of Richard Wright. That *is* what a lot of people say, and I suppose, to some degree— because of Wright's having lived in Europe, the situations under which he went there, the problems that he became involved in while there—it's OK to say that Harry Ames was modeled on Wright. But that's really the outline, and there are a lot of things that people assume that I know about Wright that I don't know.

Interviewer: You did not ever, in fact, meet him?
Williams: A lot of people are under that misconception. I never met him. I've met one of his daughters, and I know his wife slightly. Chester Himes and I've talked about him over the years, but I didn't know the man. So it was one of those situations where you have an outline and you draw upon some creative ability to fill it in. You must sort of generalize what the life was like and the problems that faced the man. And once you've done that you're able to some degree understand what motivates him, how he would react in certain situations. And that was it.

Interviewer: Is it fair to say that Harry Ames is Richard Wright to the same degree, in the same way, that Eagle is Charlie Parker?
Williams: Yes. Sure.

Interviewer: There are certain values which they represent which you are trying to re-embody?
Williams: Yes.

Interviewer: A reading of *The Man Who Cried I Am* that stresses the fact of Harry's revenge on Max in passing on this burdensome information: is that acceptable to you?
Williams: Yes, I think that is one of the focal points of the book, which most people tend to miss. What we're dealing with here is the kind of Western situation in which there can only be one black writer at a time, one figure to absorb all the praise, which is a very real situation and was during Wright's time and Chester's—you know they are contemporaries— and lots of other peoples'. We find it essentially true today. Even beyond that, I think you go back to basic human response to certain situations— the idea of revenge. I mean, after all, this guy Max has diddled his ol' lady. While Harry was not above diddling everybody else's, he is sort of in shock because he assumed that he was so great that nobody else would bother his ol' lady, that his ol' lady was beyond that kind of stuff. It's sort of like, let's say, that Prometheus, instead of going after fire, went after Zeus's ol' lady, that kind of thing. In other words, Harry kills Max for that; that's revenge. It's a point very often missed.

Interviewer: Would it be unfair to read that as an image of the relationship between one generation of writers and another? Within the same generation? Do you think writers relate to one another in this way?

Williams: I think all writers do; I think all people basically do in that same situation. Writers—they are a peculiarly vicious breed of people because there are so few prizes for the numbers of writers involved. That's one of the aspects of the terrible—how shall I say?—*antipathy* that black writers hold toward white writers and white critics. But it's an antipathy that is well deserved because certainly the white literary establishment understands very well what it's about. It propagates white values and standards, and black writers, in order to be credited and accepted, would have to displace them entirely. And this is something they will not have done, at least not now. So we find a lot of writers turning in upon themselves, on each other. But, as I say, it's one of those things you can generally apply to lots of writers, regardless of color.

Interviewer: Do you apply it to their life situations as well?

Williams: Oh, sure.

Interviewer: There seem to be a lot of situations in your fiction in which the conflict that becomes most important is the conflict between one black character and another, not, of course, separate from but somehow special within the framework of the American racial situation.

Williams: Yes, that's where I see a lot of our position today, unfortunately, and I suppose this is one way for me to express impatience at the way we seem to be dealing with each other, through betrayal or lack of commitment or jive or whatever. On the other hand, we're always talking about, "We got to get this thing together." Everybody is talking about commitment, and we are just not getting that much of it.

Interviewer: Many people have pointed out that the milieu in which your works are set are essentially middle class and urban environments—even an integrationist's environment. Your second novel dealt with a white character at the center, influenced by a group of blacks, something which seemed controversial to some critics at the time. How do you relate to that aspect of your work?

Williams: My basic feeling is that we really live in a shit society here. Many of our options have been cut off. I think any return to Africa is generations in the future. I think the idea of establishing within the continental limits of the United States certain areas for black people is foolhardy. Number one: nobody is going to give it to us. Number two: if they gave it to us, it would be for the purpose of getting us all in one place and wiping us out. I mean, those are my views, simply put. The third thing is that we're going to have to make it with this Man for some time to come, whether we want to or not. I don't see any damn choice about it. Separation, as I just pointed out, is not going to be achieved here, and there's nothing happening over there [Africa]. Given the attitude of the current administration—and the last administration—and the various police departments in the cities and in this nation, given the right provocation, they'll commence the wipe-out. So, we have to make do in some kind of integrationist establishment. I'm not saying that everybody who is black has to marry somebody who is white. That's not at all what I meant. That, in any case, is one's individual choice.

Interviewer: What is your attitude toward the fact that your imagination works that way?

Williams: Well, my imagination works this way because this is what I believe, having reached these conclusions through experience and thought and seeing and everything else. I also feel that black people generally are sources from which this particular society has drawn an immense amount of value, in terms of language and culture and even attitudes, life postures and everything else. The only people who don't reap any decent benefits from this relationship are black people, but there's not really that much we can do about it at the moment—either within the system or not. The shift from radical militancy to supporting the politics on a local level or the federal level—I think that's always been a lot of horseshit. I just see us in an area, a period of *détente*, containment. You know, we'll wait and see what happens. I think to a large extent, my work reflects this too, or, at least, increasingly so.

Interviewer: The ending of *Sons of Darkness, Sons of Light* was apocalyptic; it seemed like the end had come. Did you intend that as a warning of a possibility? Is it a prognosis?

Williams: As a warning of possibility, but that's a far cry from . . . I called it "a novel of some probability," but I think better stated it would be a "novel of some possibility." Black people aren't fools any more than anybody else, and I think to get out there and be involved in the kind of things that bring all of this awesome power down upon our heads, to eliminate thirty million black people, is something we are not about to do at this point. That book was a potboiler, in many ways; that's what I call an A-to-Z book. I sat down to it because I had expected a bit more in terms of financial remuneration from *The Man Who Cried I Am*. That didn't happen—it still hasn't happened—and I just found myself looking into a future that was notable for absence of dollar bills and the wherewithal to support my family, which is not to say that I don't believe in many things that I said in that book. But artistically, for me, I think it was a potboiler.

Interviewer: Do you have that attitude toward any of your other works?
Williams: No.

Interviewer: It's just that one that you no longer, or never did, feel any affinity toward?
Williams: Well, Joe, the response to that book sort of confirmed everything I know about this business. It got a lot of good press; it made more money than *The Man Who Cried I Am* and was reviewed in publications that I had not been reviewed in before—or since. And I know the book was shit, but all these things happened to it, which doesn't mean that I plan to sit down and write more crap—people may call it crap, but I'm going to know better. It's pretty much like Kelley now claims: since he's unable to make his voice heard and since America likes its clowns, he's going to start writing clownish books. But he has no more guarantee that clownish books are going to bring him more money than his really good, serious books. You don't know. So, the only thing you can do is sit down and do your thing.

Interviewer: Which of your books is your favorite?
Williams: Well, I like *Captain Blackman* at the moment because I think that went into still another level of convolutions in dealing with history. I've not read reviews of it yet, but the things that my wife tells me about the reviews assure me that it might—had to be—a real *bad* book. And when I say *bad* I mean bad in a good sense, you know, because all the shops close up when something like that [hits]. And it's a reaction that is as predictable for black writers to see as, like, the sky is darkening. It must be going to rain . . . these people are so goddamned transparent!

Interviewer: Is a reading of your work which sees a deepening of political themes acceptable? Is it something that you're aware of? Does it result from any kind of study?

Williams: I suppose just the study of being a guy living in these times who is aware of other times and the continuity of history—what's happened, what hasn't happened, and what one is going to do about it or suggest that other people do about it . . . to that extent, I think all this stuff is political. I'm always trying to come up with some answers—or possibilities or probabilities or problems—to pose problems that require solutions by someone. Very often I figure I've done my job once I've posed the questions.

Interviewer: Do you know James Baldwin?
Williams: I don't know Baldwin. I've met him and we've exchanged a few words, but I don't know him. I know him through his work and that's about it.

Interviewer: Would you be willing to make a literary criticism of his work?
Williams: Yes, I've spoken about him before in that area.

Interviewer: I'd like, specifically, to ask you about your view of *Another Country* as a kind of broad and general commentary, much as *The Man Who Cried I Am* is a broad and general commentary on the American scene.
Williams: To me, *Another Country* was a disappointment. I think the books that he has done after have not been the books I was looking for from Baldwin, but I again have no doubt that he has several great books in him. I think he has been afflicted by the things we were talking about earlier, the pinnacle position in terms of black writers in this country. There's no doubt in my mind that Baldwin could write several dynamite books about that whole milieu, what happens to a guy in it, what happens to the people who had helped him get and maintain that position. I know that there are a lot of people who have taken advantage of him, even now, a lot of people who believe that Baldwin took advantage of them. But hell, that's the way it goes. I don't think he's done what he can do, from *Another Country* forward. The thing is, he is a better essayist than novelist, and his last book of essays I found strangely lacking in something, too. He's going to surprise everybody.

Interviewer: In reading your work, one notices a fairly constant and consistent attitude toward the connection between sex and an authentic, useful, and fulfilled social/political life. Is that attitude—if I've fairly described it—something you have arrived at purely experientially, or had it been influenced by readings in Freud or others?

Williams: Well, I don't know. It's not a conscious thing on my part, and I was smiling because I was remembering in part the thing that Derek Walcott wrote: he said something to the effect that a good marriage equals a good life or whatever. . . . I don't know; maybe I'm old-fashioned enough to believe this. And I do believe that a healthy sex life makes for a healthy other kind of life; there is that relationship as far as I'm concerned.

Interviewer: But it seems to run the other way in your works.
Williams: I think that when one assumes certain health in terms of his sexual life and that breaks down, then his life is not going to be that healthy. On the other hand, I think a good sex life can repair broken life in other areas.

Interviewer: Would you like to comment on the kind of connection between sex, political and social life in *Another Country*, and your own novel?
Williams: No, it has been a long time since I last read *Another Country*. I think that some of these gals who are doing these books are quite right—I mean Kate Millett, "vaginal politics" and so on. I suppose all of us are therefore working toward some kind of a view of that relationship and how to make it better—the thing between the bed and what one does when one is not in bed. But I can't join comparison between the things that I do with my sex in my stuff and what Jimmy Baldwin does with his.

Interviewer: I'd like to go back to your comment about your view of *Sons of Darkness, Sons of Light* as a potboiler, in relationship now to this question. Is the aspect of sex in that novel one of the things that you feel was handled in such a way as to classify it a potboiler?
Williams: No. You're talking about the relationship between Brown and his wife? No, I feel that that was something—Well, that and some other aspects of the book had nothing to do with the fact that I needed money. Let's take two aspects of it: the guy who is out philandering on his own and comes back and finds out that his ol' lady has been philandering. And—going above the idea of sex—if he realizes, as he did when he said, "I've been alone, too," or something like that, it seems to me [then] that that kind of situation is as important because I always try to deal with the choices of individuals. Those have to be made before their acts can be effective on the group. Those two people as individuals got themselves together. Now maybe this thing going on out in the street while they're in the sack, screwing each other to death or trying to, maybe this thing that's going on out on the street will be

better the next time around because they somehow got their thing together. To that extent, I felt that was something I didn't short-change anybody on in terms of it being a potboiler.

Interviewer: At the end of *Night Song*, David Hillary is returning to Onondaga Falls to pick up his teaching career. Looking down into the Hudson River tunnel, he thinks that perhaps someday he'll understand. We see in your work a series of images of white Americans on the edge of some kind of knowledge of that situation in which the black characters operate. Lately they seem to have moved to the periphery of your imagination. Whereas Hillary is central to *Night Song*, in *Sons of Darkness, Sons of Light* we see Woody only at the end.
Williams: Yes, I suppose that's something that has come with age also. The failure of many whites that I knew—and still know and have known over the years—to, for one reason or another, come to grips with the situation in which not only I am involved, but in which they are equally involved, and to perceive that this failure on their part means that they receive less and less in terms of being characters in my books because that is the way they affect me in real life.

Interviewer: Numbers of the white characters in *The Man Who Cried I Am* seem to be stricken with a kind of neurotic paralysis, repetitive behavior— like the publisher who is constantly feeling his sexual inferiority, the woman who tries to fill her empty life with people. Do you feel that the inability of whites to cope with the racial situation is tied to their own personal, individual failures?
Williams: Oh sure, without doubt.

Interviewer: How does this relate to the social and political framework?
Williams: Well, I think they are just as unable to function in those as well. I mean, we've got this running discussion that Nixon is just beating the shit out of Congress. All right, he probably is, but it has been no news to anybody who has been a student—amateur or professional—of government and our representatives that they're a bunch of jive people and that Nixon has just simply realized it the way Hitler realized certain things. The analogy is apt, I believe. People are no longer able to control their government for the simple reason that they were never able to control, or didn't want to control, certain things that happened within their individual lives. It follows as the natural cause.

Notes

1. See Earl A. Cash, *John A. Williams: The Evolution of a Black Writer* (Third Press: New York, 1975, Chapter Two).

2. Since the time of this interview, Mr. Williams has taken up a distinguished professorship at LaGuardia Community College in the City University of New York.

3. Mr. Williams here pointed to a collage-painting on the living room wall, the work of his friend Sam Middleton, who has lived in Europe for many years.

John Williams at 49: An Interview

Dan Georgakas / 1974

From *minnesota review* 7 (Fall 1976), 51–65. Copyright © 1976 Dan Georgakas. Reprinted with permission of Dan Georgakas.

On the occasion of his forty-ninth birthday in December 1974, John Williams gave a taped talk and reading at La Guardia Community College in New York City, where he is a Distinguished Professor of Language and Literature. Williams read from novels in progress and from his poetry. He also spoke frankly about the problems encountered by American writers. The major part of the interview which follows was done in Williams's office at the college some ten days after the birthday reading. A second session took place later that spring. During the interview, Williams often looked out the window at the traffic pouring on to the approaches of the nearby Queensborough Bridge or paused during an answer while subway cars on the elevated section of the IRT line hurled by some two blocks away. He is a soft-spoken man whose manner is in sharp contrast to the violence and anger that characterize so much of his work. He was looking forward to the publication of his seventh and eight novels, *Mothersill and the Foxes* and *The Junior Bachelor Society*.

Dan Georgakas: You've spoken of the literary ghetto in which black writers are compared only with other black writers and from which only one black writer at a time is selected as representative or important enough to warrant the attention of the general reading public. Do you think this is still true?
John Williams: Without a doubt. I still see the reviews grouped together. I don't know if you can, but I know that I can't name a time when a contemporary black novelist has been given the assignment of reviewing the work of a contemporary white novelist. You'll find it can happen with children's books or academic books, but with novels it just doesn't happen. About three years ago when Watkins started with the *New York Times* he stopped

by and asked if I would do some reviews. I said sure but that I would like to review books done by whites as well as books by blacks. He said there would be no problem. But that hasn't happened, and I don't think it will happen. I don't see any chance in the near future for that breaking down. First, there's going to be fewer black writers—not because the talent isn't there but because the fad is past. The publishers have only been catering to a fad. Now, it's back to the forties and fifties.

DG: *The Man Who Cried I Am* was published at about the same time as *The Confessions of Nat Turner*. That was a period when we were celebrating a genius every year—Saul Bellow one year, Katherine Anne Porter another, and that year it was William Styron. He got the front page of the *New York Times Book Review* and all that goes with it while your novel was relatively neglected. Do you think this was part of institutionalized racism, something deliberate, or something relatively innocent such as Styron just being better known than you?

JW: Styron was certainly better known inside the literary establishment which is where it counts, and there was the obvious business of being a successor to Faulkner. All that helps. My wife believes my novel got good notices, but that was long after it got published. I had an extremely good editor, Harry Sions, who is now dead. He expressed fears that Styron's book would catch a lot of attention. He drafted the publicity blurb he wanted Little Brown to use. I remember one key word he used, *blockbuster*. Now reviewers tend to be very lazy, except when they're dealing with people they like. Eliot Fremont Smith reviewed the book with two or three others, and he used the word my editor had put into the machine, *blockbuster*. That essentially was it. Most of the reviews dealt with the King Alfred Plan. Very often I wish I hadn't put that in at all. There were other parts that were just as good. There really isn't any doubt that there is a different approach to works produced by a black novelist and works produced by a white novelist. I would be remiss if I didn't say that some of it was conscious and some of it was unconscious.

DG: How much is conscious and how much is unconscious?

JW: I think it's conscious to the point where people are aware of trends. I mentioned the fad of black writing in the sixties. Everything got published, including a lot of crap, which is all right too because a lot of white guys write crap. Like shoe styles or suit styles, we soon went out of fashion. To that extent, we are talking about conscious racism. It's still very difficult for white reviewers to handle pertinent and accurate criticism of this society because the book reviewers play an important part in the perpetuation of that racism—and they know it.

DG: In 1962 you were involved in a scandal that seems to involve overt racism. You were given an award from the American Academy in Rome that was suddenly withdrawn for reasons which were never fully revealed. Alan Dugan, who got the prize you were to receive, attacked the selection procedure and then the American Academy severed its connection with the American Academy in Rome. Do you think this has had an adverse effect on how critics, reviewers, and publishers look at your work? Has the incident given you a bad boy image, a sort of Jane Fonda of the literary scene?
JW: I believe it has. I guess, next to Nelson Algren, I have applied for a Guggenheim more often than anyone. Even a few years ago when I didn't really need it, I applied on the theory that when you don't need it, they give it to you. But that didn't work either. I suppose that's all right too. The sad thing about that kind of situation is that I have a lot of friends who are writers and who know my history of grant denials. They begin to feel self-conscious when they are offered the same grants and take them. They stop calling. I don't see them. It's all right by me that they got the grants. I understand the situation. But again, you have that awareness of the racist tendencies within the circle and a kind of indirect admission that they remain part of it by accepting the grants. To go back to the beginning of this, Dugan said, "This is wrong, but I'll take it anyway." I like Dugan. We stay in touch.

DG: I've read that you told him to accept the money.
JW: Yes, but he was going to take it anyway. He was only slightly on the fence. He told me he wanted to go to Rome, and he needed the money.

DG: Would you have advised him differently if he had said, "I want to do whatever you think is the best thing."
JW: I had told him he had to deal with his own conscience and do his own thing.

DG: It's generally assumed that most black writers know, like, read, and influence one another. How true is this?
JW: I don't think it's very true at all. I think there are exceptions too. People generally feel that I've been influenced by Richard Wright and Chester Himes. I think Wright's historical view certainly couldn't help but influence

any writer. All they teach in lit classes is *Native Son*. I wonder if they even know his other writings, his stuff on Spain, the third world, and Africa. In the beginning of *White Man, Listen*, he runs down a whole page of what reads like very good poetry about what happened in the fifteenth, sixteenth, and seventeenth centuries regarding slavery, not just African slavery, but the world picture, the kind of slavery that was part of colonialism. It's just a tremendous historical setting. I'm into that. I think history is a good base for me. Killens I admire because he has persevered. He has probably persevered beyond the point he's ever written about. I don't know who influenced Ron Fair. He seems to be coming out of a different bag. I can't define Melvin Kelly. Ernest Gaines is a purely rural, self-turning influence. And so it goes.

DG: In *The Man Who Cried I Am* you described the infighting among black writers. Does that still persist?

JW: I think it goes on with all writers. Poets like to think it's worse among poets. I think it's just as bad among novelists. And I think because of the situation of one black novelist at a time being allowed to crest the mountain, it's probably worse among black poets and novelists. This is the impression I have. While you can understand it, you can't condone it. I don't know what it's like for white poets and novelists. Since our circle is much smaller, there is an area where we do provide help for one another in regards to editors, agents, publishers, and so forth. It invariably turns out that the people you help are the very ones who are like Brutus. It's right in the old kitsch the first chance they get. I guess that's par for the course, understanding the syndrome that there can only be one at a time. That means that although you have helped me up this far, if I'm going to get over this mountain, you got to be dead. And I've done my share of it too. I understand now what the hell is going on.

DG: Baldwin came into prominence by his essays attacking Richard Wright. He didn't perceive his writing as an attack however. Do you think he was manipulated by institutionalized racism?

JW: I don't think he perceived how extensive it was and that was part of my situation too. You are lured, at least at first, into believing that we are in a totally and purely artistic situation—which is crap. Art is not pure. In this country, it never has been and never will be. It's treated as a product, a commodity, something to be bought, sold, and shuffled around. We all get caught up in this thing at one stage or another, and the determining factor for growth is if you get out of it. Some people don't.

DG: You've done a lot of journalism. Hemingway credited his journalism with helping his style and content. What's been your experience?

JW: Someone ran a tape for me from a conference where I was being raked over the coals by a critic who said my subjects were too topical. I think that's one trap you may fall into in terms of having done journalism. In terms of style, I don't think it's affected me that much. Number one, if you're doing a magazine article, the style tends to be different, tighter. Getting back to fiction is a release. You can overflow, roll, and spin. On the other hand, you can get too wild. Occasionally, I find it very good to get back into doing magazine articles where everything is more concrete. I find it works very well. Historically, I think black writers have had to do all kinds of writing in order to survive. Langston Hughes is a case in point. You do a novel. You do poetry. You do essays. This is often dictated by your need to keep food in the house, but it makes you a four letter man.

DG: If what you say is true, and I think it is, then the black American writers are more like the classical western man of letters than the white American writers who generally classify themselves as playwright, poet, novelist, or whatever.

JW: We've had a few conferences where we discussed that. Given the overall American literary situation though, it doesn't matter a good goddamn.

DG: Getting back to the overemphasis given to the King Alfred aspects of *The Man Who Cried I Am*, I'm surprised that less has been written about the nightmare elements in that book. For instance, did you base Moses Boatwright, the Harvard graduate who cannibalizes a white man, on a real person or incident?

JW: Boatwright is somebody I made up. Given the situation in which we live, I know damn well there has to be a real Moses Boatwright though. There has to be.

DG: You have a Cora Boatwright in *Sissie*. You are using a main character from that book in your novel in progress, *The Junior Bachelor Society*. Will you connect Cora and Moses somewhere?

JW: [laughs] No, I'm not very good with names. I'm really not. Sometimes when I'm coming to a character, I delay giving a name to him. I look up from my desk and see a name on a calendar or an author's name on a book, and I use it or some variation. That was pure accident about the similarity in names.

DG: In *The Man* you have a section in which the main character talks to a sort of mystical black self you call Saminone.

JW: He's talking to the tap root. There's been a lot of discussion about the black middle class getting away from its roots and how soul food has become a ritual, an attempt to find the roots. They're there though and once you break off contact with them, when you can't talk to them or imagine you can talk to them, then you're gone, just gone. Then you're like one of those Hollywood types who think inside they've always been that way, that they came out of air. Saminone is the tap root.

DG: What were the literary influences for the Saminone sequences—Joyce, Dos Passos, or Woolf?

JW: I've read those people because I had to, not so much for enjoyment. Out of all of them, I enjoyed Dos Passos the most—when he was in his rebellious period and really sitting down hard on things my father had to deal with. I've always liked him, but I don't think I've consciously copied anything from him or the others.

DG: You have said Malcolm Lowry's *Under the Volcano* was an influence.

JW: Right. I was speaking, in particular, of what you do with time in the physical format of a book. How do you put thirty to forty years within a three hundred-page book and make it work? That's pretty much what you might do with a film. An A-to-Z novel makes it as long as Joseph Heller's new book. Who wants to read it? Who wants to carry it around? It always struck me that there must be a better way of putting a novel together that works. The novel is not a tome. I tried to telescope in *Sissie*. I think it worked but not as well as in *The Man* which was a bigger book, bigger in scope too. A lot of that came from Lowry.

DG: You use a lot of flashback. Is this just a part of getting a lot into a limited space, or is it partly due to the fact that people don't come to understand things in logical 12345 order but get information piecemeal like 53214 and grope to pull it together?

JW: Do you remember the old cartoons? Whenever anyone had an idea, there was a light bulb in the balloon that went on. It was a sudden pulling together. Well, it doesn't work that way. You find out a little bit here and a little bit there. If you want to know what's going on in an English department, you talk to the adjunct. You talk to the chairman. You talk to the full professor. You have to judge expressions when people tell you things. It doesn't come all at once. Consciously, I wasn't dealing with it exactly as you said, but that's what, in fact, I was doing.

DG: If Thomas Wolfe had done *Captain Blackman*, there would have been a book about each epoch with tens of thousands of characters. Authors often talk about wanting to do a cycle of books to encompass the experience of a nation or a class. It seems to me that in *Blackman* you came up with an economic solution to that kind of problem.

JW: I'm glad you think that because I'm always accused of being melodramatic. There's really no other way to cover so much time and so much real history and still provide continuity for the reader. My melodramatic tendencies arise, I suppose, from my belief that there has to be continuity to the novel. A story must be told. The story must end somewhere near the end of the novel, not on page sixty or seventy. So if you draw a horizontal line, you get lots of vertical lines feeding into it which makes the horizontal line grow toward an end where the damn thing should conclude, not somewhere in the middle. I think I work very hard with each book to find the solution to a problem that I'm not always completely aware of. I don't like writing easy books. I don't like writing the same kinds of books stylistically or thematically. So I'm always into new things which I can't always explain.

DG: Did the massacre of black soldiers by the US army as described in *Blackman* actually happen? I know the historical material regarding the other time periods was accurate.

JW: The black grapevine says it happened. I made a lot of inquiries to find out. I even hired a guy to go back over newspaper files from the period. I got out a battle map to figure out positions in the area. Just from looking at that map, at the German installations, at the American installations, and at the swamp, I figured out how it could have been done easily. We found isolated incidents, but there's nothing I could pin down. I just went ahead and did it on the basis of the bits and pieces I had. The other stuff was all heavily researched. The exact orders described exist. Now I think I should have done more to separate the fiction from the nonfiction.

DG: You seem to like apocalyptic endings such as the one to *Blackman*. You called them melodramatic endings before.

JW: That's what the critics call them. To them they're just endings.

DG: I would agree with them on *Blackman* to the extent that if the ending had remained as a reverie or delirium rather than as an actual event, the book would have been stronger.

JW: I was trying to work out a couple of things, principally the role in American society of the mulatto, the quadroon, the octaroon. Several years ago in *Goodbye to Uncle Tom,* there was an estimate that probably twenty million blacks pass as white in America. Forget about Europe with the Moors, the Sicilians, and all that. I tried to create a role in which it would be historically sound for such people to act. The other part of it is that it would be very easy for them. There are some people who believe Eisenhower was black on the basis that his grandmother was put into an abolitionist home out in Kansas. They argue that if she wasn't black why would she have been put into an abolitionist home. Anyway, I wanted to create an element of real historical terror. The idea that there is a mulatto who has allegiance to the black race can put people into a panic because you never know who is and who isn't. It would be nice if the world as we know it ended with conventional bombs which would mean that those who survived would be able to function. It would also be nice to know that there is some human capability short of military action that can dismantle all these missile and nuclear systems and create an atmosphere in which we can work together without that fear that if we don't, the things are going to drop on us. Those were the two elements I was trying to work with.

DG: Expatriation is a theme that runs through all of your work, but the main characters always come back to America.

JW: There are many nice places to visit, but I wouldn't want to live there [laughs]. My family and I have often thought about leaving the country, but over the years it's become pretty clear that most of Europe, for example, is becoming pretty much like the United States in terms of how any one country handles different colored populations in its midst. If you go to Africa, Asia, or the Middle East, you run into a colonial experience most of those people have not worked themselves out of. In black Africa you are treated either as a colonial, with a snickering undercurrent of "we know you're really not," or as an outside observer. When you're dealing with rural people, then it's different, but after living almost fifty years in an urban situation, I don't think I want to put roots down in an African bush situation. And an African bush setting is completely foreign to me because of the colonial impact. I think, also, that one always knows the rules in America, but you are never quite sure in Latin America, Europe, or elsewhere. When you're young, I think you're more vigorous and more willing to duke it out.

DG: Gore Vidal seems to make expatriation work.

JW: I think there's a palatable difference between white and black expatriates. Now Vidal has money and a historical American position. He may be gone, but I'll be damned if he's forgotten by literary people. For black writers to be gone is to be absolutely forgotten. Out of sight does mean out of mind. That happens even if you only move to Worcester, Massachusetts. In the twenties and thirties, the literary emphasis was on what Europe had to say to everyone else. That's all changed. Beginning in the late fifties and through the sixtiess the Europeans were covering American goings-on, sending reporters over here, making films, et cetera. I don't think it's the idea of being cut off as much as the idea that Europe has become restless by the influx of nonwhites. You can talk about Paris, and of course Marseilles has always been like that, London. Something changes. The weight then falls on the black expatriate who doesn't understand why people feel this way. He always thought Europe was something else, the land of the free. So to that extent, the cultural approach to nonwhites has become almost similar. If one is a masochist and likes to feel uncomfortable abroad or wants to feel like he has to duke every time he goes down to the corner, that's fine. But if he isn't that way, he'll have to come back.

DG: Your main characters often come from lower or middle class backgrounds, but they usually have artist-intellectual values.

JW: That's a reflection of my own life. The opening chapter of my new novel begins with two guys who work in a foundry. To work in a foundry in the seventies means that the dough is good even though the work is hard, which if you stay around long enough isn't so hard either. You are in a position where you can wind up in a pretty solid middle class situation. I think we're just beginning to realize that. Because it's become middle class labor we feel we have to do something about those poor slobs who are getting bored working on the line. What about all those other generations of people, including kids, who worked in factories maybe ten to twelve hours a day, who if they got bored, it was just tough shit. Now, because of social mobility or fluidity between blue- and white-collar workers, people are concerned. This, of course, is after the fact.

DG: At your birthday reading, you spoke a lot about your poetry. Will you be working in poetry and other non-novel forms to a greater extent than before?

JW: I'm writing more poetry now but not as much as I would like to. I've always liked poetry. That's where I started writing. What I'm working on now is something I'd like to end up as a collection which has to do with the origins and experiences of black people from a mysterious past to the present. Two of the things, "Origins I" and "Origins II," were actually recently written. About two years ago, I did some other parts which fit somewhere in the middle. And that's how it's been going. I'd like to do more poetry. If I could teach creative writing absolutely the way I wanted, I'd start everybody by making them write in Petrarchan sonnets. In most of the schools I've taught at, no one would stand for that. I think poetry makes you aware of the precise word, the precise image called for, the precise impact that you want. That's why it's so powerful. Nowadays, a lot of kids start writing by writing poetry mainly I think because it looks easy. If you start knowing the tradition of poetry before you depart from it, you know what you're doing. If you want to bastardize forms to some extent, okay. At least you know what was there instead of operating out of a vacuum. In terms of doing plays, I'd much rather do screenplays than things for the stage. I've had several, probably too many, brushes with Hollywood. Film is really where it's at.

DG: Did you write the screenplay for the movie version of *Night Song*?

JW: No, I didn't try to write it, simply because those people didn't have any money. I had approval though. It was shot pretty much like the novel went with some esoteric touches. Then the director lost control, and it was cut and turned out to be an absolute bomb. I've done TV documentaries and I did one adaptation of a novel of mine for Hollywood which nothing has happened with. About once a month, someone out there calls me and asks if I'd be interested in doing a screenplay for such and such, and I'm such a whore that I never say no. But invariably nothing develops. I think film is great. If you're talking about how I break down my fiction I like to deal with new paragraphs as being changes in camera position. It works with the kids because right away they understand it. I don't like to get into some kind of composition sort of thing, however. The paragraph changes because guys are rolling on the floor with the equipment. The same scene is being picked up by a different camera or from a different angle. People have told me that

I write that way, which is true. I tend to see the things I'm writing about. I think them up visually.

DG: At your birthday reading, you said you were working on two novels simultaneously. Is that a common practice with you?

JW: It could be two novels at a time, or what I prefer is one fiction and one nonfiction book. There's a nice change of pace between fiction and nonfiction. I've got a novel going now which hasn't got a title yet. I saw *State of Siege* and thought that the same thing is happening in Africa and is going to continue to happen there. What are the conditions which bring this about? Who are the people? How do they happen to fit in? I came home from that movie and wrote a whole first chapter. Later I started doing research on a particular country, which is Liberia, and about Firestone Rubber. One thing I've learned with age is that you can think about a work and hold yourself in check. The longer you hold yourself in check the better. It's like good beer, aging and simmering. By the time you have the slot to sit down and go to it, it's there.

DG: Your nonfiction seems less intensive than your fiction. You seem more interested in persuading people to your point of view in the non-fiction while in the novels you let the situation take over and don't care who's offended.

JW: I think that's a valid observation. With a magazine you always have the question of censorship. There are damn few magazine editors who don't exert some form of censorship, whether it be their personal view or the view of the public as a whole. I can't think of any magazine that truly and freely gives the writer his full head. There's give and take. What you do is give in on the soft issues in exchange for the ones you think are the hard issues. The original writing may turn out to be hard as a nail. You've said everything you wanted to say, but you know there's going to be some retouching. That's where you begin to bargain, but I think it's always bad for a writer to prejudge his own work. You just do the first shot and take it in. Then you sit down and start dickering. The editor you deal with invariably has to go up to somebody else or if he is the editor-in-chief, there is an editorial board to consult where there is always at least one fink who feels the piece doesn't measure up to the depth of the magazine, the philosophy it wants carried out, that this reader or that one is going to be offended.

DG: In fiction, it's easier to take a character beyond a reasonable viewpoint, but in an article the author has to stand behind the ideas and to some extent the publication has to stand behind the writer.

JW: There are problems in fiction too. Many times you have a sharply drawn character. The writer views this character as being exactly as he wanted the character to be. Then he has to defend the conception to an editor who thinks otherwise. In all fairness, this most generally happens to a young writer doing a first or second novel. But even if you manage to survive the hand grenades and missiles, there may be some tentative suggestions about character and plot. When I turned in *Captain Blackman*, what are now the final two chapters were one long chapter. Some people at Doubleday felt that the material was too powerful to be in one chapter. My first response to separating them was, no. I liked it the way it was. Then I looked at it again. If I set it apart, the conclusion would be even more powerful. So I agreed. That's the kind of thing you get.

DG: Your most controversial book is *The King God Couldn't Save*. What do you say to people who charge that you didn't really present proof of sexual misconduct on King's part or proof that the FBI used it against him. One minor thing I've always wondered about is why you referred to him as Martin King. That seemed an unnecessary rebuff.
JW: Well, first off, about the name: Martin Luther King was the press name. The people who knew him called him Martin King. About Hoover: I drew a possible scene and what might have been said. *Time* ran a piece in its national section before the book was published in which they kicked my ass for lots of things, but they did say I was right about the meeting King had with Hoover. *Time* knew it all the time just like everybody else. One of the people in that meeting was a good friend of a journalist friend of mine who told me when the book came out to say that if I had any trouble he'd call Joe Blow to get an affidavit that the meeting happened. I was up in the country at the time. I would drive into town seven miles to use a pay booth to make sure no one was on the line. Eventually, the guy backed out. I had decided that if the King family sued me, I would go to jail. The people I had my information from were friends who had families of their own, who had been in different situations at the time they knew King, and who couldn't possibly spell out everything. Actually, there were a lot of things that I did not put into the book. Using editorial discretion, I came to the conclusion that they were more sensationalist than anything else.

After the King book, I was calling people from pay phones because of what happened after *The Man* came out, which was I had picked up the phone one Saturday and heard this guy talking I went downstairs to the basement where all the phones were run into my building,and asked for his identification, asked to talk to his supervisor. I called the phone company the first thing Monday morning, and they said that they had no one by that number working there. I went out of town one weekend with my family, and we came home to find all the lights on like they were telling me they could come and go anytime they wanted. I must admit that black people gave me a rough time on the King book. Some were helpful though and defended me. One person in Washington said that if I had any trouble with the family to let him know. The person said he'd use material he had in his files. I wasn't really too worried. If I needed that kind of support, I'd have gotten it. The whole thing was misunderstood. What I was trying to do was point out that no black man in America ever escapes this kind of situation, this manipulation, this drive for power. People always manipulate and take advantage of what you are doing.

DG: You've also written that King really got under your skin, which seems a more personal gripe.

JW: When I said that it was mainly because my older son, whose mother is a daughter of a preacher and whose grandmother is still with us, exerted a lot of pressure on him to be a minister. His big idol at the moment was Martin Luther King. It was all right by me that King was a national figure and had a Nobel Prize, but I didn't want that to mess up my kid. Ultimately, he decided to get a doctorate in education which he's now completing at Temple. For a while it was touch and go between preacher and teacher. That's why King got under my skin. It's like my seven-year-old watching Popeye the sailor man eating his spinach and coming over and giving me a crack in my broken veterbra.

DG: Your books often deal with violent social change. How do you feel about the outwardly tranquil seventies?

JW: The answer to the sixties was Richard Nixon. Now, the contention I hold is that all major political change in America, for the better and for the worse, and usually it's for the worse, has come about because of the black presence. Nixon's election was such an event. But he was the epitome of all the violence that was going on, except he was wrapped in White House stationery. He kept his violence undercover in most cases, except when they beat the shit out of Martha Mitchell. Violence has not left the scene at all.

DG: One commentator on your writing sees a shift from hope to despair in your work.

JW: Now you know why I don't read reviews until they've been out at least a year. I'm a very optimistic writer. I understand that there are certain fundamental changes that this society is going to have to go through if it's going to survive. When all the books are boiled down I'm saying that changes are the result of choices by individuals. A lot of people asked me why I left a white woman sitting alone at a table waiting for Max at the end of *The Man*. I thought that was pretty obvious in the sense that we have a world culture that's always waiting for something good to happen, which is not going to happen simply because it's not been involved in things which make it possible for something good to happen. In *Sons of Darkness, Sons of Light*, my potboiler—and because I call it a potboiler doesn't mean there aren't things in it I like—the husband and wife are screwing in bed while the city is burning. I don't think you can get down to any more individual choice than that. In my new book a group of guys who have been separated for twenty-five years have to come back together around an issue for the permanence of whatever they had as kids. I don't see that as despair. If I have any one problem, it's that under all the crap I'm an optimist.

DG: There's a strong radical strain in your work. It's muted, yet it keeps recurring. Do you have a developed political ideology?
JW: I don't really believe in any of them, although I'd like to see the good ones work. Finally, in 1917 we got something. That means over the previous one hundred to one-hundred-fifty years there had been attempts to get change in motion in Russia. I think the times were a bit more appropriate for certain political philosophies and the ability to carry them out before the crest of technological development. Marx and Hegel were alive during the time of lower levels of technological know-how. But they understood very well the implications of colonialism and what it does to people. It would be jive for me to say that there are philosophies I like but don't trust. There has to be one world philosophy for all of us to be part of in order for us to get along. It would be jive to say, as some do, that it's a white man's thing, and I don't want any part of it. All the great powers are in collusion and in opposition at the same time. I believe that ultimately, if things break down before we get to the more positive period, what we're going to have is all the white nations pitted against all the darker nations. Historically, I don't see any other way that this thing is really going to happen. I believe there are all these political philosophies and everyone in the world must choose one that's going to suit everybody else in varying degrees. Personally, I've always been a loner.

I went under heavy recruitment for the Communist Party when I was in Syracuse. They had a pretty good group up there. They were really aggressive. Every organization I've ever belonged to fell apart because it did not believe in its own longevity to the benefit of everyone in the group. I've gotten along very well with most radical groups because I'm not radically positioned in one party or another. Liberals tend to feel that I'm a liberal, but they used to say, "Well, John Williams, that's a very angry guy." People always say that, until they meet me. Then they say, "Gee, I thought you were a real ass-kicker, but you're really a nice guy." Well, I'm radical to the extent that I believe that large changes must be mandated for everyone in the world—equitable distribution of food, services, and peace. I'm for one people. In my more drunken moments which often turn out to be my more thinking moments, I sometimes feel that perhaps slavery may have been dictated by some greater force for the purpose of making a people's country into one people. Maybe we are allowed to develop technology so we can move back and forth, and people can mix and marry or not marry. Maybe we're only coming to the end of the first spatial Paleolithic Age.

DG: You've done two books for young adults. Do you like this kind of writing, or were there other reasons?

JW: There were other reasons, but the response to both books made me feel they were a genuine part of one's intellectual responsibilities. The book on Africa came out in '63, and we've gone through four editions, which means going back and updating. When I did the Africa book I had not yet sold the two novels that became paperbacks. I was living on Lafayette Street in the Village, and I was scuffling. Since I've always had this interest in history and since they gave me a free hand and some dough, I did it. The second book was something I sandwiched in between a lot of other things. That wasn't a question of money so much as someone wanted me to do a book on Richard Wright. I had to pull in a lot of horns on that one because it was a young adult book. I couldn't get into nitty gritty areas that would upset youngsters.

DG: That may be so, but in that book you presented a set of circumstances that hint pretty strongly that the CIA may have killed Richard Wright for exposing American black agents in Europe. Do you know anyone who has done any further research on that possibility?

JW: No. Most of the people I know go out of their way to debunk that theory. And those are the people who are given most credence, but you know there's the old adage about where there's smoke, there's fire. People keep talking about it. I don't think things were well within the family. There were a lot of other things which we may not be aware of. For instance, there was Wright's unknown connection with the CIA sponsorship of the American Society for African Culture which involved Senghor and many others. That was an example of where the CIA worked without people being totally aware of what was going on. Wright did have a big blowout with a guy in Paris who most people consider the most obvious spy on the whole continent. There is the fact of his cremation and some things Chester Himes has brought out. They keep the speculation going.

DG: Do you think there's material there for a scholar to go into?

JW: You need a broken down detective who really has to dig because it's going to pay his way. A scholar wouldn't do. He wouldn't believe it. That would upset the scholars' world, that kind of penetration into the arts. Hell, that was the new thing after World War II, that the arts could be penetrated. There was the whole business that came to light about the Encounter group. I worked for one of those magazines and didn't even know it. Just think: Wright who had published so many successful books could not get enough to do a book on Africa. Wherever he went, the doors were closed. He wound up getting $2500 for *Savage Holiday*. His editor gave him problems. His agent gave him problems. There was just no dough. Everything dried up. Maybe, he ran into the cause for this.

DG: You seem to spend a lot of time teaching. Does that interfere with your writing?

JW: Sure it does, but there's not as much time involved as it looks in the resume. It hasn't all been successive either. I find it necessary to get out and touch reality. You sit at a typewriter all the time and you lose that touch, the way language changes, what people are thinking today as opposed to two years ago. It's not a matter of money so much as that, although this Distinguished Professorship I've had this year and last at LaGuardia Community College is like super welfare.

DG: Do you think, given your writing experience, that if you were white you would be receiving bigger offers for magazine pieces and lectures?

JW: Yes and no. I've had a lot of offers that I've turned down. With regard to the lecture thing, I don't like to spend a lot of time talking to people. I do enjoy giving readings, but generally, people want a lecture. I cannot go out and give a lecture every week. To me, giving a lecture entails writing up something or making up a bunch of cards. I insist on that because, given the political atmosphere in this country, I want to have a written record of what I've said. That means taking time to do a paper, so I'd rather do a reading. I've always enjoyed hearing other writers read, and I enjoy reading.

DG: You edited two issues of *Amistad*, a magazine of black writing which was one of the best things of its kind to appear. Why did it collapse?

JW: My partner on that was Charles Harris, who was on the staff at Random House. I'd known him a long time. As far as the magazine went, we had philosophical differences, or maybe personal differences would be more exact. I took it very seriously, and I think his seriousness did not match mine. Our approaches were different. I found myself doing a lot of the reading while the material going into his office would just lie around. Meetings would be called, and he wouldn't show up or he'd come late. If you're going to have a meeting it should be conducted with a certain degree of sobriety. I'd say, "Let's drink beer; we can have martinis afterwards." Eventually we came to a parting. I resigned from the publication and shortly after my resignation, he got fired. He is now the director of the university press at Howard, and he wants to resurrect the magazine. I wish him luck. He has bought the old inventory from Random House. They always claimed the magazine didn't sell, but I never believe publishers' figures. I felt we did some good things. There was a lot more we could have done if he had just been together more.

DG: Do you think you're still locked in the literary ghetto, and if you think so, do you think you'll ever get out?

JW: Oh, I'm locked in. No doubt about that. But like the Warsaw ghetto, even when they finally levelled it, there were still people inside who came out of it.

The Black Artist in New York:
An Interview with John A. Williams

W. Francis Browne / 1975

From *Centerpoint: A Journal of Interdisciplinary Studies* 1.3 (1975), 71–76.

John A. Williams, a Distinguished Professor in English at LaGuardia Community College of the City University of New York, Long Island City, is one of America's leading black writers. His works encompass a broad range of the black experience. They include innumerable short stories, novels and nonfiction, semidocumentaries, and children's books. He is the author of one of the most provocative novels of the last ten years, *The Man Who Cried I Am*. Among his nonfiction works is *The King God Didn't Save*, which gives "reflections on the life and death of Martin Luther King Jr." The following interview with W. Francis Browne focuses on Professor Williams's thoughts concerning the status of black letters in New York and in the country as a whole. His responses, however, extend to matters that are thought-provoking and significant for the people of all our society.

Centerpoint: You live in New York; other well-known black writers, some periodically, some permanently, for whatever reasons, have chosen to live as ex-patriates. How does New York as an intellectual climate stimulate your creativity? Also, how does New York function as a special influence on black literature, as a whole—especially in the 1970s?

Williams: For generations, New York has been the intellectual Mecca for all kinds of artists, and it really hasn't changed in the 1970s. In the 1970s the movement to New York is comparable to the movement to the "Apple" in the '20s and '30s. Now, the reason for this has to be, not only the presence of other artists, but the facilities for the acceptance and distribution of one's work. Coupled with that is just the idea that New York is one of the major cities in the world and it should offer the experiences that the good artists, I believe, put themselves in the way of. This is no less true for black writers than it is for white writers. Certainly great movements in black arts, in national arts, if they have not commenced in New York City, were first recognized in New York City. Black literature in the '70s—black American literature in the '70s–of course, has reference to black American literature in America for earlier periods. I equate the black literary movement of the '60s with the black literary movement in the 1920s and '30s. The influence of New York—being in New York, working in New York—in the '70s, is, to a large degree, negative. Now, that is because black writers are not being published as much as they were ten years ago. Since publishing is a business, moving by trends in the sand, the consensus among black writers now living in New York is that the fad is over and that life is, indeed, becoming, if not already, very rough for the black writer. Now, in a way this might be good in the long run because writers black, white, or pink, tend to have an idea that the publication of one book, or a couple of books, is going to make them financially secure, and these publications will bring them worldwide recognition for all time. Now, we need to move out of this adolescent point of view, and, in that sense, what's going on today may serve as a beneficial factor in dealing with the future. But black writers have discovered that, like the black foundry worker, both step out in the world to the extent that he or she is expendable, that the best parish in the world, basically, is a kind particularity created by black writers. That is the kind of influence New York City has on black writers today in the mid-1970s.

Centerpoint: Is racism practiced in certain degrees in various major cities throughout this country toward authors? For example, are publishers' attitudes different toward black authors in New York than they are in cities such as Chicago, San Francisco, Detroit, etc.? If not, why?

Williams: The question seems to relate to influence and how black writers are reacting to that influence which is most definitely larded with racism. In New York, I think, while publishers are not publishing black writers to the extent that they were ten years ago, their attitudes toward black writers are, perhaps, a little better than the attitudes of publishers in Chicago, San Francisco, and Detroit. The reason for that is *numbers*. There are more black writers living in New York who are able to pick up the phone and curse out their editors and agents than there are in these other cities. If you're any kind of author who does not live in New York, you have some distance between yourself and your editor or your agent. If editors and agents are not doing well by an author, they would prefer that he be in the Northwoods somewhere rather than in New York City, where he or she might be able to bother the editor or agent at a moment's notice. Publishing works hand-in-hand with media, of course, and I'm speaking now about the reviewers and critics. If publishers are publishing books by black writers in declining numbers, reviewers and critics very soon get the hint—if they have not gotten it earlier in the steam baths and private clubs they all share—so that the reviewers and critics are not reviewing books done by black writers, when and if they are published. If no one hears about you, you might just as well not be publishing. And, of course, there are more reviewers and critics on the East and West coasts. Some reviewers and critics tend to be small, unimaginative people. They do not understand the works they review and take their directions from large eastern publications, like *Time, Newsweek,* the *New York Times Review,* and the *Washington Post.* When these indicate that black writing is no longer in style, reviewers in Dubuque, Des Moines, and other smaller cities, follow the program and ignore the publication of such work. There is no escaping the presence of racism in publishing, in reviewing and in critical areas dealing with American literature. It has always been there. But in the '60s, the attitude of the country, perhaps one of great fear and uncertainty, was reflected in the amount of critical attention and reviewing given to the works of black writers—all of this in no way dispelled the underlying currents of racism inherent within the system.

Centerpoint: Do you believe that the renewed interest in ethnic literatures was triggered by the outpourings of black writings in the '60s? Also, does this fragmentation of literature into special interest groups lessen the effectiveness of black writers in their efforts to achieve universal appeal?
Williams: I believe that the impetus of black studies, black literature, etc., is responsible for the resurgence of other ethnic literatures in this country. Frankly, I think that a lot of suggested areas for study in ethnic literature are silly. Much of American history and literature is, in any case, ethnic, largely white Anglo-Saxon-Protestant, but certainly Italian, Irish, to some extent, Polish, Jewish, and on and on. Many of these ethnic groups have had the opportunity to deal with their ethnicity in certain clubs, sponsored by various universities around the country. This was hardly ever the case with the nonwhite minority. Dean Allan B. Ballard's book, *The Education of Black Folks,* points out that City University has always encouraged and supported the various ethnic educational clubs within the system. With American literature as hard up for money as the reports tell us, whether they're true or not, the fragmentation of literature, as you call it, will further decrease the

amount of money to be made available to nonwhite literature studies. And that perhaps is exactly what the new ethnic literature fragmentation is all about. I believe that American literature is many interdependent literatures and ought to be taught in that fashion. I teach a course which compares one black and one white writer from the eighteenth century to the present. I would like to see the same hold for Amer-Indian literature, Spanish American literature, French American literature, because certainly we've had a number of French missionary explorers. We've had early Swedish and Irish settlements in America, and there must be some literature available. In fact, I know there is. American literature will never be truly American literature until it begins to definitely encompass the experiences in literature of all its diverse peoples. One can hardly imagine British literature without its Irish writers.

Centerpoint: At the last Pan-African Congress, a number of African writers took a position against appeals to blackness or nègritude in black letters. They felt that such an emphasis was racist in nature and tone. What is your attitude or position with regard to blackness or nègritude as reverse racism in literature?

Williams: I once took opposition to the term "nègritude," feeling that it was racism in reverse. "Racist" was, of course, the wrong term because to be racist one must be a member of the power group that can wield influence, the kind of influence which can be detrimental to you as an individual. Black people do not hold that power. Therefore, to be termed "racist" is without foundation, in fact. The popularity of the term "nègritude" in the '60s, particularly in French-speaking Africa and the Caribbean, always seemed to me to be rather elitist. The term does not have much application for the masses of black people, who are not, in fact, that involved in the reading or production of literature to begin with. Also, I think that nègritude belabors the point. There are very few black writers who have written successfully outside their skins, anyway. Now, nègritude seems to mean that those who abide by the philosophy have believed their white critics and have tried to become, in a sense, blacker than they were. I hold that black writers, wherever they are, have been, are, and always will be capable of writing universally from their peculiar ethnic situation. I know that black writers must have faith, within themselves, as individuals, that that is basically what they are dealing with, no less than Israeli writers, no less than Greek writers, no less than Norwegian writers, no less than any other writer. And any other writer must certainly come from some kind of ethnic or national strain. Our blackness is our blackness. It is not going to disappear. We must rest easy with it, see the world through these skins, and allow the world to perceive us within those skins.

Centerpoint: Since the '60s, the fire appears to have gone out of black letters. Does this mean that black writers can only respond as artists when there is a climate of protest, such as existed in the '60s, that without protest black letters will decline?

Williams: I don't agree that the fire appears to have gone out of black letters. Less attention is accorded to black writers (and this goes back to the first question, I guess). The experimentation of William Melvin Kelley, the satire of Ishmael Reed, the marvelous historical stances of George Lamming and John Killens, the rural grit depicted in the works of Earnest Gaines—all these represent a chronic attack upon the same old system, the same old enemy—with better quality weapons. As to dissenting voices? Those voices were only heard through courtesy of the white media. The sound of those voices sold newspapers, magazines and brought in television advertisers. What sold in the 1960s did not necessarily sell in the 1970s. The platforms from which to issue dissent have been removed. Finally, black letters will decline only so far. There are always going to be good black writers. Until black people themselves can manufacture the platforms for distribution and voice, then the cries of rage will come and go, depending upon white society which controls all the outlets.

Centerpoint: Do you think established black literary figures, now quiescent, are silent because they are no longer reaching the people, or because they are no longer marketable, as far as publishers are concerned?

Williams: I think with some writers the consideration of being, as you put it, written out, is quite fair. I imagine it could happen to any writer. And once again, I think all the reaching out to people should be a two-way street. People should reach out for the writers, too. I don't think black people are doing as much reaching out as they should. In reference to your first question, black writers certainly are not as marketable as they were seven or eight years ago. To a large extent that explains the kind of quiet atmosphere that you detect at the moment.

Centerpoint: Addison Gayle comments in his book, *The Black Aesthetic*, that because blacks' cultural position in America is unique, they have created a "unique art derived from a unique cultural experience" which

"mandates unique critical tools for evaluation." To what extent is it possible and necessary for blacks to develop critical tools to judge their own work?
Williams: The black man's cultural position in America is unique, I believe, wholly in terms of degree. If we take slavery as one extreme in this democratic-capitalistic society, and freedom to be the opposite extreme, then, we can readily see that black people have indeed represented the first pole. Most other white people have been deluded that they have been free, when, in fact, because of the system, they have never been free and never will be free until they manage to draw the relationship between their own positions and those of black people in the United States. We have all been economic cannon fodder, and our position has delineated the bottom. White people have not, in the main, delineated the top. Only a few white people have, will, unless some basic social and economic change is made in this country. And that change cannot be effected until black and white understand that they both have been victims, that blacks were most victimized. Whites were, but only to a lesser extent, less victimized. My friend, Addison, may have come up with some criteria to judge black literature. I think, that is to what extent it serves black people, not only in this country, but around the world, because that is the world situation. But in that reflection I would hope to see images of universality, for in the final analysis, just the primary racial characteristics of the black writer, which is his color, is a more universal color than is white, and that the route should be self to group to universe. I'm reminded of a piece of Lorraine Hansberry's, and I'd like to quote it, because I think that black writers of all people, must remember this. In one of her plays, a black man says that he wishes he could hate all white men: "That I'm afraid that, among other things, I've seen the slums of Liverpool and Dublin, and the caves above Naples. I've seen their cow and Anne Frank's attic in Amsterdam. I've seen too many raw-knuckled Frenchmen coming out of the Metro at dawn to believe that those who raided Africa for three centuries ever loved the white race either." While Richard Wright said that the Negro was America's metaphor, I would extend that and say that the Negro is the world's metaphor. If humanity, as we have been taught it or feel it or sense it goes out of our people, as we have seen it go out of other people through the historical ages, then I believe there is no hope for anyone. I don't wish to be mystical about this, but I do feel that the position that we now find ourselves in does possess fantastic mystical overtones of which we should be very aware.

Centerpoint: On Broadway, in the movies, on television, there are, and have been, several productions by and about blacks. How has New York's black literary coterie responded to this outgrowth, in terms of such media being an outlet for black writers to have their works performed?

Williams: There have not been enough productions on Broadway by and about blacks. New York's black literary coterie, as far as I can determine, begins a new scramble every time a black production is mounted. Aside from the Henry Street Settlement House and some of Woodie King's productions, there does not seem to be a continuity of black productions for the stage, and certainly not on television. And these productions have just barely begun to scratch the surface of black life in this country. At the moment I feel that many of them follow the same pattern, but this is going to change, I'm sure, as it must. And one of the dangers of mounting productions of these kinds is that they are rewritten, touched up—they become not what the original authors intended, as in *Miss Jane Pittman*, as in the case of Ed Bullins's play, *The Apartment*, I believe it was. So, again, we run a risk by not having control from the typewriter to final production. When a play is ready, whether it's television or stage, it has to go into other hands which strip the work of its guts, and we black people are left with a faint reflection of our real selves. I'm told that the newest attempt to delineate the story of Malcolm X, for example, ends when Malcolm goes into jail. Now this does not get into the essence of Malcolm the man that we all knew. But this is Hollywood for you.

Centerpoint: In your novel, *The Man Who Cried I Am*, Max Reddick was conveniently murdered because he had stumbled upon a secret plan (The King Alfred Plan) for the genocide of *all* black people. Has your outlook on black Americans and on this country's outlook toward its black citizens changed in view of the apparent quiet of black social activity today?

Williams: In *The Man Who Cried I Am*, anybody who knows American history and European history could have written the King Alfred Plan just as I did. And anybody who knows history could have also seen, or foreseen, that to have black people starve in Africa was OK—that to be fucking over Southeast Asia was OK, as long as whites do not molest each other within Western civilization. And they certainly have not. Yes, it's quiet today because they brought in Nixon to put out the fires. Everybody understood what Nixon was talking about, so everybody was cool—which does not mean that racial antipathies have changed. We are merely into a wary stage. Having done that in *The Man Who Cried I Am* and the King Alfred Plan, I wanted to do a couple of books dealing, in a sense, with more personal themes in the sense of characters. But I expect to get back on the big black scene, perhaps, in nonfiction, very shortly. My view hasn't changed at all.

Centerpoint: There has been some debate over the appropriateness of the euphemism *Renaissance I and II* when referring to the black writings of the '20s in Harlem and that of the '60s. Is such a term appropriate when noting these unique periods of black writing?

Williams: The terms *Renaissance I, Renaissance II* are ironic, having to do with everyone's foreknowledge of the fact that the good things in the '60s was going to end at one time or another. I think the term is appropriate, because during Renaissance I, white writers of the Jazz Age were suddenly copping materials from the black experience for use in their own works. We have seen this to be true in the '60s with Malamud, Styron, Bellow, Updike, Mailer—a whole host of established white writers have become so bereft of material that they had to turn to the black experience for material. In that sense, the continuum from Harlem Renaissance I and Renaissance II is a direct line.

Centerpoint: Given the history of the black man's special experience in America, is there a possibility that the so-called "black" American, because of these unique historical experiences, will come to regard himself as a new human creation—unlike any ethnic group anywhere in the world?

Williams: I would have to disagree with this view. I don't think there's any new and human creativity. And, in fact, such an assumption would effectively undercut the drive back to the roots. It's most important in these days of revisionist biology and genetics and history, however much there has been crossbreeding, that one retain the essences of those roots he or she can find. It seems to be coming clearer that the black man, in spite of the long and terrible suffering, was, perhaps, the original man. And out of this suffering I see great strength coming, our numbers and intelligence growing, our abilities expanding. Finally, no other people under such long duress have managed to increase their numbers as we have. In that increase we have affected the history not only of this nation but of the world, the politics of this nation, the economics of this nation. And in that regard we cannot in any way be considered a new creation, but the oldest of the old with much work still to be done in front of us.

Centerpoint: Thank you, Professor Williams.

An Interview with John A. Williams: Journalist and Novelist

James Hatch / 1981

From *Artist & Influence* Vol. I (1981), 183–98. © Hatch-Billops Collection, Inc.
Reprinted with permission of James V. Hatch.

James Hatch: John A. Williams was born in Jackson, Mississippi. He didn't stay there very long. He moved to New York very quickly. As you know, he is a marvelous short story writer and editor, an editor of anthologies, a writer of essays, a teacher, a professor, a journalist, and a television writer. He has written nine novels that have been published. I don't know about the unpublished ones. Some of them all of us have read: *The Man Who Cried I Am*; *Sons of Darkness, Sons of Light*; *Captain Blackman*; *The Junior Bachelor Society*; and the new one according to the *New York Times* today, but they didn't include a title. What's the title going to be?
John Williams: *!Click Song.*

JH: He has even published books of nonfiction. *This Is My Country Too*, *The King God Didn't Save* about Martin Luther King, and *Flashbacks*. He's the editor of a number of anthologies which you can see here on the table: *Yardbird* and *Amistad*. And he has written dozens of articles in magazines and newspapers including the old *New York Herald Tribune* and the *New York Post*. I counted up on the resume. He's lectured or taught in over thirty colleges across the United States.

I first met him when he was teaching at City College here in New York—creative writing. In 1965 Leo Hamalian, who is seated right there, was living in Damascus with not too much to do. He was a Fulbright. And Jim Hatch was living in Cairo with even less to do. I read a James Bond book, and I said, "I can do that." So I wrote a James Bond book with a black detective. And Leo said, "Oh, that's not too good. I can write it better." And he rewrote it. We brought it back to City College in 1965, and Leo said, "Well, let's let John Williams read it. He's a very good novelist. He'll tell us, you know, how to make it even better." I said, "Well, that man's not going to read our book." And Leo said, "Oh, yes, he will. He's a friend. He'll read it."

He read the manuscript and gave us back these six pages of typewritten criticism. And I will read to you only the first couple of sentences. "I finished your novel and found myself irritated with it. It does have the James Bond quality, and that's part of my irritation."

I knew at this point that here was a man who was honest and good and had excellent taste. And, of course, the novel was never published. But it is that kind of patience the man had with his students at that time. So, today we would like to seek out some of the people who have had patience with you. So, let us go back to—not to Jackson, maybe—but to parents or Syracuse?

JW: Well, I guess it would have to be Syracuse. I usually start my life story with the fact that I was conceived in Syracuse and born in Jackson. In some places that doesn't go down too well. But that's precisely what happened. I was the first-born of four children, so as was traditional, my mother decided to return home and my father worked with a circus to get his passage down to Mississippi. My father believed in wearing starched white shirts, even during the week. So that in that area—Hinds County—he was the only Black man who wore a starched white shirt on Monday, Tuesday, Wednesday, Thursday, Friday, and Saturday—no church days.

And, somehow, this really didn't work out too well with the local sheriff. Something happened, and he came out to my grandfather's house—my mother tells this story, and she said, "It was the only time I was ashamed of Poppa." I said, "Well, what happened?"

"Well, the sheriff came out and said, 'Some such-and-such happened in town, and Joe Jones, your son-in-law, is the only strange nigger in town. He must have done it.'" And, so my father left in a hay wagon, buried under the hay. They searched it with pitchforks and got him in the shoulder, but he didn't scream. He just stayed there until he knew it was safe. He still has that dimple in his shoulder.

But they had met in Syracuse, where my mother was working as a domestic, having been trained at Tougaloo, which is now a bona fide university college, but at that time was a training school for domestics. And they had met there: my father holding up a telephone pole—as my mother puts it—while she was on her way to church. There was that attraction, and here I am.

I don't really have any mentors, as such, in terms of writing. I am grateful to the United States Navy. Actually, at first to the librarians at Syracuse who let me read anything I could get my hands on, let me take out as many books as I could carry. This was during the Depression, and the escape was very necessary even for a kid who could somehow see pretty much what was happening.

My mother's a very strong woman. I suspect my father was a very strong man, but I have no real evidence of that other than this little story I will tell you. They used to have periodic fights, and they were pretty good. At one time I went up into the closet shelf—on the left was a .32 and on the right was a lead pipe. So I figured they must have been pretty strong people—because they survived each other.

But, I really didn't understand how strong they might have been until I was in the Navy when I had several occasions to display my own strength. It seems as though I was forever in the brig for one thing or another. In the Navy, that's what the guardhouse is, and the badder you are, the worse the brig is. The worst brig you can ever be sent to is a Marine Corps brig, and I got to know quite a few of those. While I was there—and I was still very young because I went into the service at about seventeen and a half—I started thinking of this injustice which so many young people used to write about when they began writing. They don't anymore. What they write about these days is security and money, so we're already into another age. I thought it was very unjust for the Navy to treat me the way it was, so I wrote about it . . . in poetry and things of this sort. Without any training, just an outpouring of what I felt in language that was acceptable. The language I was thinking was completely unprintable, so we reached a compromise. I came out of the Navy, and I started school on the GI Bill at Syracuse. Actually, I had gone south to play football—to Atlanta, Georgia. Time is a very funny thing because I had forgotten from the time I got discharged—January 4, 1946—until I went south—September 3, 1946—how badly those crackers had treated me. But once I was in Atlanta working out with a team—about five or six days, about two days before classes began—I said, "This is it. I don't know how to behave. I'm going to get into trouble." I left Georgia and went back to Syracuse and enrolled in the College of Liberal Arts.

I had a freshman composition teacher whose first name I've forgotten. His last name was Couchman, and he was very impressed with the composition I had done on an invasion. I think that was the first time I had ever been complimented on my writing. I had written a great deal to my folks while I was in the Navy. But, unfortunately, most of the letters came "Dear Folks, . . . Love, Johnny" with not too much in-between—all censored out.

Then, I stumbled onto this big, burly Irishman named Daniel Curley, who instead of fighting like the rest of us red-blooded American boys during the War had worked in the dockyards. He wrote short stories for *Atlantic Monthly* and was also a playwright. He taught creative writing at Syracuse. Basically his thing was discipline. You always had to produce when you got to his class. As a matter of fact, he tells me now that students—he's at the University of Illinois—his students call him Professor Cruelly—not Curley, Cruelly. And I think that discipline was very good for what I thought I wanted to do. I still was not all that sure. I knew I liked it, and I felt that I certainly could write better than much of the material I was reading. I started writing poetry when I was at Syracuse. We had a magazine called *Dilemma* or *Vomit* or something like that. And we competed to get our stuff in the magazine.

I remember submitting poetry—sending poetry—to people like Karl Shapiro and William Carlos Williams, Robert Penn Warren, Langston Hughes, some of whom were very kind with their responses. But I remember particularly the response from William Carlos Williams, who didn't answer right away. He said, "Whenever you write to an elder poet, god-damnit, you always include a self-addressed stamped envelope." So I said, "That's good to know. I'll remember that." But then, a month or so later he sent another note which was much softer and kinder in tone, and I got some nice words from Langston Hughes.

Now, the point I guess I'm trying to make is that there was no one there to whom I could show work and get any evaluations that I thought might work for me. I did have a classmate named Dennis Lynds, who writes under three or four different names today—detective novels, mainly. Dennis and I were very close. I named my second son after him. I thought I was a better poet than he, and he thought he was better—and I still believe I was a better poet. I am a better poet. But, in the exchange of manuscripts there was always something beyond the looking at the work. Dennis was white, and I was black. And some of these things spilled over into the criticism that remain there until today. So, whatever Dennis said about the work, I always took with a grain of salt. He was really quite sure that he was going to wind up being what Norman Mailer did become—the shadow of Ernest Hemingway. Swore by Ernest Hemingway. I got so sick of Ernest Hemingway, boy. . . . Until today when I have a student who wants to do an individual study on Hemingway, I ask them, "Are you sure you want to do Hemingway?"

Anyway, we remained friends for quite a few years without exchanging copy, and he was very—extremely—helpful to me during some of the frequent lean periods that I had. Dennis was important to me for another reason and that was that he gave me an area of measurement. It was pretty much like playing ball when I was a kid. I could say, "Well, damn, that white boy is not so bad. You know, I just took him out, man, made him fumble. That ain't so bad. That ain't so bad." Then I'd look at Dennis's stuff. I'd say to myself, "Gee, this isn't bad, man." Meanwhile I'd be saying, "Shit. . . ." That, I think, is very important in terms of the ego that's always involved in creative work. You have it even in the creative writing classes where one student will say, "Hey, I'm the best turkey in this class." And then you'll tell them, "Well, you're not so hot, you know; this other student has this, that, and the other going for him or her." He won't believe it. Sometimes the criticism gets so heated that you have to cut class and say, "Hey, let's have a party and drink some wine and talk about this." So it's an ongoing thing, which Dennis and I, I suppose, got over simply by dropping out of contact with each other over the years.

Another person who became important in my life for a short time—and you probably will not believe this—was my ex-mother-in-law who bought me my first typewriter. She called me a mean old son-of-a-bitch when I was breaking up with her daughter, but she knew, I think, that I was really serious about things that I was doing. So she bought me this typewriter for Christmas, and I said, "Well, she ain't so bad. Maybe I can put up with her for a little while. Not too bad at all."

And the people of Syracuse—we tend to forget that communities, even black communities or especially black communities, always had a kind of extended family relationship—people that work and people watching out for the children and people being encouraging in many, many different ways. So, we had that too. Of course, at that time all of us wanted to grow up and become like Percy Harris because Percy Harris was the numbers banker in town. But Percy Harris also bought the Boy Scout uniforms and the athletic equipment and sort of stayed out of the background—kept the cops off us 'cause the cops in Syracuse were atrocious. They would break up a penny craps game and take the pennies. I think about it sometimes . . . wow.

Then there was another man named Herbert Johnson, who we called Hoppy–something to do with the way he walked–who was at Dunbar Center. He guided all of us in many, many different ways. He was not only one of the administrators of the center, but he was the Scoutmaster. He was the basketball coach; he was the guy who gave parties when he thought we were old enough to deserve nice parties. Like my son went to his first party—second party—last night, okay? Now, I think he probably should not go to a party 'til he's about ninety-five, but that's because I'm his father. It takes somebody from outside to determine these things, and Hoppy was the kind of guy who did that and did it very well.

Billy Chiles. Billy Chiles was the welfare worker for our district in Syracuse. He was the first and only black member of the Welfare Department, I guess, until some years after World War II, so he was sort of a pillar in the community. Bill had come from the Midwest somewhere— St. Louis, Kansas City, KCMO—someplace like that. And he had tough times because you've got a whole community that's been dropped on this man simply because he's black. Bill somehow managed to survive it, and he had his own family and so on. Years later I wound up at the Welfare Department, too, working with Bill. We had a chance to talk about a great many things. Bill, like other people in town, took the attitude, "Oh, you want to be a writer? Ok. All right." Nobody said, "What? Are you crazy?" Nobody said, "No, no, it's not going to work. You don't want to be a writer. You want to work for the Sanitation Department. You want to do something steady."

I mean, some people did tell me that. But the people who counted didn't tell me that. They just said, "Oh. You want to be a writer? Well, ok. All right, now you're old enough. You're past fifteen. You know what's going down, right?" And Bill was one of those people. People like that are always important, I think, in one's life because you're always running into other people who want you to get the nine to five, who want you to wear the suit, who want you to become a trustee or a deacon in church, who want you to be in the delegation that goes down to talk to the mayor about Black History Month, . . . or whatever. There are always people like that. And, we recognize that not all of us can be that.

Another person who was very helpful to me: Wendell J. Roye, who was at Syracuse at the time I was. Together with Bob Johnson, who is now executive editor at *Jet*, and Rick Hurt, who went from there to the *Norfolk Journal and Guide* and involved me in the journalism sequence at Syracuse where people looked at you as if you might have had four heads. A giraffe with an elephant's body and four heads. "Journalism!" you know, "what the hell you people going to do?" sort of thing. But Wendell became a very close friend after I had moved to New York. We used to hunt pheasant together and talk together about problems with writing, whether it was public relations— and that was basically what he was involved in before he went to the Urban League—or other things. So, for the solitude and the space to change ideas, I thank him for that.

My first—let me call him mainstream editor, with a grain of salt because I'm sure that's the way he would feel too—was a man named Cecil Hemley, who was at Farrar Strauss and now Giroux. Cecil used to publish Noonday Press in the fifties, which was a good publication. I forget how often it came out. Anyhow, I took a short story over there and left it. And they said they were filled up and could I check back in about three or four months? I checked back in about three or four months, and they said, "Well, you know, we've been sold to Roger Strauss's outfit, and we're not doing short stories anymore. Do you have anything longer? Would you have something like a book?"

And, as it happened, I had two books, one of which had already gone over to Dell to be a paperback original and the other, something I called *Sissie*. Cecil looked at *Sissie* and said that they wanted to do it, and what else had I done? I told him, so they bought the other which was *Night Song* from Dell. And that was it. Basically it was just a matter of luck, as with all of these things.

I find it very hard to tell young people that you can have the skill, the good looks, everything. But if you don't have the luck, it just won't happen. It simply will not happen. And that's what happened with me.

Now, Cecil died swimming. But he was familiar—he was the right editor at the right time. We used to sit, and he would read my scripts word for word so that I could hear what was coming out. You can read the same thing a thousand times and still miss stuff. A thousand times. But if you hear it, you get different vibrations. He was the only editor I ever had who did that.

George and Vivian Patterson. George was a Syracusan. He was about five years younger than I was and was sort of a protégé to everybody in our group. He came down to New York and played football one year with Lou Little. He was a classmate of Frank Thomas, who is now at the Ford Foundation. George and Vivian got married. I think the day before—the night before they were going to get married—George was ambivalent about it. It's kind of funny now. I was out running through the Village with Vivian trying to find George, but we found him. We found him, and they got married. They lived a couple of blocks from me. I had fallen on extremely lean times. Vivian was working in Columbia's French Department, and George was working for the Department of Parks with Little League baseball teams and cleaning up here and there. I could not wait until like 5:30 when I knew they would both be home, and Vivian would be burning. It was eating time then. I would go over on 4th Street—they had a walk-up place—and we would sit down. It was like a whole family thing, and we exchanged a couple of very important favors for each other.

I had a cousin named Gene Williams. I tried to get him to leave Syracuse at the same time I left, and he never did. He's still there. Nevertheless, he was a good ear for me, and his mother was even better. She was sort of like a second mother to me.

And those are the people along the way. I'm sure I must have forgotten about fifty or sixty, but these seem to me to be the important ones.

JH: What about writers that you just read? Ones that you read but you never met?

JW: Well, I've always liked *Under the Volcano* by Malcolm Lowry. I've always liked Alejo Carpentier. I like Twain. I think I prefer his nonfiction to his fiction, particularly when he's into social issues. I liked Hughes, as a writer, as a person. *Invisible Man.* I preferred *The Outsider* to *Native Son.* Chester Himes, *The Primitive.* Who else? Lots of people. I can't think of them all right now.

JH: (To the audience) This is your chance to ask what you've always wanted to know.

Q: Why did you want to write? When you started . . . was it reading anything particularly, or a sense that you could write?

JW: It was not by reading any one thing in particular. It just seemed to me when I was very young that people could say things in books that were important that they did not seem to be saying in person. I think it's sort of like being a preacher or a teacher. There's not that much difference between them. I know of some writers who look at it like it was the *Wall Street Journal.* I mean, Wall Street, period. I envy them, but at the same time I don't envy the material they produce.

Q: Did Richard Wright's books affect you in any way, or what did you think of them?

JW: Well, you remember that when his early books came out—even *Native Son,* I was still pretty much a kid. And my view of the world was sort of in the *Chicago Defender, Amsterdam News,* the lousy *Syracuse Herald-Journal, The Syracuse Post,* and what the porters on trains talked about. I really didn't know that much about the world, and therefore I didn't really relate to some of those things until I was much older.

When Wright was involved with the Communists, he tried to have allegiances to both the party and the people, but the party said, "Hell, you can't have both, you know. It's got to be one or the other. And then look at *Native Son* in terms of its structure: the way he uses the media in that book—the way he uses the media in all of his books. All of that came much, much later. I think as it came later for me, Wright himself was doing different things with each of his books. So the process of growth is always there for the reader and for the writer.

Q: Aside from the development of the craft and technique, what was the most difficult thing you faced as a writer?

JW: Eating . . . occasionally. Well, I know that's funny. But, you know, within my own family I would have relatives who would say, "Johnny, are you still writing?" or they'd come in, they'd look at the books on the shelf, "You wrote all those books?" and some would suggest that black people are getting a better chance to work good jobs these days. The concept of writing as work somehow didn't really seep in until, I would say with most people in my family, until the last ten or fifteen years. Then, sometimes, they look at me funny.

Q: What was the first thing you wrote, and what was it about?

JW: The first thing I can remember writing is something I will call free-verse poetry, about how the Navy sucks. I remember getting the typewriter from the chief pharmacist's mate and taking it out to this tent and writing this poetry about how bad the Navy was. As soon as I finished—the day after I finished the poems—they sent me to the brig. So, you know, they didn't read the poems, but they had good cause to. They had *not* had good cause to send me to the brig, but I knew I was going.

Q: I'm not sure, but in the sixties did you go to Africa?

JW: I did, and, as you know, Bill (Hutson), I went back. I was back last August. It's really, really kind of a trip. I don't know how to explain it other than to say that it's complex to be there, to be with people. And a lot of that complexity deals with whether you're in the city or out in the bush. If you're in the city, it's like a city anywhere. It's filled with people who are trying to survive, who are adjusting from one environment to another. If you go into the bush, it's stable. It's always been stable. The values are different. Well, let me see if I can give you an example.

I was in Kenya with some journalists. At one hotel people said, "Oh, here come some African Nigros (sic)." I'd say, "Oh, boy!" Then others would say, "Neegroes (sic)." Now, we're into this Black Brother kind of situation. We go over there, and in many areas of the society it's just not there. I mean, we are different. We have no tribes; we have no attachments, no whatever. Now, if you're going out, say, on the main street of Mombasa to buy some curios, now those cats know everything. "Hey, Brother . . ." Everything . . . you know, "What's happenin', Baby?" And they all got caps from the US aircraft carrier that's out there. That's another thing that—the US's putting a lot of dough into Kenya. So you can go to the harbor and see carriers tied up at the same dock with Russian freighters. They figure they can handle thirty thousand military personnel out there. Obviously wherever we go with money, something happens to the local people. That's already started to happen.

But the complexity I have found—and it's, I guess, about sixteen years since we first went—I still can't put Africa down in ways that satisfy me.

Q: I notice that you have two volumes on the *Amistad*. It's the story you told me that's intrigued me. I wonder—I mean, what influence that had on you, and why did you continue that in your anthology because you brought a lot under the whole *Amistad* title?

JW: You mean, behind the actual occurrence? The actual mutiny? Well, I think it is . . . it was, at least one of the times in recorded history when slaves did mutiny. The record was kept. What happened to those former slaves in the US courts—vindication of their freedom as men who had freed themselves from slavers—that was a very important incident in a document for all Americans because we seem not to really want to close with the kind of history we actually have. And there it is in microcosm. So that's why we used it. I think that that's the only way one achieves freedom. It's not something that people are going to give you. You're going to have to take it, and that's implicit in the story.

Q: There was somebody who said the other day that if you ever wanted to understand the factions, different factions, within the black literary world, you should read certain anthologies. I was just curious to know if you had any comments on the whole notion of factionalism within the literary world and if it had had any effect on your career or your development or experience as a writer.

JW: Well, let me start with this. I know something about factionalism. I don't think it's affected my career or development too much. I can remember being very concerned when Herbert Hill, who was then labor secretary for the NAACP, was putting his anthology together called *Soon One Morning*. I was very concerned whether Herb was going to put me in it or not. I really sweated. Then I saw that develop into a very political kind of anthology. And then I started putting together anthologies myself. You can either put anthologies together and be very honest as an editor, as a creative person, or you can be a crook: which is that you don't pay the proper commissions for the material that you want to use. What you can steal is what you keep. What you don't pay these poor people or their estates—and all writers are poor people—it's yours to pocket. It's in many ways a terrible business to be into, but a lot of people do it.

Now, the factionalism does apply. Langston Hughes did—what was that in the sixties, you remember that collection he did?—*New Negro Poets, U.S.A.* in which he cut across all age groups and factions. Now, I understand that Michael Harper and Robert Stepto have an anthology out that's supposed to be a real literary black writing.

Q: *The Chant of Saints.*
JW: Now, the word started going around about that book two years ago. So we all knew what that was going to be. There have been several, and undoubtedly there will be several others, that cater to this. You are limited by the amount of money that you are given to do that. You're limited by your own perception of what it is you want your contributors to say. And then I think you're limited by where the book is going after it's published. So you accept it. The thing is that when you're starting out, or even after you're established, you simply can't be involved in all of these little things because they drain your energies. And in some very secret, nasty way we all have, that's exactly what we want the other guy to do: Lose sleep so we can steal his energy. You know, take his picture. Whatever.

Q: John, the first time I ever heard of Ed Doctorow, the author of *Ragtime*, was through you. You were preparing an anthology for Crowell, which stupidly they never published. Did Ed Doctorow have any influence on your work?
JW: No. No, as a matter of fact, Ed was acting as editor for *This Is My Country, Too*, a book which had already been beautifully edited by the people at *Holiday* magazine. So Ed had nothing to do whatsoever. But, at the time we met, Ed had done *Welcome to Hard Times*, a kind of cowboy psychodrama. He had not done any, what I would consider, mainstream writing at that point.

Q: Before, you talked about when you started writing in terms of poetry and short stories and novels. At what point does one feel that he is ready or has the form together to start a novel? I mean, that just seems very ambitious. It's very different from poetry. And, I was just wondering if there was some time when you can say, "It's got to be a novel."

JW: For me and my friend Dennis it seemed to have gone in stages. We started with poetry because that really takes the most discipline, but after a while there's something else that you want to say with words. And why in the hell should you be confined to this old jive form, anyway. So what you would have said in a poem becomes something you say in a short story. Now, our experience was that the short stories kept getting longer and longer.

Q: But a novel is not really a long short story.

JW: I know, but you see, when you take a short story, you're dealing with one or two or three primary characters. You just can't bring the whole barroom into a short story. But the minute you have created character A thinking or doing such and such and character B responding and character C thinking or responding to so and so and there's still a void there, something's wrong with your story. Then you gotta bring in D, E, and F. You gotta do something with the action. And pretty soon this little form where your short story is running like hell for 225 pages, 300 pages, and you're wondering how it got there. That's the way it goes. I don't think you can plan a novel.

Q: You don't?

JW: I've heard kids say, "Well, I think I'm going to do a novel for this course." I say, "Ok, check back with me in seven weeks; let's see how you've done."

Q: In *Flashbacks* you talk about My Man Himes—Chester Himes. Two questions: What are your thoughts about Chester's extended expatriate writings, and expatriates at large? And how is Chester doing?

JW: I don't know how Chester's doing. We had a falling out, which is not unnatural for writers. Last I heard he was thinking to settle down on the West Coast. Expatriate writers? I think some people can work anywhere, and I know the complaint with Richard Wright was that he had been away too long, particularly when he wrote *The Long Dream*. But those people who criticized him for that book didn't know the book at all because it was based very solidly on research in Mississippi at the time that Wright was growing up. You can be away and still do your job. There tends to be a kind of romantic atmosphere cast over people who are expatriates. I've heard people say, "But, boy, in order to be a successful writer you have to spend some time in Europe, don't you?" I say, "Oh, man, forget it." But there is something about being abroad that gives you perspective about this place that you could not have had if you'd stayed. So I think it's always well to get away if you can and sort of look over your shoulder, down the tunnel, and see what's going on.

Contemporary Authors Interview

Jean W. Ross / 1981

From *Contemporary Authors New Revision Series*, OE. © 1982 Gale, a part of Cengage Learning, Inc. Reproduced by permission. www.cengage.com/permissions.

Contemporary Authors interviewed John A. Williams by phone April 1, 1981, at his home in Teaneck, New Jersey.

CA: You started writing in the Pacific during World War II. Did you want to write earlier?
Williams: I'm not sure whether I did or not. I wanted to read a great deal earlier, and since I draw a relationship between reading and writing, I suppose somewhere in the inner recesses of my psyche, I probably wanted to write earlier.

CA: Were your parents in any way influential in your becoming a writer?
Williams: No, only later as characters around whom you measure other people who would be characters in your books. But direct encouragement, no.

CA: Your parents, who were then living in Syracuse, New York, traveled to Jackson, Mississippi, for your birth, then back to Syracuse, where you grew up. Was Jackson the original home of both your parents?
Williams: Jackson was my mother's original home; my father's original home was upstate New York. My mother left Mississippi to go to work in Syracuse and there met my father. I was the first-born, at which point I guess it was still pretty ritualistic to go back home to have your first child. That's what happened.

CA: Did you feel any sense of southern heritage or influence growing up?
Williams: Never.

CA: Early in your career you worked as a foreign correspondent for *Ebony*, *Jet*, *Newsweek*, and *Holiday*. Did you enjoy that work?

Williams: I like the way *I* did it, which was being loosely a correspondent with press credentials and cable cards and so on, but without the rather rigid stipulations that apply to people these days. I traveled and I sent in pieces and I wrote what I thought was worthy. It was interesting. I think if I had come to it a bit younger I would have loved it a great deal, but at the time I was doing it, I was in my late thirties.

CA: Your work as a correspondent led to your being asked to write what turned out to be *This Is My Country Too*, didn't it?

Williams: Yes, as a matter of fact, that was an assignment for *Holiday*, to do essentially what John Steinbeck had done with his *Travels with Charley*. When I had finished the trip, we decided that I should sit down and do a book and let them select the parts they wanted to run in the magazine.

CA: In the travel and writing, were you often consciously aware of the structure of Steinbeck's book?

Williams: I had read it and had consciously gone many of the same routes that he went, particularly on US Route 1 up around the northern part of the United States, fairly close to the Canadian border.

CA: Walker Percy said, "It is the very absence of a tradition that makes for great originals like Faulkner and O'Connor and Poe." Other people, of course, have made similar observations. How do you think this applies to black writers?

Williams: I think with black writers, particularly, there has been a very solid tradition which most people have never recognized. I think it goes back to something Milton discussed in his *Areopagitica* in 1644: that books, being "not absolutely dead things . . . may chance to spring up armed men"—that is, to fight injustice. And if good literature is forged in the fires of injustice, as Joyce and a few other writers have said, then that tradition seems to me to be very solid, not only for black writers but for all writers. I personally believe that all books should do things; they should make people want to do things. I would have to say that, in my judgment, Faulkner, Poe, and O'Connor were very much in touch with that tradition.

CA: What are your current feelings about the teaching of black literature as a separate course in colleges and universities?

Williams: I've always felt it was a mistake because it perpetuates the fragmentation of American literature that we've always had to contend with. Very early on in the game, I said and wrote that I was opposed to it. When I have occasion to do what is called Afro-American literature, it actually turns out to be comparative American literature because I take one black and one white writer who have lived and worked in the same time periods, beginning with, say, Phillis Wheatley and Phillip Freneau, and come all the way through up to the contemporary period. That's not at all difficult to do, and I don't understand why more people have not done it.

CA: You share with many other people a concern about the amount of money publishers spend on blockbusters to the neglect of many deserving writers. Do you think it would be even worse without the presence of the few black editors who are working for large publishers?
Williams: I know at the moment of only one, and back in the 1960s I think there must have been ten around town. One just left a major publishing house about three weeks ago. The only one that I know of now is Toni Morrison.

CA: Some people, including Toni Morrison, think small independent publishers may be the great hope for minority fiction. Have you considered getting involved in such a venture?
Williams: I would not go into book publishing unless there was a solid arrangement in terms of enough dough to take a few losses and bounce back. If I went into publishing, it would be in journalism. Years ago I wrote, edited, and published a newsletter, and I'm inclined to consider doing that in a very special way again. I'm compiling some material, formats, and so on. I'm not sure that I'll do it, but it strikes me as something that needs to be done, particularly in the area that I'm thinking about.

CA: What hope do you think there is for more publication for all minority writers?
Williams: Individual minority groups have to come up with their own funding to do their own books, or at least come together in a combine, and put up the dough to do some round-robin publishing—say, for three months of the year do black books, for the next three months do Chicano books, and so on. There has to be some balance. I no longer have faith that the publishing establishment, as it now is, is going to be at all conscientious about doing books by minority authors.

CA: Have you had much contact with the black writers in South Africa?

Williams: No. Back during the early 1960s, I knew several African writers, but the only guy I know now is Ezekiel Mphahlele, who's back there. I last saw him when he was teaching at the University of Pennsylvania. That's very strange because he vanished, and then I heard he had returned to South Africa to teach on some kind of sabbatical and was scheduled to come back to the States. But the South Africans wouldn't let him go. Then I read Joseph Lelyveld's piece that he had chosen to stay there. I still don't know which is the truth.

CA: What do you enjoy reading?

Williams: I guess that I'm reading more nonfiction than fiction these days. I find a great deal of fiction not, to my mind, calculated to make me want to explode with different emotions—anger or sympathy or compassion—but just there. Most of the writings are exercises, and that may be precisely what the author wants to do or what the publisher wants him or her to do. But I prefer work that makes me want to think or move, to do something.

CA: Have you enjoyed the teaching you've done?

Williams: Yes, I've enjoyed it, and I'm still enjoying it. I can see problems in the entire educational system, and I think they're becoming intensified. There doesn't seem to me to be as much dedication in the field as there was when I first started teaching around thirteen years ago and probably not as much as when I was a kid, and I had on occasion some very good teachers.

CA: Why do you think that's true?

Williams: It's bureaucracy. Everyone wants to make teachers responsible to him, to her, to it—school boards, presidents, deans, provosts, parents. And teachers don't seem to be able to say, "We want to be the way we were in the 1930s. We want respect. We think we can do the job if you'll let us do it, if we don't have to spend eighty percent of the time filling out papers and worrying about getting fired."

CA: What about students? Do you think they're worse than they were ten years ago, twenty years ago?

Williams: In many ways, yes, but I don't think that's their fault. I think that society has fed young people a bill of goods. For example, not every student who is in college should be in college, but there is something in the system that says you cannot move up an inch unless you have been to college, so everybody goes. Now everybody is starting to find out that this is not quite as automatic as it seemed to be. Somebody pulled the plug, so things are not so completely wired up anymore.

CA: Has teaching helped in any way with the writing?
Williams: Yes. You get lots of good characters there, lots of conflicts with colleagues, lots of situations. Everything is a microcosm of how the world functions, whether you're in school, whether you're a journalist, or whatever. You find the same types and the same situations and very often you have to try to bring to bear on those situations the same solutions.

CA: Do you get good, lively, intelligent audiences for the lectures you give?
Williams: Sometimes yes, sometimes no. I'm not really into that as much as I once was or even wanted to be because it's part of literary show biz. I think you have to decide whether you want to be a writer or an entertainer. I maybe do five or six a year, and that's about it. I am going off to England to do some things at the end of this month for three or four days. I'll be at the University of Kent at Canterbury and the University of Nottingham and maybe the University of East Anglia.

CA: You got an LLD degree in 1978 from Southeastern Massachusetts University. Was it an honorary degree?
Williams: Yes.

CA: When you're out trout fishing, are you thinking about writing?
Williams: No, I guess I'm just wondering why they're not biting any better than they are. I'm basically a mountain man—I prefer the mountains to the beaches—and it really clears my head just not doing anything except holding that pole, and maybe a drink, and looking at the reflection of the tree line in the water.

CA: Would you like to talk about the new novel?
Williams: I can say that it's a very big novel for me; it's right now almost seven hundred pages. My editor and I are working very well on it. I like the house. Houghton Mifflin is not one of those houses that allowed itself to be purchased by a conglomerate, and I like that.

CA: Are there any other future plans or ideas you'd like to talk about?
Williams: I've got another novel that I've finished, kind of a lightweight novel. I've done a full-length play which I'm having so many strange

reactions to. I don't know what I'm going to do with it. I don't want to convert it to a novel. I've got another novel that I started some years ago that's about a quarter of the way through. I guess I was anticipating that people like Naipaul and John Updike would be writing about the African in fiction, and I wanted to do this. I started it some years ago and just never got around to finishing it. I've got lots of stuff to finish up. Then I've got a big nonfiction book that I've been dreaming up for about ten years that I have half a room full of notes for. I've already started on that, but I want to go back and take another look at it and see where it is.

Cross-Country Chat
with John A. Williams

Steven Corbin / 1985

From *The Southern California Anthology* (1985): 69–73. Reprinted with permission of the University of Southern California.

"After all the marketing trends and the verbal-silicone-injected blockbusters are pulped, there will still be John A. Williams finding his way about the page like Anansi, the wise trickster," proclaimed Ishmael Reed of his contemporary whose stylized literary voice sings with innovation, daring, and piercing insight. An accomplished novelist and poet, he has authored fourteen books, among them such timeless and provocative works as *Captain Blackman, The Man Who Cried I Am, This Is My Country Too*, and his latest, *!Click Song*.

With a distinguished career already spanning a quarter century, the former *Newsweek* correspondent is currently a professor of English at Rutgers University. At the typewriter, Williams is plugging away at *There Will Come Thunder*,[1] a new novel set entirely in West Africa. He shared some of his thoughts and hopes from his home in Teaneck, New Jersey.

Corbin: What essentially attracts you to the literary form of writing as opposed to others?
Williams: I do other forms of writing—articles, poetry—and I've been a journalist. This was normal in the eighteenth century. There's very little difference between one who wrote in a literary vein and otherwise. This is true all over the world. Langston Hughes, here in the US, wrote across genres, as have (Ishmael) Reed, (Imamu) Baraka, and others.

Corbin: Could you describe the mechanism of your creative process?
Williams: Oh, God, I don't think anyone can. People who say that they know exactly how they do it are tremendous egomaniacs or just plain nuts.

I don't think that there's any way to explain this process except that it happens, and sometimes the results are okay.

Corbin: Your first novel was published when and by whom?
Williams: 1960. It was a paperback original published by Ace Books in New York.

Corbin: Who, if anyone, was the major influence on your career?
Williams: Well, I don't think anybody was consciously, but of course, that's always open to question. I read a great deal when I was a kid without any kind of discrimination; I just loved to read. Richard Wright, I feel, was an influence. I was very young when Wright's first novel came out, and I didn't read his short fiction until much later in life. I just don't know. I don't want to deny that there were influences; I'm just not consciously aware of them except in one case: Malcolm Lowry's *Under the Volcano*, from which I tried to learn something about novel structure.

Corbin: Are there any authors you admire, classic, modern, or contemporary, and why?
Williams: Yes, but I really don't want to get into picking contemporary people because if you leave somebody out . . . I've always liked the Russian writers—Pushkin, Chekhov, Tolstoy, and Andreyev—also the South American writers. Alejo Carpentier, a Cuban writer, was quite unique.

Corbin: Your name and reputation are not household words among non-black readership . . .
Williams: That's true with a lot of black writers. Oh, I don't know. I think part of it is political and the other part is, I guess, that I just don't write the same things that a Jimmy Baldwin would write, or (Ralph) Ellison.

Corbin: Black literature, historically and traditionally, is a small voice in the overall chorus of American letters. This cultural, perhaps, racist gap is bridged, if at all, by works of black authors who occasionally receive Nobel, Pulitzer, or American Book Award accolades. What are your feelings in this regard?
Williams: Well, I think it's kind of silly. The second American novelist was a black man. In other words, our tradition has been as long as America itself, but actually before America even started with people like Lucy Terry, Phillis Wheatley, Jupiter Hammon, et cetera. Perhaps, the voice is

small, and there are reasons for that, but it is certainly longer than most. Of course, racism is involved.

Corbin: Is Cato Douglass, protagonist of *!Click Song*, the literary euphemism for the fate of writers of color in a white-dominated industry?
Williams: Yes, but I think I was also talking about the fate of white writers as well. America's not a country that is terribly literary. All good writers have problems, maybe because they cut too close to the bone. This is particularly true for some black writers.

Corbin: Do you suspect, as did Max Reddick—hero of *The Man Who Cried I Am*—that there exists a highly probable governmental plan to round up and annihilate in the event of racial warfare?
Williams: I think Nixon has something called the Garden Plot. It looked and resembled, in great part, some sections of the King Alfred Plan. Governments always have plans—much of them dangerous. It doesn't take much to put such a plan together.

Corbin: John V. Lindsay, then mayor of New York City, wrote of *The Man Who Cried I Am*: "If this book is to remain fiction, it must be read." What do you believe he meant?
Williams: I guess that the more we learn through fiction, the better off we may become.

Corbin: How would you respond to the criticism—namely on the part of black women—that your protagonists tend to be intellectual black studs who invariably marry white women because black women don't "understand or render compassion for" the black-man-as-struggling artist?
Williams: Well, I don't know what I'd have to say about that except that I've heard it for so long it's like a litany. It wouldn't be such a problem if racial and sexual definitions didn't exist in this country. Is there such a thing as a black intellectual? How much does that cost? Or what does it buy?

Corbin: When citing the modern or contemporary black American writers, [James] Baldwin, [Richard] Wright, and [Ralph] Ellison are mechanically mentioned in one breath. Do you feel slighted or ignored that, in light of your prolific and equally substantial output, your name isn't among them?
Williams: I'm a little too old to be bitter and a little too wise not to understand why this situation is as it is.

Corbin: So you feel, in part, that it's another case of the system allowing us one black literary icon at a time?

Williams: Yes, and it depends on who's in favor with the literary establishment.

Corbin: You fictionalized both Wright and Baldwin as Harry Ames and Marion Dawes, respectively in *The Man Who Cried I Am*. What are your thoughts of these two writers?

Williams: I think Baldwin and Wright are both important. But, so are—and were—others. I've always liked Baldwin's essays which came at a time when black people had no other voice.

Corbin: Have you ever considered "trekking the Atlantic" in the footprints of Wright and Baldwin to become an expatriate?

Williams: No, never! I've been out of the country and lived out of the country for short periods of time. I have children, and I wasn't willing to leave them forever. Baldwin has no children that I know of. Wright took his family with him. (Chester) Himes had no children. I just knew I wasn't going to be an expatriate, and I knew in my gut that Europe was not going to be better just because it's Europe. The racism there is a lot more subtle than American racism. So it goes; Europe is and always has been racist and bigoted.

Corbin: Are anger and pain the serious artist's best friends?

Williams: That's what people say. I'm not sure. Both of them can be crippling to the point where you cease to be effective, and that's what they want—for you to get so mad that you're not able to work and you're running around at parties punching people out. Perhaps, just a *very small* dose of both would be okay.

Corbin: If you could adapt more of your pieces for the screenplay form, aside from *The Junior Bachelor Society*, produced by NBC as *Sophisticated Gents*, which would you choose and why?

Williams: Well, I would do *!Click Song* because I think that it would make the director work. He'd have to do something with the structure. *The Man Who Cried I Am* because of the exotic locales, and it would require somebody with intelligence. I'd also like to do *Sissie* and maybe *Captain Blackman*.

Corbin: Does art have a responsibility to society? And where does the writer fit in that jigsaw framework?

Williams: I'm not sure. All art is political and thus has some responsibility to society. Society, on the other hand, has a responsibility to the artist. It's important to carry the right message.

Corbin: What are your feelings regarding fiction fluctuating in the doldrums while nonfiction, the how-to, and other so-called books dominate the market?

Williams: Well, you know, publishers did that themselves. Publishers are like car dealers, car manufacturers; they can create their own markets. If they stop publishing all the crap and put good stuff out there, that's what people would read. The emphasis, of course, is on the buck, and it's a heavy instrument, but, for Chrissake . . . and everybody knows it. You hear agents and people talking about it all the time, and they're not about to change it. Nonfiction sells; most good fiction does not—a case of simply money over matter.

Corbin: Yes, it's incredible, but do you think that, as a society, we'll ever be readers again in the wake of ultramodern, technological escapism?

Williams: I don't know. I think that what's going on now is very good for the short story. Short stories are ideal because the novel demands more time and maybe a little work. People don't want to work. It happens with most people; they're just not reading long fiction.

Corbin: Why do you suppose that contemporary black women writers enjoy a higher visibility than black men?

Williams: That's American society; that's always the case. There are some very fine women writers out there, and they've always been there. The female writing tradition is much longer than the male writing tradition, but all kinds of men the world over have assumed an unnatural superiority to women. So, we understand even if those responsible for this fluctuation between black men and women writers don't.

Corbin: Would you like to go down in the annals of history as a black American writer or an American writer? Why do writers like yourself become pigeonholed in that classification, which in part I think you've already answered?

Williams: Doesn't matter a damn to me. Actually, I'd rather go down in history as having been a halfway decent father and a fair poet.

Corbin: What is the present state and future of the black American novelist?
Williams: The other day I was talking to Nathan Heard, and he said that historically we have peaks and valleys. Right now, we're in the valley—won't be the first time we've ever been in one. We usually get out of it. The whole history of American race relations has been cyclical. We'll have our turn again and again. In the meantime, we'll keep working until all fads and cycles end.

Corbin: Could you briefly describe your current project?
Williams: It's the first novel that's set entirely out of the country.

Corbin: Where is it set?
Williams: In West Africa.

Corbin: As a professor at Rutgers University, what do you hope to impress upon your students?
Williams: Just the need to know—to know anything. Part of the students' apathy has to do, I believe, with superpowers waging threats of nuclear war.

Corbin: What advice would you give to the first novelist?
Williams: Before or after it's finished?

Corbin: After.
Williams: My advice would be to get an agent, which would be very difficult unless you've published somewhere else. It wasn't like that twenty-five, thirty years ago. I would get some kind of system down to get the manuscript around. I wouldn't let that take more than ten percent of my time. Then, I'd write my second, third, and fourth novels. There's nothing like sort of filling up your own bank. For somebody to do one novel, then wait twenty years to get it published doesn't make you a writer—it makes you something else which is probably closer to an asshole.

Note

1. The working title for what would become *Jacob's Ladder*. (JAT)

Interview with John A. Williams

John Albert Jansen / 1988

From *Plantage Magazine*—VPRO (November 15, 1988), Hilversum, Netherlands. © VPRO.

VPRO: John Williams, born December 5, 1925, in Jackson, Mississippi, grew up in Syracuse, New York, and is now professor of English and journalism at Rutgers University, New Brunswick, New Jersey.[1] At the beginning of the sixties, Williams was the first black correspondent for *Newsweek* in Africa. He is the author of an extensive oeuvre which is mainly concerned with the experience of black Americans in a white-dominated society. That is the case, for instance, with his jazz novel, *Night Song*, an homage to the late Charlie Parker, and in *Captain Blackman*, which deals with the position of the black soldier—Williams himself served in the US Marines in the Pacific.[2] In addition, Williams has written such pieces as *The Angry Black* and *Amistad 1 & 2*[3] as well as a great deal of nonfiction: a history of Africa, a biography of Richard Wright, and *The King God Didn't Save*, reflections on the life and death of Martin Luther King. You will hear John Williams reading an extract from *The Man Who Cried I Am* against the background of the Childrens' Sunday School Choir of Birmingham, Alabama . . .

"I am the way I am because I'm a Black man; therefore, we're in rebellion . . . ," "I want trouble to be my middle name . . ."—these statements—in what way do they still fit in the eighties, where we live now?

JAW: Well, I guess I've had a few problems because of my books, what I say in my books. There's even a black playwright who was asked to do a TV version of a book of mine and said, "No, he's—John Williams is an angry, bitter black man." He didn't even know me!

VPRO: You're not a bitter man?

JAW: I'm not a bitter man. I don't really have time for that kind of bitterness—so even with some elements of the black community I'm still viewed the way people thought they saw me in 1967. But let me tell you about bitterness, OK? It's crippling; you can't do your work if you're bitter. You are incapable of seeing those areas, those slight areas when things do appear to be better. You have got to train your children, you have got to train your grandchildren, and you can't do all of that if you spend time on bitterness.

VPRO: So, it was not bitterness but struggle and indignation that made *The Man Who Cried I Am*, published in 1967, a document of its time. It was also an indictment against the society which, through racial segregation, caused a large group of black intellectuals from Richard Wright to James Baldwin to leave for such places as Paris or Amsterdam.

JAW: Well, at that time I was just recovering from about nine months of travelling through Africa for *Newsweek*, and I was resting before returning to New York. That's where I met Sam Middleton, Paul Carter Harrison, and some other people in Amsterdam.

VPRO: To speak in the words of—to use the words of Max Reddick, "What did all these niggers do in Europe?" He wondered when he's still in New York. What was the reason for all these black Americans to go to Europe after World War II, in the fifties and the sixties?

JAW: To escape America. I mean, that's why people went to Paris. That's why people went to Amsterdam or Italy—to get away, to feel more human abroad than they did at home.

VPRO: *The Man Who Cried I Am* was first published in 1967. It's a book about the black experience after World War II. It's also a book which is full of anger.

JAW: I don't know if it's anger—except he's a man who is totally aware of American history. All of the people in his group do not believe that the Supreme Court decision of 1954 outlawing segregation in schools and public accommodations—that sort of reflects my view and the view of others that I knew at that time: that America would not make a great deal of progress from that point onward because historically speaking it never has. It goes forward, then it backs up, just as it's in the process of backing-up racially right today, 1988. So my view is/was sort of projected on to those characters, and I know that to be an accurate view.

VPRO: But what were your roots? You had had the same kind of experiences with segregation? Where did you grow up?

JAW: I grew up in Syracuse, New York, which is a town of about forty thousand—maybe three thousand black people.[4]

VPRO: A university town too?

JAW: It's a university town; that's where I went to university after the war on the GI Bill. Not many black people were well-to-do there. But I did grow up in a relatively integrated community of whites and Jews and Irish and Native Americans and white Americans and a lot of some of the immigrant peoples who had come to America then, so my experiences were far different from those of, say, the late John Killens, who grew up in the South, or Jimmy Baldwin's in Harlem; mine were entirely different. So if I was angry, it was a different degree of being angry. If I was bitter, it was a different degree of being bitter. But during the war—to speak of how things never change—the closest I ever came to being killed in the war was not by the Japanese, but by a white American.

VPRO: Tell me about that.

JAW: Oh, he was just saying things that I didn't like. I told him to stop it, and he pulled out a .45 and threatened to blow my brains out. But he thought better of it!

VPRO: That was when the Army still was segregated too?

JAW: I was in the Navy, and the Navy was segregated. This was out in the South Pacific, and I think it was in the New Hebrides or the Solomons somewhere—I think it was the Solomon Islands, yes.

VPRO: So that's one of the many experiences from which you also took your ambition to write about this situation—a black man in an overall white society?

JAW: Well, yes, that was one of many situations—that perhaps was the most dramatic—also the shortest! But very often you write about these things in the hope that intelligent people will understand what's going on and do a little more in trying to alleviate that situation.

But America is America, and again I think it's very important—racism is very important to some people in this world because it does set a class structure. It is profitable for some and not for others—and that's the way it is. One hopes that it will not be around forever, but I don't see the situation changing in my lifetime nor in the lifetimes of my children, nor grandchildren—as a matter of fact, I see it spreading quite rapidly throughout the world.

VPRO: Through the eyes of Max Reddick, the alter-ego of Williams himself, we experience the sixties: John F. Kennedy, Martin Luther King, Malcolm X, Black Muslims, the CIA, the March on Washington on August 28, 1963, and the racial disturbances such as the attack on September 15, 1963, in Birmingham, Alabama.

As well as being a document of its time, *The Man Who Cried I Am* is also a historical novel: Minister Q in the book is certainly Malcolm X or, to be more accurate, Al Hajj Malik al-Shabazz. Earlier, we heard his voice in an extract from the LP *Malcolm X: The Ballot or the Bullet*. He too met a violent death: in 1965 he was shot dead in a ballroom in Harlem. Williams met him exactly a year earlier in West Africa and is still convinced that the CIA had a hand in it.

JAW: I was in Lagos, having returned from Ethiopia and the Sudan and Egypt, and I was making my rounds in Lagos seeing what was now, as you do when you're a reporter. There was a man at US Information Agency who said, "Would you like to do an interview with Malcolm X?" I said, "Yes," and he said, "Well, he's coming in . . ." I'm sort of making this part up 'cause I don't remember precisely—he said, "He's coming in day after tomorrow, and he'll be staying at the hotel. . . ." There are two hotels, the Bristol and the name of the other one I forget now—and I said, "Yes, thanks." I didn't ask him how he knew when Malcolm X was coming in or what hotel he'd be staying at, but I can assume now that he had been tracked very carefully by the CIA. Anyway, I called him up, and he asked if I had—if I was the John A. Williams who'd written a novel called *Sissie*. I said, "Yes," and he said, "Come over and talk." So I went over, and we talked. He was going on to Ghana to talk to Nkrumah, and then he was going back to the States. And that was the last time I saw him.

VPRO: And how did you react to his death? What was your reaction?
JAW: Oh, I was angry. I mean, that was when I was really angry because the pattern had been . . . We'd seen Black Panthers who had been assassinated. We'd seen the kids in Mississippi who'd been killed, and I was just angry that people were not angrier about the situation. And, yes, I did then assume that he was killed by the government, and I have not changed my opinion at all.

VPRO: And the same thing about Martin Luther King—but that's maybe even a more dangerous assumption.
JAW: I don't see why it's a dangerous assumption because there are a lot of factors that have not been cleared up in that situation. They got somebody.

They got somebody in the case of Malcolm X. They got somebody in the case of John F. Kennedy. They got somebody in the case of Bobby Kennedy. They can always GET somebody, but that doesn't change my opinion.

VPRO: Apart from the larger politics, with Williams it is also the personal experiences which are almost always political. The passage from the book where Harry Ames—incidentally, a portrait of the Godfather of Black American literature, Richard Wright—is refused a grant, is autobiographical. The incident took place in 1962, when a grant awarded to Williams by the American Academy in Rome was suddenly withdrawn—partly because of a rumor that Williams was having a relationship with a white woman. Williams commented then, and I quote, "It is a naked fact that the Negro is superfluous in present day American society." Here Williams speaks of this incident.
JAW: Well, it happened in 1962, and I feel—not bitter— not really angry, but I feel that was one of the experiences that gave me so much knowledge about America that I didn't really want to know. Yet I suppose I had to, and once you have one of those experiences, you can say with some degree of certainty that things are bad. And they're not getting better. That I know.

VPRO: One of the subjects in the book is definitely also women, and especially the relationship between a black man and a white woman.
JAW: Yes.

VPRO: That was one of the reasons all these black men went to Europe . . .
JAW: [laughs]

VPRO: [embarrassed laugh] Or not?
JAW: I think—I don't know because I didn't ask them—but I do believe that the first instance, the first *wish* to go for those that I knew, had nothing whatsoever to do with women. It was to get out from under American racism. Now, if they were attracted to European women, I think a great deal of that had to do with European women, not so much the men—or maybe it was a fifty-fifty proposition.

VPRO: I'm asking it because in the book there is a lot of talk about—the focus on that is very much there.
JAW: Yes, but the focus is there objectively. It is not as though the black men were going to be used by European women as they were used by white American society. They see the women as desirable objects—things, if

you will—and these things or objects are attracted to them, simply—no, I shouldn't say that, that's unfair—in large part because they're exotic. They're not European; they're different. They bring a whole new atmosphere to the European scene, and I suppose we could take that back to World War I when James Reese Europe, a black army bandleader, took jazz to Europe. And the army band played jazz, and Europe never got over it. Europe fell in love with jazz—and with black people.

VPRO: Well, I'm asking the question also because we talked before about the grant which has been withdrawn from you, and I heard mention that one of the reasons could have been that, the relationship in the early sixties—black man/white woman.
JAW: I was engaged to a black woman at the time that happened.

VPRO: So there's nothing with that?
JAW: Well, the people at the Academy may have thought otherwise, on the basis of the book that won me the grant—in which there was an interracial couple, and it's got a jazz background. They may have made the assumption that my girl was white, but she wasn't, not at that time.

VPRO: Yes, but I think you made the assumption that they made that assumption, or not?
JAW: Well, that's what I was told by people who were close to the scene, so it wasn't an assumption on my part. It had to do very much with what I learned.

VPRO: But still, it was very much an issue.
JAW: It was an issue—on their part, let me say, on their part.

VPRO: OK, that's what I wanted to make clear.
JAW: I think there is something else too, and that is, as I've explained in some pieces I've written: when I went in for this interview I had a beard, I wore a cap, I was black, and there was this rumor. I had written this book about jazz and dope and so on and so forth . . .

VPRO: Which book was that?
JAW: *Night Song*—published in Holland as *Synkopen in de Nacht*. So the director made certain assumptions, and everybody that I spoke to about this incident told me that he had indeed made those assumptions. And

it developed later that there was a problem with dope at the Academy in Rome, even that someone had died of an overdose of dope in the Academy, so they didn't want to take any chance of this new "dope-hippie-with-the-beard" type cat coming in there and further polluting the Academy.

VPRO: A friend of John Williams, the painter mentioned briefly earlier, Sam Middleton, came to Amsterdam at the beginning of the sixties from the ghetto of Harlem, via the mercantile marines. Middleton recognizes himself clearly in the group of black Americans portrayed by Williams, who were tossed back and forth in Europe between their own careers and the enticing call of home.

Sam Middleton: I recognize very much of myself for being a part of the same group—of leaving and watching from afar the developments that were building up through Malcolm X and through Martin Luther King with his marches. I also was aware of having to choose, of either returning and joining this contingent or staying where I was and becoming more proficient and more professional, as an example, a living example of the possibility— someone children or teenagers or school-age students could identify with. There are two ways of fighting. You could go—I could forget painting and go and help Martin and carry banners, but then I get no painting done.

VPRO: But you see it in *The Man Who Cried I Am*. It's a continuous struggle, always looking back to the States, what's happening there.

SM: It's the not knowing what's happening there. I have to call John often to find out what's really—because what I read in the newspapers isn't really what's happening there. I have people who keep me in some form, but I've often asked John, "Do you think it's time that I should come back?" And he says, "No, stay there and do what you're doing." So I'm staying here—not that I take his word that way, but I understand its affirmation. I was right. I still am a good example.

VPRO: *The Man Who Cried I Am* is the history of the black man; it's also in a way documentary. It reflects the death of Martin Luther King and the death of Malcolm X. During such events it must be even harder to be so far away from where it actually happens—how did you experience it?

SM: In both occasions, an absolute . . . solemnity. I remember when Martin was assassinated, I took some days off and went to Paris to a hotel room and stayed for a couple of days with myself. I didn't want anybody that I knew around me at that point. I just wanted to be left alone for a lot of soul-searching and deep thinking. And it's always easier if you go outside of everything that you know for the moment—just completely away where nobody knows you. The phone doesn't ring, nobody's after you for information . . . I wanted to be left alone, completely, to relive the Harlem I know, the Harlem I tried to forget, the Harlem that was supposedly growing . . . and then cutting off the head of the movement in such a brutal fashion left me with many questions I had to ask myself about—how I felt about a lot of things.

VPRO: At the end of *The Man Who Cried I Am*, the novel develops into a real thriller—the scenario of a James Bond movie with, for example, Sidney Poitier in the leading role.

Max Reddick receives documents of the so-called King Alfred Plan— plans for the internment of black leaders in concentration camps in the event of increasing racial violence. An entirely fictitious plan, but according to Williams anyone familiar with US history could set up their own King Alfred Plan. Williams cites the Garden-Plot Plan set up under Nixon, which has many similarities to his own King Alfred Plan.

JAW: That was history, and I think anybody who knows and understands the way American history works could have sat down and planned the same thing quite easily. It was all fiction. I used the names of some real organizations. I used the names of some phony organizations. Now, that list turned up in some FBI documents, even with the phony names there—even with the phony names. I don't know if you're aware of this, but under Nixon there was something called the Garden-Plot Plan. And it was almost like the King Alfred Plan.

VPRO: Tell me more about it. I don't know it.

JAW: It was a plan to contain civil unrest, and it had structure to it by hour and areas in the country where people would go . . . And there was a man named Fred Allan, I believe, who did a monologue that came out after my book came out, dealing with concentration camps which would actually be the camps where they had held the Japanese during World War II—and these in themselves were concentration camps. They weren't like the German camps, but people were confined to those areas. And once you understand all this history and the way the country historically has worked, then you could very easily have sat down and done your own King Alfred Plan. This is not hard to do.

VPRO: So, it's fiction but with some big clues to reality.

JAW: Well, the FBI did send me some stuff under the Freedom of Information Act, and J. Edgar Hoover was very concerned that the public know that this King Alfred Plan was taken from a work of fiction. It seems to have been a high priority of the FBI that the public be educated that this was not, in fact, a government plan. On the other hand, I had friends who were reporters, who laughingly suggested that I had stolen the plan out of some government file or wastebasket. [laughs]

VPRO: But both could be true.

JAW: Both could have been true except that I didn't steal it out of anybody's wastebasket, and, well, again, it was fiction. It was fiction. Over the years I've spoken to a number of people, or a number of people have spoken to me, who had been in various positions when that book came out—one of whom was in Army Intelligence, and now a teacher of English. He said, "When that book came out, the whole department just went ape-shit! They could not believe it." And I said, "Well, why?" And he said, "I can't tell you, but you can guess that we probably had something like that already planned." That's from Army Intelligence!

VPRO: John Williams, now sixty-three, lives in Teaneck, New Jersey, and teaches at Rutgers University—New Brunswick. With his oval face and gray beard, he looks the part of the friendly professor. I came directly from Harlem when I met him and told him how shocked I was by the social misery I had seen there. Williams has the same experience: twenty years after *The Man Who Cried I Am* he too is in a very somber state of mind.

JAW: We do have the same kind of experience except that it's been speeded up, and I think it's fairly easy to lay that on Reagan and maybe his administration is a part of that. But a great deal of that has to do—that situation in New York City—has to do with the politics of New York and the emphasis on big money. In two years you've seen that there are more new buildings in New York City than you've probably seen in twenty years visiting New York. So instead of serving the entire New York City community, city hall has chosen to satisfy the needs of landlords, the property people, and the real estate people at the expense of communities like Harlem and Queens and the South Bronx.

VPRO: I had to think about the words of Max Reddick in *The Man Who Cried I Am*. He wondered when there would be a riot again, and sometimes I wondered about that too. People *have* to turn radical and militant again.

JAW: Well, I think the elements of the population that normally would have turned radical and militant are the very ones that the system has poured crack into—the dope which keeps coming. And therefore you render a lot of young people, who otherwise would have been militant, harmless. As Jesse Jackson said, "You know, it's very easy to talk about addicts and dope-pushers on the block, but these are not the people who are laundering the money. It's the bankers who are laundering the money; it's the police offi-cials in some cases who are letting the dope go through. It's government officials who are closing an eye to the influx of drugs, and since a lot of these drugs are going into minority communities, you render them harmless. So you never have to worry about militancy or rebellions—even down to the age of twelve or thirteen because you've got these kids hooked on crack. The problem they have to worry about is old guys like me!

VPRO: How?
JAW: Because we're not hooked, we're still thinking. We still see that things are wrong. We are still searching for ways to make things right.

VPRO: But on the other hand, you seem to be very pessimistic now. I mean, *The Man Who Cried I Am* was a very powerful and very angry book, but we're twenty years beyond that period. And things seem to be even worse.
JAW: Well, pessimism and optimism are first cousins . . . Of course I'm pes-simistic, but I'm alive. I'm working. I have family, quite a large family. I have friends. I have neighbors, and I can be pessimistic and still work as though I were optimistic. I have to; I have no other choice . . . Otherwise, I would do what Primo Levi did—or a lot of other people, Pavese, you know—you commit suicide if you feel that you can't help change things. And I'm not ready to do that.

Notes

1. Williams actually taught at Rutgers–Newark. (JAT)

2. Williams actually was enlisted in the US Navy. (JAT)

3. Williams coedited *Amistad* with Charles F. Harris and edited *The Angry Black*. (JAT)

4. The information here is inaccurate and perhaps mistranslated. According to biggestuscities.com, the population of Syracuse, New York, in 1990 was 163,855. (JAT)

An Interview with John A. Williams

Kay Bonetti Callison / 1989

From American Audio Prose Library, Inc. 1989. Audiocassette 536. Used by permission of American Audio Prose Library, Inc. All rights reserved.

The following is an interview with John A. Williams conducted by Kay Bonetti for the American Audio Prose Library in May 1989 at the author's home in Teaneck, New Jersey, where he is chair of the Creative Writing Department at Rutgers University.

Born in 1925 in Jackson, Mississippi, Williams grew up in Syracuse, New York. After serving in the Navy during World War II, Williams graduated from Syracuse University with a degree in Broadcast Journalism and worked at a variety of jobs before publishing his first novel, *One for New York*, in 1960.

Since then, he's published ten other novels, among them *The Man Who Cried I Am* and *!Click Song*, and seven volumes of nonfiction. His poetry, along with dozens of essays and other nonfiction pieces, has appeared in a wide variety of magazines and periodicals, including *Ebony, Village Voice, Holiday, Yardbird, Callaloo,* the *Saturday Review, Negro Digest, Swank, Nugget,* and the *New Leader.*

During the 1960s, he was posted by *Newsweek* in West Africa; and, as you might guess from reading his work, he has traveled widely in Africa, Europe, and the Middle East. Since 1965, he's been married to Lorraine Isaac, and they're the parents of one son. Williams also has two other sons from his first marriage.

AAPL: Mr. Williams, could we just put some things in context for our listeners who maybe haven't read *!Click Song,* a few of the things that led up to what happens in the last segment that you read from *!Click Song?*[1] For instance, who is Amos Bookbinder to Cato Douglass?

JAW: Amos Bookbinder is a very close friend of Cato Douglass's and, actually, when he first appears in the novel, is the first black editor in publishing in New York. Since there're so few black writers, it's sort of natural that they would gravitate toward each other.

AAPL: Why is it that, all those years, Amos has been begging Cato to let him publish his books, and Cato won't let him do it?
JAW: Because Cato, like a number of black authors, always felt that he could deal with editors who had more power than Amos would ever have, being a black editor.

AAPL: Do you think that the new surge of small presses—and by small presses I mean like Thunder's Mouth Press and Algonquin Books of Chapel Hill—do you think that they're doing anything at all, that their presence is being felt at all to rectify the artist-commodity scene in publishing that you describe in *!Click Song*?
JAW: Yes. Sure. The big danger there, however, is that if the small publisher and the independent publisher do very well, then the traditional publishers are very much tempted to buy the imprint and add it to their house, as with North Point Press, as a case in point.

AAPL: Oh, really?
JAW: Yes.

AAPL: Who bought them?
JAW: I forget who, but a—

AAPL: Is this recent?
JAW: Oh, yes. It's been at least a couple of years. Oh, yes. Sure.

AAPL: When that happens, does the editorial autonomy and the integrity go?
JAW: Well, if I remember the drill right, the editorial autonomy is there for a little while, and then it begins to dribble away in favor of command decisions from on high. That's not unusual.

AAPL: I guess I was trying to find some—for my own sake, as a lover of books—to find some way to look at this all to see if there was any kind of hope, in your opinion, in terms of the publishing industry, that perhaps things come full cycle.
JAW: I think they do represent a hope. They have a real problem, however. That is distribution. As long as major publishers are tied in with these major

distributors who just keep swallowing up smaller distributors, you have a sense of the same situation. But there are ways, I think, small and independent publishers can get around that situation. They'll find it, obviously. I think they will.

AAPL: What are some of those ways, do you think?
JAW: Well, at Thunder's Mouth Press, they do quite an extensive amount of publicity. They've set up quite a university and a lecture and reading circuit. They are known to be fairly reliable as people who will send books for exhibit or books for sale at conferences, and that reputation is, so far, untarnished. There are other smaller publishers who do, essentially, the same thing.

It's sort of like running between the legs of a giant to get to where you're going since you can't go around 'em or over 'em, you know.

AAPL: The situation that you describe in *!Click Song* still was not the worst, as yet to come, was it, in publishing?
JAW: Oh, no. No. The worst, of course, was the continued conglomerate buying of large houses buying smaller ones. That's continued. [Inaudible] has some numbers that are just absolutely amazing, and sad, about the number of publishing houses that control so many others these days. That's going on, okay? I think even the writers' organizations have taken a back seat to the power of the publishers, as most unions in this country have taken a back seat to the corporations.

I've had an example with one book where the publisher backed out of a contract, that didn't finish paying off, and would not go to arbitration as the contract said. The attorney for one of the writers' organizations said it would cost you more money to go into court than you could get in the deal, but no one offered to take the case for me. I'm paying all of these dues, as are lots of other writers, and we need a hell of a lot more support than we are getting from some of our organizations.

Third, I guess, is the favored few who will always get published and get good reviews, although, now and again, you see that there are quibbles with some of the work. It's—what can I say, without sounding like a jerk?—that some writers become part of the establishment, part of the corporate image. It's not literature anymore; it's something else. It's literary writing with the literature left out.

AAPL: Yet, as a writer, your vision has always seemed to take in the possibilities of accessibility. That's important to you, isn't it?

JAW: Sure. Yes. I don't know. I'm getting a little tired, though. I suppose that that's the vision that I'm sort of locked into, and that's where I'll have to go. That's where I'll have to stay.

AAPL: Do you have any particular philosophical feelings about the deeper levels of communication that are in storytelling genres, such as spy books?
JAW: I think some of those genres are very deceptive. In other words, you can use them to get across ideas that might be unwieldy in another form—in poetry, for example—and a different kind of novel. I've used jazz. I've used a spy-thing, if you will. I've used the neighborhood thing. All of those are basically popular forms, I would imagine, since a lot of people have used them, but you want to do something else with the content. It's sort of like jazz. You know, I'll give you the melody in the first run-through—

AAPL: "When You Wish Upon a Star," say.
JAW: Yes. And if you don't know what I'm gonna do when I finish the melody, I can't help you because I'm improvising from there on out. But the melody is the familiar—is the popular genre, so, yes, these forms are accessible, but I want to do something else with them. If we talk about the spy novel, I really do think that the popularity in this country has had a great deal to do with the Cold War attitudes sponsored, in part, by us and the Soviets. With our agencies, the more our people understand how evil these other guys are, which they can understand through spy novels, the more we can do in terms of telling them we need their support.

AAPL: So you see the spy novel as a tool?
JAW: As a tool.

AAPL: For the writer?
JAW: It can be as a tool for the writer. Obviously. Sure.

AAPL: To expose . . . ?
JAW: To expose what's wrong with spying, for example.

AAPL: Yes, and the general spiritual bankruptcy of the times.
    You also use the spy genre in *Jacob's Ladder* to tell a tale of an American black man who goes back to his first home—which had literally been Africa because he was the son of a missionary—and climbs a ladder, I would gather, into heightened consciousness.

JAW: Exactly. See, that's very good. People keep saying, "Why did you use that title?" [laughs] They don't understand what's going on. On the other hand, I think, many times people don't want to understand what's going on in a given novel. They just simply refuse to. I mean, most Americans would never think that a black African country would seek to build a nuclear weapon. It's totally beyond their imagination. They just do not think that way. I'm afraid most reviewers cannot conceive of this either, as part of a literary plot, part of a literary device, you know.

AAPL: To just play devil's advocate for a minute, one thing that I wonder about is, the situation that is portrayed in your novels over and over again is that when a driving, ambitious, black person—and it's usually male in the case of your novels, with the exception of, say, Iris Joplin, who goes overseas to find her world over there—when they become successful, they have to deal with racism, both overt and subtle, from the white community that they live in. But then they're also turned out by the black community. What does that say about black culture?

JAW: Well, the Bible said it better. You know, there's no honor among prophets who return home, and I'm paraphrasing. I don't know that that has so much to do with black culture per se as with the natural reaction of people who look askance at those who've gone from the group, gone out into the world, and then return to say, "Hey, I've got the message for you." The answer, invariably, is "Well, we're not interested." That seems to happen to everybody, regardless of race. I suppose what it says is that if you break the connection with this group by departing and leaving for one reason or another, it is going to be damn difficult for you to get back into it.

AAPL: In your position as a writer, do you feel this dilemma in terms of audience? Like, who are you writing for?

JAW: I'm writing for me. Fortunately, I've picked up readers who understand what it is I'm saying, whatever that might be. That's always very gratifying, where you go, and people say, "Oh, I read *Sissie*. I loved it." Or *!Click Song* or *The Man Who Cried I Am*, and so on and so forth. That is extremely gratifying because, actually, you spend most of your life as a writer feeling that you're in a total vacuum. You're writing, and then these other people who are publishers are doing certain things that you don't always approve of. Then there are people who are jumping on the book, and so on and so forth. Isolation seems to be one way of persevering or surviving, but then you get these voices of people who say, "Hey, that's okay. Write. Write on!"

You wish this extended to the people that you grew up with, your friends, your first real friends. Very often, it doesn't.

AAPL: Well, one wonders. Do you think that you, as a writer, . . . when you decided this was your vocation and what you wanted to do, did you feel, like Iris Joplin says in *Sissie*, that you always knew that suffering was an element of learning things but that you never realized how much you were still going to have to pay?

JAW: No. [laughs] I never believed that I would have to suffer in order to learn. I never believed that.

AAPL: So that's Iris's perception, not yours?

JAW: That's Iris's perception, not mine. Obviously, whether one is suffering or having a high old time, one learns if one is perceptive and is willing to learn. There are many different ways of learning, many different conditions under which one does learn. Suffering is not the favorite method of mine for learning. [laughs]

AAPL: Well, what seems implicit in *!Click Song* and in a lot of your work is the notion that there's just really limited possibilities in this world in the subject matter that you talk about, which is the situation of race. What does a black person in this world, in this culture anyway, do? That it comes down to a close individual relationship and a lot of isolation, and that's just the way it's gotta be. Are you comfortable with that?

JAW: No, I'm not. Of course, it can be far worse, and may well be, at some time in the future. I'm not sure what the solution to all this will be, but obviously this world does have a very serious problem with race, racism, and races. I can't help sometimes but consider that this is somehow a challenge that we are supposed to face and master, and we are not.

There are certain very obvious things that one could do, like, teaching history well and properly, which we don't even bother to do. We don't really need to isolate people by race because everybody, actually, undergoes the same thing to differing degrees, clearly. But we're not really interested in telling people that, so racism must be important to some people for some reason. Unless we come to grips with that reason, we're gonna be in trouble.

AAPL: When we talked to James Baldwin, I asked him if he'd ever thought about the fact that if the world turned around the way that his writing was geared toward, seeing it happen, then in fact, he would have written himself out of a job as a writer. He said, "I'd love to have that happen." Do you feel that way?

JAW: Well, yes. I think if my vision of the world and its peoples and politics and whatever, could suddenly be achieved through one means or another, I wouldn't mind not writing. I would love to go fishing all day or just sleeping and drinking beer and smoking a good cigar all day.

Basically, I write because I feel that I must. I'm trying to understand. I'm trying to explain. I'm trying to, I suppose, guide, advise, support, warn, and, perhaps, even threaten; a lot of those things may appear in the work. None of those, I don't believe, stem from negative impulses. If I have a peculiar, by that I mean particular, knowledge of the world that I think may be important (if it's important to me) and I presume that it may be important to other people, I would use it and hope that that knowledge will be of some value to them. So I will use it, as there were so many things in *!Click Song* that a few people know, but most people, generally, do not. I think that's a part of my function, too, as a writer, to teach whenever I can.

AAPL: Now, a lot of people have also described *!Click Song* as being very autobiographical, that dread word. You have admitted that there are elements out of your own history and your own life that are in that book. Now, I wonder if we could use that as a way, though, to show how a writer works because I feel sure that life being chaos, that this book is by no means the story of your life. Is that true?

JAW: Yes, that's true. I try to tell my students that—and young people tend to do an awful lot of autobiographical stuff, as well as they should, because they don't know that much else about the world—but to try to take what you know about yourself, your life, and your world a few steps beyond. Imagine something beyond the area in which your life and imagination are already defined. Go beyond that. I think I followed that precept with *!Click Song* and most books that I've done. I begin with what it is I know and imagine something far greater.

AAPL: Is there any particular thread or section or scene in *!Click Song* that you could use to illustrate how something might have started out of your own personal experience and then was completely transformed into something else?

JAW: Well, I think the scene of Cato in the mountains when he is ill, obviously having a breakdown and reflecting at the lakeside with his son, which breakdown never occurred. I do like to hang out with my sons when they join us up in the country. It just seemed to me such a very pleasant scene and association with promises for this family relationship that I, personally, want to build or rebuild or whatever. I could see taking that through other sons as characters in the book and their friends and some of their experiences in growing up as children of a broken family where the father has remarried, and everybody's gotta try and make peace.

But if I may, just briefly, come to an experience that leads to the creation or, at least to the beginning of the creation of a book, the thing that I'm working on now, *The Book without a Title*,² actually is the first book that I can really pinpoint its beginning in just a visit, a trip. Lori and I were driving through Germany in 1966. We stopped at Dachau, which had only been open a year as a museum. We didn't even know that at that time. When we went in, we saw a collection of ID photos of some of the inmates. Among the collection, there were two black men. I said to myself, vaguely, "Gee, I wonder how they got here?" I really didn't give it that much thought. Over the years, the idea of them being there sort of bothered me. At the same time, over the years, I was not sure whether I had seen them in the first place.

I wrote to the Dachau International Committee and asked if they knew about the photos and if they could tell me something about black inmates. They didn't know about the photos, but they did give me the name of a black inmate who had lived in Belgium, who had been in Dachau, with his address. Well, I didn't need his address. I just needed confirmation that I had seen whatever.

Through further research, I discovered that it was a matter of routine that they did, indeed, photograph every prisoner who came through, every person. From that, one thing led to another, and I hope, by this summer of 1989, I can finish this book about a black inmate in Dachau, which I've been working on, now, about six years. But I can really pinpoint when that started.

AAPL: Over the years, you have had an incredibly varied life and career. You have traveled as a reporter for *Newsweek* in Africa. You did go on a journey throughout the American south and ended up writing a piece that was called *This Is My Country Too.*
JAW: Not my title.

AAPL: I know. I read it was not your choice of a title. That's happened to you as a freelancer a lot.
JAW: [laughs] Yes.

AAPL: Are there any general statements that you can make about how the work you've done in nonfiction—the kinds of straightforward reporting, or interpretive reporting, article writing—have related to the fiction that you do, if at all?

JAW: Well, I think, in some sense, the structure, which is to get yourself a great hot paragraph to open a book or a chapter, a short, concise paragraph filled with punch, you know. On the other hand, you can get so involved in writing news copy that you feel as though you had been released in heaven when you sit down to write fiction, and you are not bound by the rules of journalism. I've experienced both. I enjoy doing both. It's been the kind of thing that I've done without problem. I've known journalists who, over the years, have wanted to write fiction and simply can't do it. They look at me as though I had three or four heads, and I could do it. Well, I think I've been lucky, and for that, I'm grateful. But what I've learned is to observe, keep your mouth shut, listen, and ask the right questions, make sure you understand why the reaction is the way it is.

AAPL: Did Bud Powell really slug George Shearing in a bar?

JAW: That is a story that I've heard several times. It was on Broadway. I think it was—it wasn't Birdland, the Roost; I think it would have been about the high 40s, on the west side of Broadway.

AAPL: Well, you cite that in *!Click Song* as being the inspiration, or the germ, for Cato Douglass's first novel. And I couldn't help but wonder if that was, of course, a sideways reference to, not your first novel, but your second novel, namely, *Night Song*.

JAW: *Night Song*. I hadn't thought of that. Who knows? Maybe. [laughs]

AAPL: Well, you did get interested in—here's a case where you were interested in doing some kind of a book about Charlie Parker, a factual sort of book. How on earth did you and that other writer get a copy of Charlie Parker's psychiatric report?

JAW: I'm not sure how that happened. Maybe Bob had gotten it, or—

AAPL:—and who's Bob?

JAW: Bob Reisner,[3] who is now dead. He was the guy I was going to work with on the Charlie Parker book. On the other hand, I think there was a doctor that we knew who was a jazz nut who got that for us. I forget his name. That was a long time ago. We had marvelous stuff from tapes from

Babs Gonzales and other people. I mean, we would play these tapes and fall out laughing because they were just so funny—some of the things that happened with the detectives taking Billie Holiday to the precinct house and what she did with the dope that she had with her, you know, [laughs] and hiding it. It was very funny and also very sad; but when it became clear that Bob and I could not work together on the book, then I decided to do *Night Song* as a novel.

AAPL: Was the germ of *Night Song*, then, just the idea of doing a book that would center around a Charlie Parker–type figure?
JAW: Well, there were a lot of other things too.

AAPL: I would think so from reading it. That's why I'm wondering.
JAW: Yes, there was a question about—the big question was the cabaret card and how clean you had to be to keep it. A lot of musicians were worried about that. Then, whether you were clean or not, a cabaret owner could see that you didn't work unless you agreed to work for his money. It was a very nasty business. A lot of guys were complaining, but there wasn't a hell of a lot they could do about it. It was a question, once again, of being at the mercy of the powers-that-be for good, creative people. Many of those guys and women, singers, basically—Melba Liston, blew a trombone, sort of an oddity—but they didn't have a hell of a lot of help. They were just struggling, trying to get by, trying to do the best they could. Most of them were clean.

AAPL: In *Night Song*, there is just a beautiful crossing; that book strikes me as really informed by a tragic vision. It's really, almost, a classically tragic vision because as Dave Hillary is rising, with the help of Eagle and of Keel and Della—and they form this foursome, this friendship, this very dear, sweet friendship—as he is managing to pull himself up with the help of these friends, he goes back to Onondaga to get his teaching job. He's to meet Eagle on the street corner, and it's his fault that he's late making that appointment. As he's rising, he sees Eagle on the corner, and there's this just wonderfully enmeshed rising and falling of fate. As you rise materially, you are falling spiritually; as the other is falling materially, he is rising spiritually. How does magic like that happen in a story, in a book? When you're working, you know, at what point do you have the vision of that denouement, or did it just—?
JAW: I'm not sure. It just happened. If I could explain it, I guess I would be a critic instead of a writer. I'm not sure I believe critics' descriptions of how

things occur in art that much. I don't know. It just seemed quite natural as I structured the book, that it's happened to a lot of people that I know of consciously, or unconsciously, or have heard about. It's one of the problems in life. You know, one goes up; one comes down. One betrays somebody else. Essentially, I think, we are talking about betrayal in that particular scene. It's something I deal with quite a bit in books—betrayal.

AAPL: Then you have at the very end, just like in the end of *King Lear*, you have the question of the tragic insight, you know, that's left ambiguous on the part of Dave Hillary.

JAW: Yes, as he goes into the tunnel. Well, I suppose the tunnel should tell you enough about [laughs] where Dave Hillary is going. He's going into the tunnel under the river. We don't know if he's going to emerge or not, but given that scene on the corner with Eagle, not coming to his help, then we have a pretty good idea of his direction.

AAPL: Except that he has come back and with Keel and Della.

JAW: He's recovered himself, but he has not recovered the kind of humanity that Eagle and Keel had, in the sense that they rescued him. He has been rescued and, as far as he's concerned, okay.

AAPL: Do you like to think—I mean, do you have a feeling about characters at the end? Do you like to think that maybe he's going to come up on the other side of the river into an enlightened consciousness?

JAW: My sense about Hillary was that he wouldn't.

AAPL: Really?

JAW: Yes.

AAPL: Oh, that's sad.

JAW: Yes.

AAPL: Where did *Sissie* come from?

JAW: *Sissie* came, in part, from my mother. As a matter of fact, she asked me, oh, I guess, within a year after the book was out, "Who was that little colored lady in the book?" I said, "Oh, just a character." In part, she would have had to be molded on someone that I knew very well. Iris was, like, whole cloth. Ralph is partly me. You've got that mix of fiction and reality. It seemed to work very well.

AAPL: Why did you decide to use part of that Charlie Parker psychiatric report with Ralph in *Sissie*?

JAW: Because I couldn't find anything better that would have—Parker's psychiatric report would have covered a lot of artists, whether they were musicians or writers or painters or what have you. So I used it without any qualms.

AAPL: But Ralph is, fundamentally, so much healthier a person than Charlie Parker was.

JAW: I think Parker had some very healthy periods too. And I think one cannot view the world that he lived in as a healthy person for very long because it was just too damn threatening. It was too evil.

AAPL: Was *Sissie*, in any way, meant to be a celebration of family again?

JAW: Oh, yes. Very much so.

AAPL: Of your family in particular? Or of black families?

JAW: Well, I—all black families that struggle to maintain some semblance of a relationship. As a matter of fact, the Joplin family goes through three or four books.

AAPL: Why do you keep coming back to them?

JAW: I like them. I would like to bring Iris home in a book at some point. I did go back to her, but set back in time in the sixties, in *Jacob's Ladder*. I think, in many ways, they reflect the Afro-American family.

AAPL: Is there any general thing that you can say in terms of where your characters come from, where you find your people for your novels?

JAW: Well, they come out of reality and whole cloth and combinations of both. I don't know that I've ever really come up with a Stephen King—a totally fantastic kind of character, which I would really like to try sometime.

AAPL: Well, what about *The Man Who Cried I Am*? What were you trying to do in *The Man Who Cried I Am* with the, obviously, very allusive creation of characters that resemble actual people, such as, of course, the Harry Ames figure, the Richard Wright–type of figure?

JAW: Well, with that book, I suppose, I was trying to tell people something about the probable future for black people. You can't talk about black people in a vacuum, you know. Whatever happens to black people, there's going to be some reaction among the rest of the population. And it seemed to me that the business that happened in Europe with the Jews and gypsies and the politicals—we're talking, what, eleven, twelve, thirteen, fourteen million people?—was something that just didn't happen overnight. A lot of things contributed to that and made it okay. It made it okay for people to say it didn't happen, or "I didn't know what was going on over there." I could very well see this happening here because there was already a trade-off in terms of what the Nazi spokesmen said we were doing to our minorities: lobotomies, the law breaks down when you deal with these people, so on and so forth. They took the lesson from us, or at least, part of the lesson. So I felt that if I use real characters in a situation that really smacked of a reality that had already occurred, but somewhere else, that perhaps people would think more about the future. I know that the FBI did from the file that I got.

AAPL: Now, what's this again? The FBI did what from what file that you got?
JAW: Well, I know the FBI was very concerned that people understand that the King Alfred Plan was fictional, so they had memoranda flying all over the place.

AAPL: You mean when that book came out?
JAW: Yes. Uh-huh.

AAPL: Oh, is that right? [laughs]
JAW: I got a copy of the file that they sent me that I requested. They said they had not been maintaining surveillance, but they had a file.

AAPL: On who?
JAW: On me.

AAPL: On you. What about on Richard Wright?
JAW: Oh, yes, he had a file. He had a 227-page file.

AAPL: Did you ever actually know or meet—?
JAW: No, I didn't.

AAPL: Never did.
JAW: No.

AAPL: How did you base your portrait of him?

JAW: Well, you do a lot of reading, and I knew a lot of people who knew him. I had heard things.

AAPL: Did Chester Himes know him?

JAW: Chester knew him.

AAPL: I'm sounding brilliant here, but I read someplace where you admitted to the fact that you said that, in a way, you were really thinking of Chester Himes in the character of Max Reddick?

JAW: Yes. Right. Yes, I did say that.

AAPL: Is Chester Himes still living?

JAW: No, he died in 1985.

AAPL: 1985?

JAW: Yes.

AAPL: Boy, I wish I could have recorded him! Where was he, and how old was he?

JAW: He was seventy-five, and he died in Spain, near Alicante. It was in Alicante, Spain.

AAPL: What aspects of Chester Himes did you use to create Max Reddick? Is it physical, psychological, chronological, or historical?

JAW: Well, the witness, the witness. If you read Chester's two-volume autobiography, *The Quality of Hurt* and *My Life of Absurdity*, the first volume particularly, you get the impression once he gets to Europe, he's spending an awful lot of time studying Richard Wright and other things that are occurring there. That's essentially where I drew that from. Max Reddick is the observer. I think, in one part of the book, Harry Ames says that he is the observer just sitting around digging people, watching people.

AAPL: Did you feel like in that book you were taking a risk at all, that people would be reading that book just to name names and figure out who was who?

JAW: No, they do that with any book. It never entered my mind.

AAPL: Really? That's a good tune.

JAW: [laughs] Yes, it's a great standard. Let's do the melody, and then take a—but then I started reading reviews, after about three years, about the roman à clef, and so on and so forth. You can look at it that way dismissively or say, "Well, look, you've got people like Malcolm X, people like Richard Wright, people like Martin Luther King." King was assassinated, we know. Malcom was assassinated, we know. There is a school that believes that Richard Wright was assassinated, and I'm with that school. If I use these three people as characters in the book, I'm also saying that if you propose a viable leadership it is liable to get wiped out. So it's another reason for you to consider the situation we're in here.

AAPL: We've brought up before in the interview the fact that a lot of the things you write fly in the face of assumptions about things. Other readers have described you, you know, described your vision as essentially an iconoclastic vision.

JAW: Could you define that for me, please? [laughs]

AAPL: Breaking down of icons, you know. Exploding expectations.

JAW: Yes.

AAPL: Telling it like it is.

JAW: Well, that's probably closer to it. I don't know that I'm tearing down anything that hasn't already been torn down by others before me.

AAPL: Well, certainly, I think your book on Martin Luther King could be described as iconoclastic.

JAW: Well, not really, because didn't the FBI reports bear me out on every detail?

AAPL: Well, it doesn't mean that an iconoclast isn't telling the truth. I mean, they are telling the truth, usually. They tell truths that people generally don't like to hear.

JAW: Well, that seems to be a bad habit I have.

AAPL: Why do you, as Max Reddick did—why did you, or do you, admire Malcolm X more than Martin Luther King?

JAW: Well, it's not a question of more because I understand where Martin was coming from; a lot of people think I don't. But I think that Malcolm X was closer to the way black people really wanted to be perceived, except that it was probably more dangerous to embrace that completely so that one accepts the vision most acceptable to the people who can kick your ass, and that is a church-going, hymn-singing, marching kind of thing. I've never made any bones about it. If that got us ahead, okay, but if it came to choices—we had to choose—for me, it would be Malcolm.

One has to look at it in the long run. I think it takes a great deal of courage to be a nonviolent person, and I'm not saying, "Down with Martin! Down with Gandhi!" But I'm not sure that the world understands nonviolence the way they wanted the world to do so. Hell, I'd much rather have nonviolent change, but given the history of the world, that's really not to be assumed at all.

AAPL: At the end of *The King God Didn't Save*, you say, "To what constitutional, to what moral authority, do the black, the poor, and the young now appeal? This book, the book for Martin Luther King, is basically addressed to that point." I wonder what you would say now, in 1989.
JAW: Well, I had eight years of appealing to zip in Washington. I believe there is still some great moral authority to emerge. From where this moral authority is going to come, I simply don't know. It does seem to me that the whole world needs some kind of moral authority. It's very much in the state of flux. We're talking political systems. We're talking changing populations. The Europeans can't get over the fact that they got so many colored people living there now. Americans, here, can't get over the fact that in 1990, a third of the population will be nonwhite. Everybody's going slowly bats. We need stronger moral authority. Where is it going to come from? I don't know.

AAPL: We went through a period, historically, of—at least I feel in my generation as someone in my forties, that we went through a period, through the 1950s and the 1960s, with the Civil Rights movement, you know, that things were getting better. It has . . . at least to me, it really looks likes things are worse now than they ever have been. Does it strike you that way?
JAW: Well, yes, but I said that in *The Man Who Cried I Am*, when they're celebrating the 1954 Supreme Court decision—

AAPL: Yes, you did.
JAW:—saying, "Well, let's celebrate just in case it's for real, but we're not really gonna buy this." One of the problems with this country is that you take one step forward and two steps back. We're not satisfied with the moral

progress. I assume that any other progress must follow that. That should be basic. We don't trust it. And I do feel it's worse. It's more subtle.

We've got American Nazis, Aryan nations, and—I don't know; nobody seems to be that concerned. We've had KKK flyers at school at Rutgers. I asked the dean, "What's going on?" He says, "We're looking in to it."

AAPL: Well, I'm not so sure it's so subtle.

JAW: Well, when I say subtle, I mean on the part of the establishment, whether you're talking education institutions or governments, whichever level. Everybody's got these affirmative action proposals, declarations flying around. "We believe in it. We're gonna do this. We're gonna do that." Flying out with the left hand, and with the right hand, they're probably as active as some of the people with the flyers and the hate letters. I see it in the schools. I see it in the businesses. I see a duplicity on those levels that didn't exist before because it didn't have to exist before. People could just go ahead and be what they were, say what they wanted to say. Now they're under some constraint to be nice, at least those kinds of people, so they are duplicitous. Younger people who are writing the letters, or just the guy on the street, that's different. It's worse in the sense that people are becoming more vocal on one level, and more duplicitous on another. It all adds up to total disaster.

AAPL: You have written pretty extensively about the ghettoization of black writers. You know, that all black writers are talked of in terms of other black writers and rarely, if ever, is a black writer asked to review a book by a white writer. That has carried over, now, into the schools where we have departments of black studies segmented off. Yet, the argument on the other side of that is that these books are now being read by a lot people. How do you feel about that dynamic?

JAW: I'm not sure they're being read by a lot of people. If they were, the publishers wouldn't be so reluctant to publish black writers. They may be being read by a few black studies departments, and they are shrinking around the country. They're shrinking every year. They don't attract the students. They don't have the faculty that they had, say, in 1968 and 1972. They're just really hanging on. I think that—I've always been opposed to separate departments like that because I felt it the responsibility of any decent university or college to have enough curriculum to include that material, without establishing new departments. But they knew what they were doing. They left them out there to wither on the vine, cutting faculty, students losing interest, and now they are just about—I shouldn't say that—but they're nowhere near as strong as they were in, say, 1972.

AAPL: So you don't see it as having been a flourishing thing at all.
JAW: No. It couldn't flourish unless all of these studies become a part of what are the major elements of any decent, good, maybe even a great, curriculum. They're not interested in dealing with black history as a part of American or world history or black literature as a part of American or world literature. They're just not interested in doing it. Listen, I've been working with these people for twenty-five years. I know where their heads are. [laughs] It's not where, I think, they ought to be.

AAPL: You're a very productive writer.
JAW: Compulsive.

AAPL: You describe yourself as compulsive. Okay. Do you read? Do you have much time to read books by—?
JAW: I read every day. Yes.

AAPL: When you read fiction—
JAW: I don't read that much fiction anymore.

AAPL: What do you read?
JAW: Nonfiction. I read science, prehistory, what's going on in the Third World, a lot of publications from the third world—Cuba, Africa, the Middle East. I've read—the last work of fiction I read was Ngũgĩ wa Thiong'o's *Weep Not, Child*, in preparation for a panel that we're having next week with four East African writers. I've read two novels, one from Mozambique and the other from Angola, this year. I haven't read that much western literature, not because I'm turned off by it, but because I'm interested in getting into new forms and new people, new views of the world. I have a fairly good idea of how most western writers view the rest of the world.

AAPL: At what point can you say that—is there a point at which you can say that you now remember first feeling the impulse to start really, seriously, writing fiction?
JAW: No, because my first impulse to write was poetry, not fiction. Then I went to vignettes and short stories. Each form seemed not to be large

enough to express what I wanted to say. I think I started my first novel about 1955, when I had been out of school about four and a half years.

AAPL: Had you gone to California at that point?
JAW: Yes.

AAPL: So you didn't finish high school. You went to the military. Then you came back and did finish high school.
JAW: Yes.

AAPL: Then, did you go on to Syracuse?
JAW: That's right.

AAPL: Where you grew up.
JAW: Yup.

AAPL: After that, you married young, and you—
JAW: I married while I was in college.

AAPL: —you worked at a lot of jobs to keep ends together, foundry work and things like that.
JAW: Foundry, supermarket, yes.

AAPL: And eventually—then, how did you come to go to California and start selling insurance?
JAW: Well, I didn't sell insurance. I was writing speeches and doing publicity.

AAPL: Oh, you were doing, like, essentially, technical writing and promotional writing.
JAW: Well, my first marriage, it had busted up. I just needed a new place to be and a new view on the world.

AAPL: That's when you started really beginning to work, in literary writing anyway, in terms of—
JAW: Well, it was writing. I was doing a lot of news writing out there and some public relations for CBS and NBC. I should qualify that. The PR I was doing, it actually was more publicity, and that happened whenever they had a black actor on a show. [laughs]

AAPL: I have read that you did—you've mentioned that you grew up in an integrated community and that you're first real sting, as far as the subject of race and race relations, came in the military.

JAW: Yes, that's true. I mean, a kid has things, when you're a child, that turn you off, but I know they were not as bitter nor as filled with hatred as some of the things that occurred in the service. I mean, I can't imagine anybody threatening to blow my brains out in Syracuse as they did in the Navy. You know, that kind of thing. It was a real change. It was like instant coming-of-age.

AAPL: Was that at all related with your—did that at all tie in with your deciding to write?

JAW: It may have. I do recall going to the brig one time, and I just felt I had to sit down and write something about this business. It was poetry, free verse, I suppose. Not very good, but I thought then that it did express what I wanted to say, what I felt.

AAPL: Is there anything really important that you think we've left out of this discussion?

JAW: You know, it's been very good for me to be married as a writer—a sense of teamwork that we've always had, a sense of sharing, doing well with all the kids, and knowing where each other's space was, space and time, and understanding and respecting that. I had twelve years between marriages, and, I suppose, there were times when I could have married earlier. Something just was not as right as it should have been in those instances. In this case, it was pretty good; it's worked. I think of so many friends that I have who are writers, whose marriages have not worked, and they have never remarried. I just think of the terrible loneliness they must have and how it must, in some way, affect their work. I think it's really good to be together. [laughs]

AAPL: Well, thanks for talking with us for so long today.

JAW: Boy! You're welcome. [both laugh]

Notes

1. The audio of this interview is preceded by Williams reading from *!Click Song*. (JAT)

2. The working title for what would become *Clifford's Blues*. (JAT)

3. Robert Reisner published *Bird: The Legend of Charlie Parker*, a compilation of interviews with those who knew Parker. (JAT)

Black Authors: John A. Williams

Charlie Rose / 1990

From *Nightwatch* (February 27, 1990). Footage supplied by CBS News. CBS Television. Permission granted by CBS News.

Charlie Rose: John A. Williams has been a writer for some thirty years, more than thirty years. In that time his work has received a lot of critical attention, but it has not had the widespread success that many believe it deserves. He is most noted for the book *The Man Who Cried I Am*, published in 1967, and his most recent work, *Jacob's Ladder*. He has written novels, nonfiction, poetry, and short stories, but until recently, all of his books were out of print. Joining us now is John A. Williams, the writer. Also, he is a professor at Rutgers.
John A. Williams: Rutgers University.

CR: Welcome, first of all.
JAW: Thank you.

CR: Teaching I guess creative writing or . . .
JAW: Creative writing and journalism.

CR: . . . and journalism. Boy, we need all the help we can get.
JAW: I'm telling you.
[laughter]

CR: It certainly would be a lot better when you know how to write better.
JAW: That's right.

CR: I've got some of them here. I've got *!Click Song* here. I've got *Sissie* here. I've got *Captain Blackman*. When I saw that, it made me think about *Glory*, and I said to you, "Have you seen it?" and you liked the movie.
JAW: Yes, I did. Actually there's a section in that that covers the same battle.

CR: Because what? It's a breakthrough in . . . ?
JAW: It's a breakthrough in terms of the way the country perceives the participation of the black soldier in American wars.

CR: Here is *The Man Who Cried I Am*. This is the one that most people think is your best, but that's 1967.
JAW: Sixty-Seven.

CR: Do you believe it is?
JAW: No.

CR: Which is the best?
JAW: I tend to say the one I'm working on now—

CR: Yes, I know you do.
JAW:—but actually I think *!Click Song* is the better one.

CR: Really?
JAW: Yes, 1982.

CR: Why is that better?
JAW: Because I had the sense of having done everything in that novel that I set out to do.

CR: Which was?
JAW: I'm not really sure. I was going after a certain sensitivity, instinct, and I felt that I had captured those things.

CR: Sensitivity and insight?
JAW: Insight, structure, characters, what the characters meant, what the characters do.

CR: I have not read *!Click Song*. Tell me about it.
JAW: It's very different—it's longer to tell. It's quite a story—

CR: What's the story?
JAW: Well, it's a love story, and it's a story of writing. It's a story about publishing.

CR: Autobiographical?
JAW: In part, yes.

CR: Also reflecting your own sense that there is, in the publishing industry, a censorship and a discrimination against black writers?
JAW: Oh, yes.

CR: More about that later for sure.
JAW: [laughs]

CR: All right. *Sissie* is about—
JAW: It's a black family: a very strong mother, a father who's unemployed, and two children who are challenged to go out and make something of themselves, by their mother.

CR: Written in 19—?
JAW: It was published in 1963.

CR: And *Captain Blackman*?
JAW: Seventy-two.

CR: Seventy-two, and you talked about the same battle covered in *Glory*. Magnificent film.
The Man Who Cried I Am.
JAW: Sixty-seven.

CR: It's about—?
JAW: Politics and the possibilities of disaster.

CR: Here is *Jacob's Ladder*.
JAW: African American and African possibilities, plus US intervention in the whole business.

CR: How do you feel about the fact that a lot of people don't think that you, and other black writers, have received attention, fame, support of the publishing houses, support by the book reviewing community that you deserve?
JAW: Well, I'm glad people think I deserve it, and I'm gladder that they're finally starting to think about it.

CR: And you're a little bit angry.

JAW: That's what they say. I think I'm more than a little bit honest, which people transpose into being anger, but then—

CR: No, no. I'm not trying—I don't want to put words in your mouth, but I'm trying to say *I* would be.

JAW: I've been pretty lucky in the sense that I have a fairly good job, got a solid family. It's true that I have a great deal of antipathy for some people in the industry, and in fact much of the industry itself, but I understand what's going on. It's not a puzzle to me, and it's part and parcel of the whole program that we have here in America.

CR: Let's get on with it then.

JAW: Okay. Well, I think obviously you cannot have no racism in publishing while racism exists everywhere else in the country. It's part of the total package.

CR: Publishing is not an island that has not been touched by racism—

JAW: That's right.

CR: —and it's manifest by . . . how—in what way?

JAW: Number one, you will have noticed that black writers do not interview the works of their contemporaries who are white.

CR: In other words, a major white writer is coming out with a book. It's unlikely you're going to see a review given in the *New York Review of Books* or in the *New York Times Book Review* section to a black writer to—

JAW: Who is a contemporary, yes.

CR: —who would be eminently qualified to do that—

JAW: That's right. That's not going to happen.

CR: —except for color.

JAW: That's right.

CR: Doesn't happen.

JAW: Doesn't happen.

CR: As soon as we say this, somebody from the *New York Times Book Review* or somewhere is going to call and say—
JAW: I've been saying this for a number of years.

CR: And they never called up.
JAW: They haven't called yet. Okay?

CR: Why? What is it?
JAW: Well, obviously people have some perception of basic differences between white and black writers, and as much as they say this is not true, the fact remains that those perceptions persist.

CR: What about when someone, like the other side of that coin, when someone like Toni Morrison comes along? Who gets to review her?
JAW: Generally speaking they're always white—I would imagine; don't hold me to this—

CR: All right.
JAW: —but my impression is that they're essentially white feminists.

CR: I would think so too. How about Alice Walker?
JAW: Essentially the same.

CR: Rather than, saying, a black literature professor in journalism and professor at Rutgers to review Toni Morrison, they'd more likely assign it to a white feminist.
JAW: Yes. Well—

CR: Or a black feminist.
JAW: Yes. Okay.

CR: There are less of those.
JAW: That's right. I don't think you're going to get too many of those reviewing people like Toni.

CR: You've made speeches about this. You've written about it.
JAW: I have not made speeches. I've written about it. I've included this in some speeches that I've made that dealt with other issues.

CR: Nothing has changed.
JAW: Nothing's changed.

CR: What happens when you bring it to the attention of the literary establishment?
JAW: Nothing.

CR: Well, do they say, "Mr. Williams, you're right," or do they say, "Mr. Williams you're . . ."
JAW: Let's take one of the organizations I've been associated with for thirty, thirty-five years.

CR: PEN.
JAW: That's PEN. Okay? One person called me from PEN on the basis of an article I did that was, once again, surveying this whole business of racism in publishing. One call from one writer. Two, two calls. Let's see what will happen now. Well, nothing happened, but I've had experiences with PEN where I expected them, as a member of the organization, to go to bat for me. But PEN didn't, so I was not expecting anything. Other people tend to be more hopeful about this situation, the possibility of change, than I could ever be.

CR: They will get excited and go active on human rights, censorship, and issues like that.
JAW: Censorship elsewhere, outside the country, but censorship within the country is not something that PEN, nor some of the other organizations, want to handle.

CR: Why not?
JAW: [laughs] Again, for the obvious reasons. It's too close to home and their involvement in that because you can't stand at the scene of a fight which involves you and your life and your country and say that it has nothing to do with me. That's essentially what's going on with the organizations that I belong to—the Author's Guild and PEN.

CR: John A. Williams is here. We'll talk more about his life and his work and his views and other subjects, and we hope you'll stay with us. Back in a moment. [commercial break]

We're back with John A. Williams. This issue has come up with me before, in terms—I never know how to raise the question. If I say to you, "John A. Williams has been a black writer for thirty years," that limits you.
JAW: Yes.

CR: This has occurred before in conversations with other people. I'll say, "He's a black musician," or "He's a black politician." They say, look, you know, if I say "He's a well-known black politician," why not just say "He's a well-known politician"? Right?
JAW: All right. What you're saying is that how I feel—

CR: Why does that limit you? Explain that because I know you're sensitive to that.
JAW: Because within the publishing world, within the multiple worlds that make up the US, that is limiting in a sense that here is white and there is black. If you are a black writer, that presumes that there are certain things you cannot write about, will not be allowed to write about. That presumes that you will accept smaller advances, smaller printings. It presumes a lot of things that actually take place. Now, obviously I am a black writer. I cannot change that. It's like sixty some odd years too late. Because I am a black writer, I think I bring to literature a certain sense, a certain way of expression that a white writer most times could not do. In other words, my view of the universe is still a view of the universe, perhaps slightly different. Therefore, I maintain that I am of extreme value to the society.

CR: Help me understand this.
JAW: Yes. Okay. I am. I am. I'm trying to get there.

CR: I know it. I'm a slow student. It is the difference—though on the one hand you want us to say—I mean—you and lots of other people say, "Look don't define me as a black writer. Define me as a writer." On the other hand you want to say, "Look, recognize my unique experience as a black man."
JAW: Define me as a black writer, but when you define me, make sure that it's not negatively. That's essentially what happens, what's been going on.

CR: Are you optimistic this will change?
JAW: No.

CR: Because?

JAW: You look at the generations. Nothing has changed. You know, we go from the Taney court in 1895 to the Warren court in 1954, and now we're back to another court, which is saying, "Hey, we like Taney better than we like Warren" kind of stuff.

CR: Roger Taney is a Supreme Court justice, and—

JAW: Yes. Right. We keep moving in circles rather than making straightforward progress.

CR: Who reads your books?

JAW: I'm not sure. Not enough people obviously.

CR: Well, let's take *The Man Who Cried I Am*. How many copies?

JAW: Well, I have no idea because I've had problems, as I usually do, with royalty statements. Over the years I can't begin to estimate, but I would imagine hundreds of thousands.

CR: Hundreds of thousands?

JAW: Yes.

CR: That's a runaway bestseller.

JAW: Over the years, maybe.

CR: Who published it?

JAW: It was published initially by Little Brown.

CR: And then by Thunder's Mouth Press.

JAW: Then New American Library, and now Thunder's Mouth Press. New American Library went through about five printings of the original paperback edition.

CR: *Jacob's Ladder* was published by the same—

JAW: Thunder's Mouth.

CR: Thunder's Mouth there, rather than by what you have referred to as a mainline publisher.

JAW: That's right.

CR: Why?

JAW: I had difficulty securing a mainline publisher. As a matter of fact, with *Jacob's Ladder*, the situation got so bad I began to use a pseudonym, but people wondered who this new writer was and so I went back to my old name.

CR: What happened when you used the pseudonym?

JAW: Well, no track record. Why be concerned with this guy who's anyway writing about Africa in 1966.

CR: Part of what you have written about and talked about, in terms of discrimination, you make the point that James Baldwin, for example, never received the recognition that he was due.

JAW: Yes.

CR: Same forces?

JAW: Same forces.

CR: A lot of people say his later work was not as good as his—

JAW: Well, there are a lot of things that Jimmy did early on that certainly deserved prizes, and he was completely overlooked. It was almost as if the powers that be in publishing said, "All right, let's give Jimmy lots of money but no prizes," and that's essentially—

CR: We'll give him fame but will not recognize him with the kind of artistic awards that say you are the best among us.

JAW: Precisely.

CR: And it's because of racism.

JAW: Of course. I don't think it has to do with anything else, anything else. Don't forget the time when Jimmy was doing his absolute best work was a time of great ferment in this country. People were looking for answers from anybody who could put them together.

CR: This is what, the late fifties, early sixties?

JAW: Early sixties, mid-sixties, yes. Sixty-three say to before, 1960s to—

CR: He was the angry young man then too.

JAW: Well, everybody kept saying that he was angry. There's something about the language. Maybe—

CR: *Angry* is a bad word?

JAW: Well, I think sometimes. Maybe Jimmy's attitude in person was that way, but I think certainly his language was used to express certain things in precisely the same way, perhaps the only way they could have been expressed.

CR: There was a time he came—didn't he come back from Paris then to work with Dr. Martin Luther King at that time?

JAW: I think he did. He volunteered to do some things.

CR: You were the first to talk about Dr. King, before Abernathy, before— who was the fellow who won the Pulitzer Prize, David Garrow?

JAW: Garrow.

CR: Before Taylor Branch. Here is a man who should be recognized for his genius and his leadership and his contribution, all the honors that have come to him, but also he was a man, with flaws and frailties. Did the black community come down on you for that?

JAW: Everybody came down on me for that. *Time* magazine broke a story before the book was published saying I was a rat and a traitor and this, that, and the other, but in the same story they said, "However, we have learned what happened in the meeting with J. Edgar Hoover . . . ," which was exactly the same stuff that I had gotten. Most people, to be honest, who finally got around to reading the book said, "Well, you know, all of this extracurricular publicity and media hype just was not deserved."

CR: Okay. Thank you very much, John A. Williams. *Nightwatch* continues. Back in a moment.

On *If I Stop I'll Die: The Comedy and Tragedy of Richard Pryor*—Interview with John A. Williams and Dennis A. Williams

Joe Hunter / 1991

From *Changes*—WPVI Television, Philadelphia (August 11, 1991). Reprinted with the permission of CBS Television. The views expressed do not necessarily represent those of WPVI-TV, its employees, or advertisers.

Joe Hunter: The comedic genius of Richard Pryor. Good morning, I'm Joe Hunter. This is *Changes*. Recently, a biography of Richard Pryor came out, and it's called *If I Stop I'll Die: The Comedy and Tragedy of Richard Pryor*. It was written by my guests, and the first one I'll introduce is John A. Williams. John has been on my program many times before; I'm sure everybody remembers him. He's a Paul Robeson Professor of English at the Newark campus of Rutgers University. Of course, he's also author of a dozen books, more than a dozen probably, that are very well-known to readers like yourself and myself. My other guest is his son, Dennis A. Williams. Dennis is a former *Newsweek* reporter, and he teaches writing at Cornell University. This was a joint effort, father and son. *If I Stop I'll Die: The Comedy and Tragedy of Richard Pryor*. We'll return with our guests and talk to them about this book right after this message. [commercial break]

My guests, John A. Williams and Dennis A. Williams, the coauthors of Richard Pryor's biography, *If I Stop I'll Die: The Comedy and Tragedy of Richard Pryor*. Gentlemen, I'm going to start off by asking, "Why did you decide to do a book on Richard Pryor?"

John A. Williams: Well, let's do the history first because the book had a second life. The first life was that I finished the book in 1984. It had been commissioned by New American Library. When I turned the book in, my editor had left. The man who replaced him suggested a few more changes.

When I made those, he had left. The third editor, who was actually the managing editor, didn't want to do the book at all. Now they owed me, I wouldn't say a considerable amount of money, but they owed me money which they were refusing to pay. According to our contract, they were supposed to go into arbitration. I filed my papers; they simply refused to do anything. I couldn't get the support from the Author's Guild to back me up. The lawyer said that it would cost me more money to go through arbitration in court than I had coming, so it was a dead issue. A few years later, I guess about two years ago, as a matter of fact, maybe two and a half, somebody suggested reviving the Richard Pryor book. A lot of water had gone under the dam as far as I was concerned. I was tired. I was working other things, and it occurred to me that this was perhaps a golden opportunity to do something I'd always wanted to do, which was to work with my son on a book. The second generation of writers in the family. The book needed updating. It needed a younger view than mine, I felt. I called and asked, and he was raring to go, and he can take it from there.

Dennis A. Williams: Well, the timing worked out well for me. I remember when he was working on the book the first time, and I was into it then. In fact, we went to a concert together.

JAW: The last concert he did.

DAW: Yes, at Radio City in New York. I was very interested in the subject. I thought it was a great idea for a book. I was disappointed when it didn't come out. In the meantime, after the book had been done the first time, I had stopped working for *Newsweek*, had moved upstate, and was teaching and doing more of my own writing. I had more time, and as it turned out, by the time everything fell into place, we got the go on updating the Pryor book. I had just completed my own first novel, and I had some time. I also appreciated the significance of the opportunity to do a joint product—project.

JAW: Product, did you say?

DAW: Product. [laughs]

JAW: Okay. All right.

DAW: A project to produce a product. [laughs] And there we are.

JH: Dennis, I gotta ask you this. Did you feel at all—how should I term this?—nervous about working with the master here? I mean, that would throw me if he said, "Joe, let's do something together." I would be completely floored.

DAW: Well, it was a bit daunting. It would have been more daunting if it had been fiction, and if it had been fiction, he wouldn't have asked me.

[chuckles] He wouldn't have invited me in the first place. It was more along my lines. It was more the kind of writing that I had, you know, nonfiction reportage, more the kind of thing that I had been doing, so I felt a little more confident in my contribution. It also helped that, as I said, by the time I got—I was ready to start work on this, I had finally finished something of my own. I felt that I had earned my wings, and I was ready to copilot.

JH: Okay. John, you mentioned that you felt that it needed a young voice in there. Now, what do you mean by that, and just exactly how did that weave itself into . . . ?

JAW: I felt that I was being perhaps too critical and too cynical because obviously—

DAW: What else is new? [chuckles]

JAW:—I'm older than Pryor by twenty years plus, and I knew that he always had tended to have younger audiences. I just felt that my cyanide needed some leavening with something else, and I feel sure that this was the right thing to do.

DAW: You're not that much older than he is.

JAW: He was born in 1940.

DAW: You said "twenty-plus years." Never mind. [laughs]

JAW: Yes, okay.

JH: I wanted to get back to something that you said because I'm afraid I'll let it slip by and forget. You just had a novel accepted by Simon and Schuster.

DAW: That's right.

JH: Called—

DAW: It's called *Crossover*—

JH: —*Crossover*.

DAW: —and it'll be out, I guess, late winter, sometime after the first of the year. I don't have the exact date yet.

JH: I can hear viewers saying, "Wow, you know, John A. Williams, he's published all these novels and everything. I wonder if he got his son's book published. You know he knew somebody; therefore, he could get the book published for him." Because people are always saying you gotta know some-body in order to—you know how it goes.

DAW: He does know a lot of people, but it didn't help.

JH: It didn't help this time.

JAW: I can't even get my own books published. [laughs]

DAW: In fact, it was actually gratifying after we'd signed the contract, and I had a—the first time I had a face-to-face meeting with my editor, I guess he knew who my father was, but he had no idea that he was my father so that was good.

JH: Okay. All right, we'll pause here for a message and return with our guests John A. Williams and Dennis A. Williams right after this. . . .

Back with our guests, the coauthors of *If I Stop I'll Die: The Comedy and Tragedy of Richard Pryor.* I think they're showing that on the screen right now. The authors—coauthors, John A. Williams and Dennis A. Williams. People always want to know how collaboration works. I'm sure that a lot of people tried that at one time. In fact, I was asked about that many times myself in prior years. "Let's do this together. Let's write this together." I've always said I don't even know how that works. What does that mean? I'm going to sit down and write a certain part, and then you're going to write the next chapter, or what have you? How does collaboration work? How did you guys get together to collaborate on this insofar as the actual work?

JAW: I think you gotta have confidence in each other to begin with. Then there has to be a chief and there has to be an Indian, so to speak. I think I knew those—

DAW: I let him be the chief. [laughs]

JAW: I think I knew the parts of the book that needed working on, and the interviews that I hadn't been able to do at the time I first did it, needed doing. That worked out perfectly because Dennis filled in all of those spaces and got those interviews that were crucial to the book because they tended to support things that had been said by other people in the book. We talked to each other on the phone. We exchanged Xerox sheets that were adds, and what was it I was always saying? Please mark your . . . [chuckles] please mark where this 'graph goes in the end. [laughs]

DAW: Yes, there was a lot of that. Mix and match, cut and paste. I think it helped that there was, by the time I came to the project, a text, that the first version was there as a guide. That made things a lot easier because it's like the basic track had been laid down, and I was working with that as opposed to, well, where do we begin? We didn't have to deal with that. Also, with my experience of having worked on a news magazine—which is all collaboration, you know, and you have to submerge your ego quite a bit—I was used to that in just doing things, fitting things in, making the—making not only the facts match, but the tone match so that it sounds relatively seamless. So I was used to that.

JH: I think the thing that amazed me about the book when I read it, was the evenness of it. Why that strikes me, is because when I was, oh, very much younger, I used to read books by Ellery Queen. Those were two authors who wrote those Ellery Queen detective novels, and I used to read books by Nordhoff and Hall. I could always tell where one writer was writing and the other one came in. I picked that up very early. I could tell the unevenness, but I didn't see that unevenness in this particular book that you guys have written. It was very seamless, as the word you used.

JAW: That may have been because of our facile use of the language, and I mean street language. [laughs]

JH: That did amaze me—and I remember asking you about this a little earlier, Dennis, and you said you're a good mimic.

DAW: I also think that the subject matter makes that sort of thing easier in the sense that—well, not so much the subject matter, but the fact that it's nonfiction. It's much harder to achieve that effect when you're telling a coherent story. In this case it's not one straight narrative; there are different sections of the book and different incidents and different time periods that we're dealing with. It's a little bit more episodic, I guess, in that way. It's easier than picking up the thread of a narrative and trying to weave them together.

JH: Right. The research aspect, that gets to me too. I'm very curious about that because when you're writing nonfiction, you can't just take it out of your head and put down what you think or feel. You've got to really dig and find out the facts about what happened. How did you go about the research? I'd like to hear about that.

JAW: Dennis had an interesting experience last year at the National Association of Black Journalists.

DAW: As it happened I was in Los Angeles to talk to some people for the book. I talked to several people, and I didn't talk to several people because they didn't want to talk. This National Association of Black Journalists convention was being held in town at the time, so the place was crawling with black reporters, a lot of people I knew. That was—it was helpful. I made some contacts, and I also chased some people around for three or four days, trying to get some interviews. As I said, some I got and some I didn't.

JH: Were there any particular stories about getting these interviews that we would find interesting?

DAW: I don't know.

JH: I'm sure there must have been.

JAW: There was one with—not in LA last year—but the one with David Franklin, which was so crucial to the book. Franklin had not responded to me at all when I first did the book, but I think over a period of time he obviously had a change of heart. Maybe it was Dennis's good looks. I don't know. [laughs] He agreed to talk to Dennis, and he got some very great stuff, very important stuff.

DAW: I think the timing was crucial because the first time around, they had maybe just begun litigation or were in the midst of litigation between Franklin, who was Pryor's former manager, and Pryor—this was a few years later, and that had all been settled. Going through clips and other published reports, I hadn't seen much from Franklin commenting on either the time he spent with Pryor or the breakup. I assumed that he didn't want to say much but I gave it a try, and the response was almost as if he'd been waiting for someone to ask. You know, reporters often encounter that. [laughs] People wonder why these people talk to reporters, and sometimes people are just waiting for somebody to ask them. So he was very helpful.

JH: Yes, but at the same time too, a lot of people in a situation like this are afraid, I think, to be quoted about because they fear it'll come back on them in some kind of way, the suits and so forth.

JAW: That's one thing that didn't change between the time I first worked on the book and when Dennis joined me. People would not talk about Richard Pryor. They would first ask, "Did Richard say it was okay?"

JH: That's what I heard.

JAW: Then I'd say, "No," and that was it. As you know from reading the book, we never did talk to Pryor, though I made several contacts. All of them turned out to be negative, and I spent part of one afternoon parked outside his house in Northridge, but without any luck. I mean, I had a question as to whether it was his house or the house next door. Then I saw a mailman, and I said, "Where does Mr. Pryor live?" He laughed, "Hahaha. I can't tell you that." [laughs] Sucker.

JH: Okay, we'll pause for another message. We'll return with our guests, John A. Williams and Dennis A. Williams, right after this. . . .

Back with our guests, the coauthors of *If I Stop I'll Die: The Comedy and Tragedy of Richard Pryor* by John A. Williams and Dennis A. Williams. Pryor never has seen this book then, so far as we know?

JAW: Well, we don't know, but we suspect that he probably has by now.

JH: I would think so. Just out of sheer curiosity, he'd probably want to know, but he has never contacted you to say, "Hey man"—in his own way, he'd probably use some choice language, you know [chuckles]—"what did you do to me?" et cetera and so forth.

JAW: He hasn't yet. I really don't expect him to.

JH: Did you think that you might be able to get his authorization at all before you did this, to do this?

JAW: Well, when I first was commissioned to do the book and we discussed it at the publisher's, it was felt very strongly that it would probably be a better book without contact with the subject.

JH: Why so?

JAW: Well, because people out there, and I guess people who are big or whatever, have this little game of seduction. They want you to like them, and because it's important for them to like you, you would find yourself in a situation, perhaps saying yes to things that you ordinarily wouldn't say yes to, or whatever. It's a whole seductive relationship that's, I think, bad to be caught in. I spent three days interviewing somebody who's very famous now in showbiz, and I still admire the guy. I don't know anything negative about him, but when I look back on my situation with him, I know that for five to ten years after I'd done that interview, he couldn't have done any . . . I would have punched out anybody who said he was wrong or bad. It's that kind of situation.

DAW: Pryor is an interesting subject in the sense that there isn't—or I won't say that there isn't a lot of dirt about him, but there's certainly an awful lot that's public already. He's hung out plenty of his own dirty laundry in public. It would be hard to imagine something, some embarrassing detail that one could unearth, that goes beyond any of the things that he's already told us about himself and his own problems. That kind of personal, the sense of personal revelation really isn't important to this book. We don't want to find out something titillating about a famous person because one of the reasons he's famous is because he told us all that. We really don't need to be concerned with those kinds of things.

JH: Yes. Quickly. We have less than a minute. You didn't do much interviewing of women who knew him, or know him, in this. It's all males.

JAW: No, the women that I interviewed who had known him were just as cautious about what they were going to say as the men. Perhaps even more so.

JH: Right. Okay. Just about run out of time here on this particular show. We wanted to deal with the mechanics involved in putting this biography together, and that's what we've done on this particular show. I hope you'll join us next week for part two, next Sunday at the same time. Then we'll talk about the book itself and some of the very interesting things that went on in Pryor's life. Our guests, John A. Williams and Dennis A. Williams. I'm Joe Hunter. Good morning.

John A. Williams

Wolfgang Binder / 1995

Interview of John A. Williams from pp. 167–84 of *American Contradictions: Interviews with Nine American Writers*, edited by Wolfgang Binder and Helmbrecht Breinig. © 1995 by Wesleyan University Press. Reprinted with permission of Wesleyan University Press.

John A. Williams was born in Jackson, Mississippi, in 1925. Today, after several guest professorships at various American universities, the novelist, dramatist, essayist, nonfiction writer, and publisher lives in New Jersey.

John A. Williams achieved fame with his novel *The Man Who Cried I Am*, in which the author addresses the race problem in the United States. Several other novels followed, among them *Sons of Darkness, Sons of Light* and *!Click Song*. In 1983 he received the American Book Award of the Before Columbus Foundation. His work is distinguished by a rejection of the literary cliché, whereby the African American protagonists appear as the victims of society because they do not know their own history. It is this subject—the overcoming of the past along with the intentional theme and the plight of the African American family—that are the dominant themes in both his fictional and nonfictional works. As an author, he sees the possibility of a new aesthetics for African American literature in the mixture of history and fiction.

Wolfgang Binder: John, could you tell us when and where you were born?

John Williams: I was conceived in Syracuse, New York, because my mother had gone up there to work and met my father whose family was up there already. And because I was the firstborn, she returned home to Mississippi, and that is where I was born and lived for the first six months of my life.

WB: So your family was actually not a southern family?

JW: Not on my father's side. If it was, we don't know. They may have preceded the Underground Railroad. They couldn't wait for it. As a matter of fact my father's family is probably in part related to the Onondaga Indians of the Iroquois Nation.

WB: What kind of family was that? How many kids were you?

JW: Well, four of us, two boys and two girls, survived. Two died in infancy. It was a Depression-time family, which meant that it was kind of tough. I was just thinking the other day about the most pleasant place we lived during childhood, and it was a giant four-family house in Syracuse. The neighborhood was very integrated then—a Jewish family, a peddler and his daughter and son on one side; an Italian family above them; and a black family upstairs over us—but the whole block was pretty much that way.

WB: When did you start writing seriously?

JW: I guess I started writing seriously—I'll put that in quotes—while I was in the Navy because I had such a rough time in the Navy. Whatever my reaction was to the Navy only got me in more trouble; so sometimes when I was in the brig I just got pencil and paper and wrote down all this crap and called it poetry, which, of course, it was not. But I think that's where it started.

WB: Were books important at home?

JW: No, books were not important. As a matter of fact, reading back over Richard Wright's life in the family and his interest in books, I think his family, like mine, essentially felt very threatened by books and my interest in them. With the exception of the Bible, books were considered to be pretty much troublemakers.

WB: And too worldly?

JW: Well, I don't know if they were too worldly or not. They may have had the sense that if this kid grows up reading books he's got to know more than I do, and then where in hell am I going to wind up, you know?

WB: And where did you go from Syracuse?

JW: I stayed in Syracuse until 1953 or so. I had gone to the junior high school and high school, and I played on the high school football and basketball teams and ran track. Then the war came, and I went off to war from '43 to '46. I hadn't finished high school before I went into service because my parents were divorced, and I helped out working. But when I got back and the GI Bill was available, I went back and finished that last semester in high school before I started college at Syracuse. Actually, I went south to start. I had gotten something, a kind of a promise of an athletic scholarship.

Anyway, so I went down there about two weeks before classes started to Morris Brown College, and, if you know Morris Brown, you can imagine what it was like in 1946. I had forgotten how bad it had been in the Navy with southerners. So I guess a week before classes started I was in the train coming back north, and I just enrolled in Syracuse and finished up there, did some graduate work.

WB: Apart from your literary work you have always also been a journalist and a teacher. Could you sketch that triple career briefly?

JW: Actually, I was doing some teaching at Syracuse with labor unions. I don't know why they asked me to, but I would go and talk to these labor groups. It may have been because I also did a lot of factory work in Syracuse. My first job when I came out of school was at the foundry, where I had worked summers. Then I also worked as a caseworker for the Welfare Department and then as a worker for the Children's Protective Service, which was a pretty grim job. Talk about children today being abused. It was just awful. And then I guess I had written for the *Post* in Syracuse and occasionally for the *Progressive Herald*, which was a black weekly. I know it sounds cliché, but I had always loved the smell of newspaper, you know, and being able to produce this stuff and to put words together to tell a story—this I was always in love with. But what I discovered was that when I was of age and had had some training to do this, doors were pretty much closed to me. Although even in Syracuse I wound up as a copywriter for a white public relations agency. They were very nice guys. So I was getting all kinds of experience but not being able to really put it into practice. Then I think after I did *The Man Who Cried I Am*, I was asked to go up to City College and teach. So I said, "Why not?" I enjoyed it immensely. I think I did two years there.

WB: Was that in '68?

JW: It would have been '68/'69. Then I was invited to teach a summer at the College of the Virgin Islands at St. Thomas. I'm saying to myself, "Well, hell, if it's going to be this exotic . . ." [*laughs.*] So we went down there for a summer, and after that I did a year at Sarah Lawrence College. Then I was offered a CUNY Distinguished Professorship at LaGuardia Community College. I think that's where I really got sucked into the whole teaching thing. Then I left there and went up to Boston, then did a summer at the University of Hawaii as well. I was also a Regents lecturer at UC–Santa Barbara.

WB: When was that?

JW: That must have been about '74. Then we moved to New Jersey, and I got tired of beating my head against the traffic getting into Manhattan. I sort of put the word out, and then I got into Rutgers. I've been there now for fourteen years.

WB: What do you teach there?

JW: I teach undergraduate journalism and graduate creative writing. I really have not taught literature in a number of years now.

WB: What are some of the key impressions of American students in those fields for you? Are there certain trends, group mentalities that you can decipher as being part of a racial setup or functioning on a class scale?

JW: Let's start with undergraduate journalism. On the whole, people have fallen in love with television. When they think about journalism, they think in TV terms. There are very few people who look forward to going into print. They are ill-prepared in terms of language and history of politics, economics, all the things that you really should know. Younger journalists don't seem to be as eager today to know as much about the world as possible. What they want to know is what will get them over and that's it. In graduate writing we get a lot of people who apply, and it is my job to say yea or nay. And I like to keep the class at about ten people. That's very difficult to do. Now, as any teacher of creative writing will tell you, if you get one or two people out of three or four years you are doing pretty good. And that's about what you get. I will tell you one crucial thing that has changed for me in terms of being a teacher, and that is it seems as though all freshmen or sophomores would want to do papers on injustice. Nobody does those kinds of papers anymore. They just don't.

WB: Even though it should be obvious to them that that would be a great topic. At this conference,[1] in the mass media, and I'm sure in the US, the term *multiculturalism* has been used and abused over the past few years. How do you feel about this term? Do you think it is covering up things? Do you think it is homogenizing things that are not really in harmony?

JW: Luci Tapahonso said something yesterday that I thought was quite apt. She had no qualms with the term, but she said it is this kind of study that is going to help bring her work to the fore, and to that extent it is very good whatever the title is. But titles become slogans, and slogans become clichés. And they go the way of the change in the weather. But I think for the time being we're sort of stuck with it, and most people are going to use it. Hopefully a lot of people understand what the hell it means, but that is the problem with coming up with a heading for any kind of new venture. By the way, it is not a terribly new venture because, as we mentioned earlier, there have been a lot of people who've been working in this area for quite a while without being labeled as multiculturalists but just people who are involved in literature.

WB: Just mention a name or two.

JW: I would say Bruce Franklin, who is my colleague at Rutgers; Jim Hatch at City College; Michel Fabre; Ishmael Reed; a teacher I had at Syracuse named Dave Owen, who is now dead. So there've always been teachers who have been ahead of the field in terms of decades, not just years. I haven't said a lot of the textbooks, but publishers are using those terms interchangeably—multiculturalism and diversity. I suppose as long as they sell books they'll be happy, but I think those of us who've been involved in the field for a long time have a right to feel or hold reservations about what these labels actually mean.

WB: Into which literary tradition would you put yourself? In which literary context do you feel at ease?

JW: I'm not sure. Certainly not all the terms that are being knocked about in postmodernism. I feel more closely related to the people in the Progressive era. I have always found that to be a very impressive period and probably too short a period in the way we form periods in literature and not give half enough credit.

WB: You would see the term *protest writer* as limiting you?

JW: Well, when many people use that, it is a limiting term, but I nevertheless feel that for a long time it was a label of honor.

WB: Do you feel a special closeness and special allegiance to the so-called Third World as a black American? Is that included in your vision of things? Do you also apply your criteria to the US or not?

JW: I have to admit that one of the things I have always been a sucker for is the underdog. I mean, I can watch a boxing match and see the poor guy getting beat up and say, "Come on, do something! Help yourself! Whatever!" But as soon as he starts winning, that changes. So to answer your question, yes, as long as people cannot help themselves or defend themselves. Yes.

WB: Would you say that in particular it is Africa that you would relate to most intimately?

JW: It's not only Africa. It is my people in the United States and by extension other people who don't even know they're in the same situation in the US and around the world.

WB: Do you think your journalistic career has strengthened that tendency or developed it even?

JW: I don't think so.

WB: You don't think so?

JW: I don't think so, no, because the pieces that I have really wanted to do on that situation are pieces that most editors are not very interested in, and I could give more voice to that situation in fiction than I ever could in journalism.

WB: Do you see American society holding together or falling apart today?

JW: I think it's falling apart, and I am not sure what it would take to find adhesive to put it back together again. In a great part the media is to blame for that as well as the politicians. Spengler always said that the journalist just obeyed the masters. I think a lot of philosophers and contemporary ones said essentially the same thing, but they still do it. We talk about the Watergate business and how great the press was, but actually there was only the *Washington Post* and two print reporters and CBS and a couple of broadcast reporters. Harry Ashmore, the Pulitzer Prize winner from Atlanta, from the *Little Rock Gazette,* said that if it weren't for these four or five people we wouldn't have had Watergate.

WB: Do you feel that since Nixon, Reagan, and the Bush administration that tendency to be separate and unequal has been enforced rather than easing up?

JW: Yes, it has been enforced in a way that's not as subtle as that. I try to explain to students that if you go to a press conference and you start asking tough and nasty questions, they're going to pull your press badge. You'll never get into another conference. They know who you are. They're just going to make it damn difficult for you to get any information from the White House. And that's the game, whether it is the White House, the state house, city hall, all in the same way.

WB: What about race relations between the different ethnic groups? Have there been changes in the eighties?

JW: Well, I think the press tells us that there've been changes and great antagonisms, and we know that the Hispanic community is growing by leaps and bounds and that it'll probably be the largest one in the country by the year 2000. That may be true between some Asian ethnics and black and Latin ethnics, but I'm not sure that the antagonisms are that deep between black and Latin because now they share so much of the same history, so much of the same blood and things of this sort, so Asians tend to be newcomers who don't have that particular history. In fact, they are very often placed in a position that in order to survive they must sort of economically bleed out these communities. I just find it incredible, for example, that in south central LA there are seven hundred liquor stores. More than any other number of liquor stores in any other community in the whole of the United States. But we've always known that in Harlem, in Southside-Westside Chicago, you find more liquor stores and churches than elsewhere in the city. But to return to those antagonisms: The individuals who understand that for anything to really work for ethnic groups there must be cohesion between them, and once that is achieved, you make your political move. Then you can divide the spoils. I mean that is what the Brahmins did when the Irish came and the Irish did when the Italians came, and on and on. So it is a pattern we have to learn to repeat. And I think the press is not our friend in this situation.

WB: How do you see the events in Los Angeles? I have the impression that the press was in part very unfair, attributing everything at first to the black community, whereas I think there were fifty percent Hispanics involved and quite a few whites in lootings, et cetera. It was a multiracial riot. Would you agree to that?

JW: Yes, I would. I think it was very important that the press worked very hard to create the impression that it was a black revolt, for obvious reasons, because if you have all of these people in rebellion that says something very, very bad about the system. Extremely bad. But the problem with Los Angeles—I have relatives there still—is that in that particular community there are practically no services. Now this was before that happened. There were very few banks, very few supermarkets, lots of check-cashing places, little fast-food shops, lots of churches, lots of funeral parlors, lots of liquor stores. But the services you need to have a viable community just really did not exist for that large number of people. So there are a lot of antagonisms building up there, not to mention the fact that the cops are always cops.

WB: So you would not say it was simply a repetition of Watts?

JW: No, I would not. No, not at all. We may get a book or two on it later on, but it is not going to be right now. A former student of mine at New York University who works for *Esquire* in West Hollywood came and visited a couple of weeks ago. He said he could see the fire from his apartment building. One would start here, the next one would start a bit closer to his neighborhood, a little bit closer, and he said it was just awesome. It seems they could not contain the fires. Now, in the neighborhood itself I have two sisters and a brother living. One sister is very close to USC—that area was pretty much devastated. As a matter of fact, USC was sending out notices to parents of potential students saying, "It is okay. It is all right. Don't worry." Another sister lived a bit further to the west toward Hollywood, and they just burned down a supermarket across the street. It was gone. There was no postal service. People had to go to the post office to pick up their mail. And since she gets a widow's pension—her husband had worked for the city—she had to go get that. My brother, who's not well, had to have friends come and get him and drive him to a market in some other neighborhood.

WB: The year 1992 is one of the big dates for commemoration and celebration. Do you have feelings about this year of Columbus as it is termed very often? Does that tempt you for a piece of journalism?

JW: Yes, it does in a way. I've been looking to see pieces on the twenty-ton Olmec heads that they've found from one side of Mexico to the other, for somebody to do a review of Alexander von Wuthenau's book, *African Faces in the New World*. All we're going to get out of this is what Columbus's journey may have done, but there are a lot of other things that could have come out of this. It is a celebration; it is not an occasion to learn anything. Celebrations engender money, and that's it.

WB: So you would keep festivities low-key?

JW: I would. I would throw in as much education as I possibly could get away with.

WB: You don't see that?

JW: I don't see that happening.

WB: How do you see, if that's possible at all, your function as a writer in American society? I mean both in black and white society. I hesitate to use those primitive terms, but they are very American. I prefer the concepts of culture to that of race because I think it is very demeaning, but anyway, this is couched in American language.

JW: I understand. I think my central function is to tell the truth to myself and, in extension, to my fellow human beings. I just find the truth is so hard for people to absorb, particularly if it is an unpleasant truth. You will get—somebody mentioned this the other day—you get a lot of facts, but facts are not necessarily truth. That is basically what I see as my function: to deal with these truths and have people respond to them—to at least give them alternatives so they can see that what they are living is not the truth but a lie. And I am not sure if a writer can be sure he or she is doing anything more than that.

WB: Let me ask you about the politics of American publishing, the conspiracies or just the interest.

JW: I can remember that when I first started writing there were editors who were very concerned that the work would offend the southern readers. It sounds like this was five hundred years ago or so, but it wasn't. We're talking about thirty or thirty-five years ago. The mentality of the editors then—let me say that I think there were better editors then—is not, in my opinion, very high. I was lucky enough to get one of my magazine editors who moved to books to do a couple of what I thought were important books for me, but the level of intellect in understanding the world has diminished tremendously. There has always been a sense that if you have a Richard Wright, you don't need a Ralph Ellison; if you have a Ralph Ellison, you don't need a Jimmy Baldwin; if you have a Jimmy Baldwin, you don't need an Ishmael Reed; and on and on and on. That's the one-at-a-time syndrome, which has been pretty much destroyed when it comes to black women. We have seen this repeated with Asian American authors—the women versus the men. But those are some of the problems we have. And the hard currency issue—the purchase of American publishing companies by some of the European companies like Maxwell, Bertelsmann—they have really made the Americans start to look to the absolute bottom line. We are not talking about literature, serious literature, that makes people think about who they are, where they are going, or where they came from. We are talking about writing where people get in a sack and romp, and serial killers.

WB: Sensational material?

JW: Right. So we are getting a lot of that to the detriment, I think, of a considerable number of very good writers. Then they go to the small presses if they are lucky, and because small presses don't have the money to publicize except in a general press-release way, we seldom hear about them until it is too late. They become famous suddenly, or they are gone suddenly. So we have a real problem, and I think it is based on the fact that nobody takes books seriously in America anymore. I do textbooks occasionally, and I have always felt like an idiot when the publisher's editor says, "Well, how are we going to structure the teacher's guide that goes with the textbook?" I'm always thinking, "A teacher needs a guide to teach this book?"

WB: Do you feel that since the mid-eighties the male African American writer has it harder than before to come to the foreground?

JW: Yes, I think it started a little bit earlier than that, but yes, generally speaking. One of the reasons may be the proliferation of women editors, but that's not necessarily the case. I think there were fewer before, and they tended to do all kinds of books, males, females, or whatever. But I think right now there are a lot of female editors who feel safer dealing with what it is they know, what it is they best know.

WB: Is there something like an American mainstream literature, or is that fictitious? Is that created by the media, by vested interests?

JW: Oh, I think it is created by vested interests, and I think the mainstream keeps changing. You could go from a WASP mainstream in which Hemingway is insulting Jews and blacks in every corner and not in the voice of the characters but in the authorial voice. Then you would move to a situation where you would get Jews at the bottom rungs of the literary establishment. And now that has changed, so a lot of Jews, not all, are at the top of establishments. I am not sure who comes next, but we can see the ethnic changes occurring quite clearly. Then you take publications like the *New York Review of Books* and the *New York Times*—they both certainly have a powerful role in creating this mainstream group. Who is in the mainstream, and who is not? And, of course, *Esquire* comes out with its little charted thing, who is hot and who is not. So there are a lot of factors, but I believe there is a mainstream and a no-stream.

WB: Could you comment on generational shifts in African American literature and its production?

JW: Yes, let me try if I can. Well, the newest application of a black aesthetic as I understand it is that the younger writers now represent a second generation of the black people who have been to college, and having done so and experienced things different from their parents, feel no constraint and just write about whatever it is they want to. That is well and good, but I think the old black aesthetic essentially felt the same way. The problem was that editors were not about to let you write of white love. That simply was not going to happen. Now, beyond that I am not sure what the difference is because publishing tends to keep people and groups in certain molds and channels, so we will have to see how that develops. If you wanted to talk about the progressive protest school, then, of course, we have got a long tradition from the nineteenth century on, but we are now getting some postmodernist works of new structures in literature, new narrative points of view. I am not sure if that's good or bad, but I do think, in view of our inability to change the language any more than we have, that there must be something else we can do to tell the same old story. And essentially stories are the same.

WB: Would you say that what has been termed "the double consciousness" is both a burden and a gift but, above all, a great potential for a black writer in the sense that you can command more than one cultural discourse?

JW: I think it is a fantastic gift. Maybe during his time Du Bois saw it as a curse. Don't forget, he was also one of the talented tenth, which made his group even smaller, more singular, so it became a curse among blacks who thought he was too high and mighty. But I think it is an incredible gift to be able to describe not only white society but black society or any society that you are perceptive enough to understand what the hell is happening in it.

WB: I have always felt that this was one of the blessings of so-called ethnic writing as long as it is not stuck within the confines of an ethnic group, which is hard to define anyway.

JW: Well, as you know, an African American can go to Africa, and I don't know what it is like these days, but when I first started going, around '64, in some places Africans would view you as an American even though you were black.

WB: Would you situate your work in general as an urban literature or as a regional literature?

JW: I have worked very hard in an unconscious way to bring the world into my small urban setting, trying to think international. *Captain Blackman* certainly is. *Jacob's Ladder* certainly is.

WB: I notice you bring in Europe here.

JW: That is one thing that I would like to see more of; that is, the less personal setting, whether it be urban or Caribbean or whatever, and relate those settings to the rest of the world because, actually, that is the way the world is. The world is already impinging on those locations. I can begin in an urban setting, but the characters are moving in and out of the world. I feel very comfortable with that. I think of the great writers whom I have loved who have always been internationalists.

WB: Could you mention a few names?

JW: . . . the foremost of whom would be Alejo Carpentier. You know, he is just incredible. If you take Chekhov, he's talking about Russia, but his characters are always going to different parts of Russia, seeing different kinds of people, people who have been influenced by places and people outside of Russia and things of that sort. If you take Richard Wright's nonfiction, you have got essentially the same thing. There is William Attaway, who is doing the same thing on a small scale in his dealings with other cultural groups within the US and saying, "These people are doing this the way we do."

WB: Do you have any literary relationship with German writers?

JW: No; I mean I did some reading on Schiller and Schopenhauer, on Nietzsche, the usual abridged editions, and I have read Grass and Böll and *All Quite on the Western Front.*

WB: Do you have any feelings about Germany as it is today, the so-called unification?

JW: I worry about Germany. I worry about the US. I really do. I mean, there are so many places that seem ripe for the resurgence of fascism, and right now we can sort of see or hear echoes of Hitler, of Pilsudski in Poland, and Doriot in France; and I am saying to myself, "I think I have done this before," and I am not sure—I know I don't want to do it again. That is pretty much my impression, not only with Germany but with many places in the world.

WB: Do you have—if you do not wish to call it a theory—a certain concept of what human tragedy is?

JW: Yes, I think I do. The thing about human tragedy is that it occurs without the individual having any degree of hubris whatsoever. I mean, he is not flying in the face of a god. He is just trying to get by, and in that sense it becomes not classical but neoclassical tragedy, like *Death of a Salesman.* I think it is just merely while hoping for the best that one understands within one's capability—not only for oneself but one's family, one's country, one's world—and in finding out that life is pretty impossible through no fault of your own. The more you fly in the face of that impossibility, the more you get hurt because you don't have sense enough to say, "Oh, this is bad business. I am going to go back and do an Uncle Tom, and maybe I will survive."

WB: Do you find that the naturalist novelists' theory of class, immediate conditions, and racial makeup is essential for some kind of tragedy in the sense that it was for Dreiser and Norris?
JW: No, I don't think race or class necessarily make up those key essentials. One could look at the work of Flannery O'Connor and not find those things and still find very, very deep tragedy. I think it is the self-perception of the character that really causes that tragedy.

WB: To what extent did you leave the limits of the black community and have avenues that lead into white European and even other countries? How much was that a consideration of yours?
JW: I think if you look at a lot of that stuff there are always two or three minor or major white characters, and I usually try to have one who is good. If one is not good and able to help the black protagonist, at least he feels badly about not being able to help because that has been their experience. And I think that is absolutely valid, and more than valid, in my sense that it is fair, so I have done it. Most critics have not noticed the continuation of the black family that has appeared in about three or four books. If my name were William Faulkner, they would all say, "Look at what he's doing! Great shit with that family! Good stuff." But that doesn't happen. I know what I'm doing, so I don't mind that much.

WB: What about language? Was that a concern of yours to use black English, colloquial levels of various strata of society?
JW: Yes, if I have to have the character to fit the language but the more I write, the more I really do realize how limiting the language is for me. My sense was that *Beloved* had reached the point where Toni Morrison was straining to reach something else in the language, and at times this strain is quite visible.

WB: In *Jazz* it certainly is.
JW: . . . and detracting. But yes, it comes as a relief when I can deal with a character from the mean streets who is talking a language that I understand,

and it can denote very simply and broadly some of the things that it would take character by character, say, at another level, three pages to do.

WB: In most of your novels your heroes, especially black men, are portrayed as marginal, beginning with your first novel, *The Angry Ones*, and its protagonist Steve Hill. Could you comment on this?
JW: Black men, generally speaking, have always been marginal.

WB: I do want to ask you about the book on Richard Pryor you did together with your son Dennis, *If I Stop I'll Die*.
JW: It is badly edited, but don't blame me. He was so much of what the people are in his language and his thoughts; he was just an incredible comedian. He did and said and thought everything every black person in the twentieth century must have said, thought, or did or wanted to do. He was just the complete comedian. Besides that, he revolutionized the whole comedy approach for whites as well. Language that was deemed unseemly became, not unlike household words, words that no longer shocked people. In terms of revolutionizing comedy and reflecting the black community, and to some extent the white community, I don't think he has a peer. He is a different comedian from Bill Cosby, who is very funny in his own way.

WB: And Redd Foxx, whom I like a lot.
JW: But he is brash and bold and a victim, while he victimizes people too.

WB: Into which genre would you put the book? Is it a biography? Is it a study of his art?
JW: I would call it a study because we never saw him. He just would not give us an interview. It just didn't work out. For that reason I would call it more of a study than a biography because I think a biography has a hell of a lot more depth. I don't think it is all that popular a book either. I think there is a lot of black history in there because we felt we had to place Pryor against the backdrop that explained his situation and the limitations that he had to perform against.

WB: In 1982 your novel *!Click Song* appeared, which, apart from being a political text, is one that deals with the topic of what it means to be a black novelist in New York. How representative a life would you say is that of Cato Caldwell Douglass? And could you briefly comment on those three loaded names united in one person?

JW: I hope very representative of black male writers. Cato refers to a republican (Roman). Caldwell is merely alliterative. Douglass refers to Frederick Douglass, the black abolitionist.

WB: In *!Click Song* and in *Sissie* the issues of race, beauty ideals, black family life, the relationship between black men and women play an important role. Do you see, both in real life and in African American fiction, a continuum of those issues and constellations?
JW: I believe I have finished with these issues in my writing. Now it's on to gloves-off political writing on contemporary America.

Note

1. Williams was one of a number of American writers invited to speak on the topic of multiculturalism in Erlangen, Germany. (JAT)

An Interview with John A. Williams

Dennis A. Williams / 1995

From *Forkroads: A Journal of Ethnic American Literature* 1.2 (Winter 1995), 37–50. Reprinted with permission of Dennis A. Williams.

For me, at first, he was always, above all, a writer, a romantic figure, a world traveler, Greenwich Village bohemian, jazz aficionado, peace activist, outdoorsman, lover of art, and an impossibly well-read man who could turn the most casual conversation into a teaching moment with references to obscure philosophers and historians. That he was also my father only complicated matters. It took many years—and reading between the lines of many novels—to know him, as well, as the fun-loving, rambunctious kid from my own Syracuse, New York neighborhood: an easygoing, would-be jock with whom I could watch a Super Bowl, fall out laughing to Richard Pryor, and, in time, get drunk. Those split images began to come together as I grew to adulthood and—both because of and in spite of him—ventured to become a writer myself. His legacy, however, remains daunting and secure from filial challenge: thirteen novels, eight nonfiction books, ten edited or coedited volumes including two literature texts, and a forty-year history of publishing short fiction and poetry. *The Man Who Cried I Am*, published in 1967, cemented his public reputation as a compelling and uncompromising chronicler of politics, race, and the human heart. Yet his wide-ranging interests have always eluded easy categorization. It is to his credit and my enduring pride that one of his nonfiction books was also the first to bear my name, *If I Stop I'll Die: The Comedy and Tragedy of Richard Pryor*, which we wrote together at his suggestion. His invitation to me to conduct this interview was but the latest expression of a generosity that has evolved from paternal to collegial. We spoke in the spare living room and on the perfect porch of his upstate New York hideaway, where he had taught my younger brother, as well as my older brother's children and my own, to shoot, play, and understand that they have a special place in the world. It is the place where he is most at home, where all the parts of him come together, from the book-lined writer's studio to the fishing dock, where both the collection of jazz records and the telescope aimed at the clear, rural sky can transport his spirit, and where his mother's ashes are buried. Because it was an official, taped interview, the occasion seemed oddly formal, but because it was also a synopsis of forty years of such conversations, it was entirely natural. He doesn't change: the Syracuse kid, the poet-philosopher, the compulsive teacher, student, parent, and bop-cool hang-out buddy are all alive and well in John A. Williams.

Dennis: When did you know for sure that you could do this, that you could be a writer?
John: I never knew for sure.

Dennis: You're still not sure?
John: I'm still not sure.

Dennis: When were you sure enough to commit yourself to it?
John: It wasn't a question of commitment, Dennis. It was a question of doing something that I thought I might possibly be able to do in order to maintain sanity. I know Baldwin has said that and I have said it before myself. In a world which really, given certain situations, doesn't give a shit whether you exist or not, it is very important that you create yourself, and you do that by—or at least I think I did—by writing.

Dennis: You recently completed your thirteenth novel, *Colleagues*, which you said would be your last. Talk about it a little bit.
John: Well, it's set in a university, and it's told from the point of view of an African American professor. There've been a number of novels about university life, but Ishmael Reed's *Japanese by Spring* is the only one I know of where you find African Americans. For me it's a new area stemming from one more experience in my life. Anyway, it's something I wanted to do and it's done, so now we'll see what happens to it.

Dennis: Why is it your last novel?
John: Because I don't see fiction doing anything, at least not the way I think fiction should do things, and it's true that when I begin a book it's usually something that I want to say. I don't have a fixed audience. I hope the audience, like metal scraps to a magnet, become attracted to it, but I am just

really disgusted with publishing in general, the quality of editors, the whole who-struck-John that makes the writing of fiction not anything I want to do anymore. I've always looked at fiction as being a corrective force, an enabling art form focused on an angle of truth. I feel now that that's a view that is not popular.

Dennis: You have another one, the one before that, number twelve, *Clifford's Blues*?
John: *Clifford's Blues*, yes. Now there is some mild interest in it. It's amazing what's happened to that book.

Dennis: What kind of reactions have you gotten?
John: One guy found no fault at all with it—loved it, he said, but didn't offer to publish it. Another editor seemed piqued because I hadn't written extensively about what was happening to Jewish people in the East, the ovens, the genocide. All in all I came away with the clear impression that I, a black writer, was not supposed to be doing this kind of book.

Dennis: What kind of book is it?
John: It's a novel centered on the diary of a black musician in Dachau from 1933–1945. His diary's discovered in Denmark by a black couple there on vacation who get it to the only black writer they know. The trio is comprised essentially of Clifford, who is the musician; Jay, the writer; and Bounce, who is the guy who discovers the diary.

Dennis: Do you feel you have left any stories untold?
John: Yes, probably a novel about aliens who actually turn out to be black people from somewhere manipulating these little people everybody claims to see these days. [laughs]

Dennis: Good idea, I'll do that one. How would you evaluate your career as a novelist?
John: I don't think I'd even try.

Dennis: Okay, what would you consider your best book?
John: I like to think *!Click Song* is the best book. I think I did things with structure better than I did with *Sissie* or *The Man Who Cried I Am*, and it seemed to work best. I think I got into a writer's life pretty good, yet that was not the key element of the novel. That was the marriage of Cato

[Caldwell Douglass, the protagonist] and Allis, and secondarily the rivalry between Paul and Cato, which in a sense is like another marriage. The secondary theme was very painful for me because it reflected an experience I had with a very dear friend, Dennis Lynds, for whom you are named. We just stopped maintaining contact because he thought I was getting more applause than he was as a writer, which was not necessarily true. He has done very well as a writer and produced more books. But that led me to thinking, and I never wanted to think this, that he was like so many other white people I have known who, if they think you're getting ahead of them, the play ends. So that aspect of it was painful, but that's the way it is. Some things I wanted to say about kids and family and the world in general were there, too, not to mention the anthropological elements and the jaunts through the museums. I don't know that I'm that unhappy with any book. I may be unhappy with the reception a book got, but I've said what I wanted to say in every book. Few people have heard of *The Berhama Account*, but I thought that was my funny book along with *Mothersill and the Foxes*, which of course was a bit deeper than *Berhama*. I learned early on you just can't do a book and sit around waiting for good things to happen to it. The sense should be, fuck it; let's get on to the next one. And that's pretty much the way I've been working.

Dennis: Is that why you won't read a review until a year after the book has been published?
John: That's right.

Dennis: Can you talk a little bit about your approach to work? I've always thought of you as a lunch-pail kind of writer. As far as I know you have never not been working. You've always got something going on; you've always got a project. One foot after the other. Why?
John: Writing's become a way of life, and I'm not sure it's not also seeking shelter from storms—that could be a part of it. But I write practically every day. For me it's like putting on my pants. If I'm not writing I'm taking notes while watching TV or something else, but my mind is always somewhere in the production of something or finishing something and sometimes starting something new.

Dennis: The Joplin family appears in several of your books, the first time in *Sissie*, I believe, and right up through this last one, *Colleagues*. What is the meaning for you of that fictional family?

John: Longevity and some depiction of family ties through the generations and what happens to them. In the case of the Joplins, not much spectacular ever happens, they're just grinding it out generation by generation. I like to think that's pretty much what African American families do, for better or for worse. As a matter of fact, all families. And of course I guess it's not so amazing, but I don't know of any reviewer who's picked up this family and followed the continuity through all of these books. But then I tend to put critics in the same category as editors. Maybe I'm spoiled because when I began I met some really fine editors and critics as well. My sense is that people like that are not out there now.

Dennis: I'll say this so you don't have to: I never thought your work has gotten the respect that it deserves. Any ideas why not?
John: I've got a few.

Dennis: I thought you would.
John: I've written about this before, so I don't want to belabor a lot of dead horses here. But I think it began with the publication of *Night Song* in 1962 and the American Academy in Rome and the National Institute of Arts and Letters. I was the first writer ever to be rejected for the Prix de Rome, after being unanimously selected to go there. Subsequent investigations seemed to have tied me to drugs, jazz, and white women. The rest, as they say, is history set down elsewhere. On the other hand, I've done my share of stirring shit, having had run-ins with people at the [*New York*] *Times*, *Newsweek*, publishers who resent my having accountants check their books, publishers who won't arbitrate problems as most contracts call for, and editors who get pissed because they've lost your manuscript and you call them on it. Everybody wants you to kiss their ass, and I'm not going to do that. There are people out there who simply have not forgotten. An editor at one of the literary publishing magazines told me about five years ago that he thought it was a shame what "they" were doing to me. When I finally got around to asking him who the "they" were, he wouldn't respond. But that's life, you know.

Dennis: What do you most like and dislike about being a writer?
John: Oh, I most like language and ideas and weaving cloth from them as well as from experiences. The creation of a whole from fragments of ideas. I can't say I dislike anything about it, even now. I like the idea of being a writer. I am very proud to be a writer.

Dennis: What would you say in terms of a literary career has been your biggest thrill, the high point?

John: Literary career? Well, I never looked at life that way, but I can tell you I did a play, *The Last Flight from Ambo Ber*, which was read in a little theater in Cambridge. I thought that was the most exciting thing that has happened to me as a writer, to hear these words coming off the stage, and they made sense. I found that pretty astounding. That was incredible.

Dennis: Was there a low point?

John: Low point. Yes, I had a low point before I really got into writing, but it didn't have anything to do with writing. It had to do with what was going on in my personal life, and I think the writing helped me get out, get over that. It was a lifeline when I was drowning, really, really headed for the bottom.

Dennis: Poetry is your first love.

John: It is.

Dennis: Why?

John: I don't know. Because I've never been good at math or geometry or algebra, any of those things, poetry for me comes closest to becoming as concrete as numbers in terms of language and rhythms and cadences and images—a certain precision. And I like the compression of ideas that poetry demands, which is not to say that all of my poems are that short—I've got some that go three or four pages long. I've a poem called "Journey without Name," and that's about the family. It has an ending that really is just the beginning. I love poetry the way I love painting.

Dennis: You've also done, obviously, a lot of nonfiction. You mentioned the play. Any screenwriting?

John: I did a bad screenplay for Clarence Avant for [my novel] *Sons of Darkness, Sons of Light*. Nothing ever happened to that, but the world is so filled with shits that as soon as Clarence's option was over people started calling me up in the middle of the night from Hollywood. I would say to them, "Talk to Clarence," because Clarence had been very decent with me. You don't find a lot of that in Hollywood. I've started dabbling with another screenplay based on *The Man Who Cried I Am* since I saw you last.

Dennis: What different kinds of satisfactions do you get from the different kinds of writing?

John: Each has its own kind of discipline, but if you asked me to name what each was, I couldn't. The basic discipline is just sitting your butt down and writing. Each provides you with a different way of seeing, thinking, and feeling. I love them all for the challenges they provide. That's the kind of satisfaction I get from doing different kinds of writing.

Dennis: What about straightforward nonfiction prose as opposed to fiction? Obviously they are different, but are you aware of any particular difference in your approach?

John: Yes. Most things I want to say and share quite openly with readers, and very often when I approach nonfiction it's with a club in each hand. I know that's not always good, but there you are. With a novel, there are elements I want the reader to have to work to find. With any genre, I always want to write the best I can.

Dennis: What would you say to Johnny Williams if you had him in class now, as you were when you took the class with [Gordon W.] Couchman, the professor who let you know that maybe this was something you could do? If you had somebody who was like you were then in your class now, what would you tell him? Would you encourage him to become a writer?

John: I would encourage his writing if it moved me, but at the same time I would tell him how damn difficult it is to become successful, whatever that may mean to him. Discouragement doesn't deter people who want to write, but it's only fair to tell them what they are going to face. There would be no armies if every person in them believed he or she was going to get killed. Armies exist because every person in them believes if anyone is going to get killed, it's not him, but the guy next to him. So it is with young writers, and maybe that's a good thing.

Dennis: What do you think about MFA programs?

John: They make more sense than the PhD programs, but I'm wondering, out of all the people now attending MFA programs, how many are actually going to end up being writers? I guess, oh, about twenty years ago you could count the number of people who did well coming out of those programs on two hands. I don't know what the figures are now, but those programs are getting very, very crowded. I tend to feel that the old school is somehow best and closer to where a writer should be—formally unschooled in creative writing, just out there in touch with the world. I once suggested to a very good student that he hit the road and experience life. He signed up on the crew of a yacht. It went to the Caribbean and then back north. He jumped ship somewhere along the St. Lawrence River. The captain had turned out to be another Captain Bligh.

Dennis: You've had several trifling encounters over the years.

John: Yes. *Trifling* is a term meant to define irresponsibility, laziness, incivility, things like that. My mother used it when I was a kid. I get a number of requests from black people doing magazines or books and stuff, and they ask for things and I send them. It's more of a case of responsibility to the community rather than a matter of money. So, when I follow up on what I've sent and say, "Look, it's been nine months since I sent you these poems. Are you going to run these or not?" Or, "What do you mean you can't find the manuscript I sent eighteen months ago?" With certain editors who are putting anthologies together, it's essentially the same thing: they won't tell you that you've been dropped from the table of contents. You find out inadvertently and call for an explanation, and all they've got to give you is some trifling crap. And I want to make clear that black people aren't the only people like this. Courtesy and civility are the cheapest kinds of human intercourse; it doesn't cost anything to be courteous or civil. I'm not interested in your power trip, and I'm sure you don't give a damn about mine. Don't be trifling.

Dennis: What do you enjoy reading now?

John: I'm reading a hell of a lot more nonfiction than fiction, but I'd like to finish reading all of Alejo Carpentier's work. He's my kind of novelist, historic, sardonic, subtle, whatever. I do read a little fiction—*Losing Absalom* by Alexs D. Pate, I thought that was a very fine book, and these books by this young Williams. I think his first name is Dennis.

Dennis: Is there any author or works that were particularly influential in terms of your own work?

John: Probably Richard Wright. I can't nail that down because I read so damn much, but Wright, when I was going to school, was not one of the authors you'd automatically get to. You were pretty much on your own. Every writer who excited me influenced me in some way, I'm sure.

Dennis: Right now what would you say is the best novel you've ever read?

John: I'd have to give you two: *For Reasons of State* by Alejo Carpentier and *Bound to Violence* by Yambo Ouologuem. I reviewed that book for the *Times* almost thirty years ago. I think there was some controversy about the book as to whether he wrote it or not, and I don't think that was resolved. The novel dealt with the experience of being educated in France and returning to Africa, and I must have read about a dozen books like it since then. It was a great book.

Dennis: I thought you might have said *Under the Volcano.*
John: Malcolm Lowry. That was my teaching novel. I learned much from it in terms of structuring time. How you can confine it, shift it, weave it back on itself, whatever. I guess it's the same thing painters do when they have a canvas, space. How in the hell am I going to fill all this blank space?

Dennis: You first wanted to be a trumpet player.
John: Yes, actually I first wanted to be a great athlete and then a trumpet player when I discovered how well I could play the bugle. There were no programs at Dunbar Center where you could rent musical instruments or anything. You could go to a music shop and rent them but that was far too expensive, so I just didn't pursue it. And I wasn't encouraged to.

Dennis: Are there other people that you particularly admire in other creative arts, other than writing, such as musicians, painters?
John: I've always liked Charlie White, who has been dead for quite a while now. His art always struck me as my nonfiction writing, clubs in both hands. And Tom Feelings, he has a new book coming out called *The Middle Passage: White Ships, Black Cargo,* and it's fantastic. It's all done in black and white and grays and suggestive swirls, yet it's a very graphic, tough book. Feelings is very good, and Romare [Bearden] I've always liked. We met him I guess in the early seventies. Jacob Lawrence, especially his Toussaint series, I've always liked. I like [Sam] Middleton. I like Van Gogh, got Van Goghs all over the house here. Lots of other people.

Dennis: What about musicians?
John: Too numerous to name. There is this cat on guitar from Boston, Adam Williams, and lots of new young people coming up. Maybe I'm just an old fogey. I've got to get with these young people, but the old stuff I'm content with.

Dennis: Such as?
John: Well Bird, of course, and Diz. Ellington when he isn't so busy being dissonant. There're those long, stagey lines and lots of brass and stuff like that.

Wes Montgomery, Ron Carter, Chubby Jackson, Bud Powell, Teddy Wilson, just a whole bunch of people. Miles, you've given me a couple of Miles's albums. Benny Carter—oh, man, armies of cats. Ben Webster. God, dozens.

Dennis: You, like a lot of folks of your generation, went to college after the war on the GI Bill, and in doing that you were already kind of changing your life in terms of careers and class, that sort of thing, from the family in which you grew up. But then to go from that leap to ending up becoming a writer, it's one thing if Johnny is going to get a college job, but now Johnny is going to become a writer? What the hell is that? Did you have any awareness at the time what an absurd leap that was?

John: It wasn't absurd in the beginning. You know, when I was going to school I was also working as a night orderly at Memorial Hospital. I was working at Oberdorfer foundry during the summer, and I was so good that they gave me a regular job on the night shift. I was a vegetable clerk at Loblaw's, and I only wound up getting a job at the welfare department after a back injury. But for a time it was like falling back into the swamp, like everyone else in my family. You took any job that came your way.

Actually, I didn't do that. I remember there was a job at a tuxedo rental place on the corner of Montgomery and Warren Street, just off it. I remember I went down to apply for a job, and there must have been five hundred pairs of shoes on the floor that needed shining. I turned around and left. See, in a sense, the idea of having gone to college didn't make a real dent in anyone's head but my own. I could understand that the important thing was to have a job to bring in the money, but here I was with a college degree and a half shining shoes? What was it all for then? [My mother] Ola wanted me to learn how to become a florist with Al Markowitz. This, too, was after college. Al Markowitz and his wife had a son, they actually had two sons, but Bernie was a pain in the ass. My brother, Joe, would go with me and we'd work around the shop, and Bernie would tell Joe to take a bucket of water and go out and wash his car wheels. The first time he did that I couldn't believe it. I went out there and said, "Wash your own fucking car wheels." I threw the water out and dragged Joe away, and that was it for Markowitz.

So that was a long time getting to that welfare gig, and even then it was doubling up. I was running an elevator in the Loew Building at night when I got on with Doug Johnson Associates, public relations. Then the world fell apart and I went to California. That was like trudging through the Mohave Desert at night. That was an incredible year for me, Jesus Christ. Out there one job I held for a couple of weeks was as a butler-chauffeur in Beverly

Hills—cleaning, serving meals, driving the kids to school and back. I discovered that black people were generally uneasy when they discovered I'd gone to college. Go figure. But I got back East and latched onto a job at a small publishing house, and after a year I asked for a raise and they said that's it, you're fired. But I survived. Everybody in the family could understand what you had to do to survive, but of the writing, as you know, a lot of the relatives would say, "Are you still doing that writing?" like it was a part-time job or something. And I said, "Yes, sure." My father never spoke to me about writing, never asked for a book, and I never gave him one. He was not a reader. As a kid I had a feeling that books were dangerous things to have around, but Ola seemed to catch on faster than anybody else. When I visited her and we went out, she'd tell complete strangers, "This is my son. He's a writer." And these folks would look at us like we were both crazy.

Dennis: What was it like growing up in Syracuse?

John: Well, that was an experience. I remember living in a place when I was very small down on Washington Street, two houses from the old Rescue Mission. The New York Central Railroad trains used to come right down that street, so you'd see the redcaps getting ready for the station, hanging out the doors, waving. The first time I saw that train I was scared shitless. I hit the steps screaming, and my mother rushed out of the house and picked me up. I don't think I have ever felt so safe in my life.

At the time I started kindergarten a number of black folks must have moved deeper into the center of the 15th Ward. I still remember the first day of going to kindergarten, being lifted up by Miss Riley, whom I last saw when she was in her eighties. I had things a little screwed up in that kindergarten class because some kids would get little containers of milk and graham crackers, and I would say to myself, "How come I'm not getting some of that?" And it later developed in 4th, 5th grade this was for really poor kids. "Oh," I'm saying to myself, "I guess we were not that poor." But that changed overnight, it seemed. The schools were then involved in the subtle kind of hygienic existence. They would pass out little bars of Lifebuoy soap and Dr. Lyons tooth powder because there were a lot of immigrants coming in, and they had to somehow measure up to American standards.

I remember the gym teacher, Mr. Andrews, a mean motherfucker, boy, and that gave me my first clue as to how rotten some teachers could be. That man kicked ass. But most of the other teachers were pretty good. And I loved the English teacher, Miss Lloyd. We all did. The last half hour of class she would read from adventure novels. She had us so much under her spell that when she'd ask a question we kids would race each other to the front of the room to answer. I was a musician at that time. Whenever we had an ice cream social I would play the triangle and the water whistle.

Dennis: What is a water whistle?
John: It's an odd-shaped object that held water with little holes and made a sound like beep beep.

It's become kind of cliché now because everybody my age speaks about it, that kind of cohesive element you had on the block. Everybody knew everybody else, knew everybody's children, and everybody would squeal on you if you hadn't behaved when your parents were gone. I am not sure what was wrong with me, whether I was unhappy or just restless or stubborn or whatever, but I would take off at a moment's notice, just hit the bricks, man. Everybody would be looking for me through the night.

Dennis: Where did you go?
John: Up on the hill, Thornden Park, just hang out, sleep under the bushes. I never did this in the winter. Come home and get my ass beat, and things would be okay for a while. The church was very important. I would wind up usually getting the longest poem to read—speeches we called them—Christmas, Easter, whatever. I remember I got a poem in which the speaker was some kind of warrior. I was really innovative, so I went out and got the top of a garbage can, painted it. That was going to be my shield, and I got some old lathing and made myself a sword. So I'm standing up there, and the paint hadn't really dried. I'm in my Buster Brown suit, and the paint from my sword is getting on my pants. I could tell that Ola was going to cut my butt a duster when we got home. She did.

Then we would go to the Rescue Mission in the afternoon and these ex-drunks would get up and tell how God had saved them and stuff like that. At one point religion got to me (I may have told you this). We had this china closet that I had learned to pry open with a knife to get peanut butter and tiny slices of cakes and pies, while Ola wondered why the cake was shrinking, why the pie was shrinking. My old man used to keep his booze in there. I pried it open one Sunday after a fire-and-brimstone session at the Rescue Mission, got the booze, and poured it all down the toilet. "So what the fuck happened here?" my father is screaming. I said drinking is evil so I threw it all away. "What!" Pow, pow, pow. That taught me about the dangers of being too religious.

Dennis: I've always gotten the impression, on some level anyway, that your Syracuse was more integrated or multicultural than mine and certainly more than it is now. What do you think?

John: It was. One of the things that happened was the federal government came in and built Pioneer Homes, the project with housing on a segregated basis in the heart of the Ward. The Jewish people began to move out; the Italians moved to the North Side, the Irish to Tipperary Hill, and so on. The Depression and later the defense industries also brought in many more black people though industry in Syracuse didn't open for them until FDR came down with the Fair Employment Practices Act. There was still agriculture in the area, and a little later you had an influx of black migrants from the South who some old black residents called pea-pickers or bean-pickers. By that time Syracuse had changed forever.

Dennis: Where did you get the sense of family pride that you conveyed to us?

John: I'm not sure where I got it from, probably my mother. Pride came way behind survival, but it was, I guess, survival that was the tap root of family pride. It was tough. I mean, you got to have some pride when you look around this motherfucker and see where we began and where we are now. I had an uncle who spent most of his life in jail, another uncle who everyone in the family agreed was close to being a certified nut, and people whose marriages have always been suspect, though no one ever said anything about them. We've got family that just vanished, and family bound together tighter than a steel band. I miss not ever having a real bond with my brother and sisters, all of whom are younger than I, so I've tried, with some failures, to urge out the importance of family with my own without belaboring the issue. If you don't have family, with all its strength and weaknesses, in the end you don't have shit. Period. My mother's family looked down on my father's family, which didn't have diddley, while they, down in Mississippi, owned eighty-eight acres and were pure-dee-black, none of this Uncle Bernie–white folks or Aunt Viola-just-off-the-reservation business. But all the fighting and fussing didn't completely break off the branches, and you guys see that they never do. Please.

Dennis: We go back to, what did you figure, 1832 in Syracuse?

John: Well, that was the 1803 thing, and you said look at it again and maybe it's 1863, but then that would eliminate my father's great uncles, who were in the Civil War. Gorman Williams married Margaret Smallwood in 1838, when she was eighteen. My mother's family we can trace back to 1830.

Dennis: Have you any idea how those folks got to Syracuse, and what they were doing there?

John: No. After *Roots* everybody started talking about where they came from. Ola was filled with stories, some of which I have on tape. She came north about 1922–23. My father's family Bible has that 1803 entry and many, many more. I do recall him telling me when I was a boy that he swam in the Erie Canal. For years I thought, "Hey, he must be some swimmer, swimming in the Canal, damn!" A couple of years ago I discovered that it was only four feet deep.

Dennis: Up here I am reminded of the line in *Mothersill and the Foxes* about black folks being jived off the land and into the cities. Where did you get your appreciation of land? Certainly it wasn't from moving from house to house in the 15th Ward in Syracuse?

John: I like being outside camping. There was nothing romantic I got from Ola about those eighty-eight acres down there; she was talking about the rattlesnakes all over the place and up in the chimney. Picking cotton. Chopping firewood. Walking miles to school. Mean, murderously mean white people. I have never heard anyone on that side of the family say one single good thing about white people in Mississippi. If this love of land came from Ola, it was the land without the people she knew. Or maybe for me it came also from one of those shadowy Indian relatives on my father's side, but he hated the country. You know, you walk outside on a sunny day, and there's a miracle: here's this ball up there, 93 million miles away, and your life depends on it. We take it for granted, like so many other things that nature sets out for us, like a Thanksgiving feast. I cool out in the country. My head clears. Food tastes better, whiskey's smoother. With my scope I can see the same four moons around Jupiter that Galileo saw, though we know now there are eight more. Ola loved this place and usually came in time to pick crab apples for jelly or when the blackberries were ripe, and she could toss a mean fishing line into the pond, too, or get in the rubber boat, paddle to the middle, and just lay there.

Up here you can see weather coming, fog settling or lifting, autumn colors on the other side of the valley like some giant Monet dripped paints there. This is it, man. Care for it.

Dennis: How did the war change you?

John: In Syracuse the kind of racism you got was not really worth mentioning compared to what I found in the Navy. You wouldn't even call that stuff back home racism; you'd call it pique. The fact is that one way or another, everybody got along. That was not true in the Navy, and I think for the very first time I came in contact with deadly, gonna-kill-yo'-ass racism. And, of course, I couldn't manage to stay out of trouble. Sometimes it just walks up to you, says, "Yeah, it's me; what you going to do about it?" So I had some problems in the Navy but managed to get an honorable discharge. I've written about all that. The war created in me an absolute hatred of racism, of intolerance, of injustice and were it not for my experiences in the 15th Ward and meeting a few decent white people while in service, that hatred would have eaten me alive.

Dennis: What did you learn about yourself in those times?

John: Well, in retrospect I kind of liked myself for surviving, for one thing, and for not putting up with too much shit. That may have come naturally; I think it probably did. I still did not know a great deal about the world when I went into the Navy, but when I came out, I certainly knew the world. It was not like the one I grew up in.

Dennis: How and why did you get started teaching?

John: Quite by accident, I think, although recalling a couple of things even when I was in Syracuse with the welfare department, I had sort of flirted with the young progressives, young communist league or something. I say flirted, without going to a single meeting, but I could always talk to those people. Someone from Cornell asked me to address a couple of groups of workers. I don't even remember what I said; I was just nervous as hell.

Dennis: When was this?

John: Right after I got out of school. I don't remember where the meetings were held, but I do remember talking to a couple of them. Before that, I would coach the Dunbar Center football team. I was in the Scouts for so long as a troop leader and then camp counselor, so I guess in some ways the teaching thing was always in there. But, academically, that started at City College in '68.

Dennis: How? You needed the job? You were interested?

John: I didn't need the job, but I was interested in it. It was teaching article writing, so I went up and met people like Jim Hatch, Leo Hamalian, and

Jim Emmanuel, who moved to Paris after his son got killed by cops in New Orleans. I had class the night or the night after Martin Luther King got killed. I stood before the class—I was really pissed—and I told them I didn't think I should be teaching white students anymore. There were about four black students in the class. Silence. But that anger soon passed.

Dennis: You have written about academic politics in *Colleagues*. What was your worst experience with that?

John: My worst experience was working with a totally incompetent man. Not only was he incompetent—I don't see how he lasted in his field. He was an evil man. He played around with grades, made students do certain things in order to get grades, and I'm not talking about sex or anything like that. I mean they had to really kiss his ass in order to get decent grades. His student evaluations were always bad when they showed up in the file anyway. Even when he was caught in a criminal act the administration pretended it hadn't happened. I said, "Shit, forget this."

We had people there who had been associate professors for over twenty years. You looked at their publication record, and they were about as slim as a book of matches—didn't seem to matter. And meanwhile, there were minority faculty, who always had a rough time with promotions. If they got one bad student evaluation, everybody was on their ass, and I said, "Oh, Christ."

Dennis: What were some of your more satisfying experiences as a teacher?

John: Well, to see some kids really get through it. To see kids who had managed to get good grades and survive all the academic crap and the politics and graduate. I went to only one graduation while I was at Rutgers. I was invited to weddings, and kids would come back and bring their children and stuff like that. So that was pretty cool. I had a couple of good colleagues, and we bitched on each other's shoulders. Otherwise, it was a jungle. The whole thing was another experience to be explored in fiction.

Dennis: I asked you about students in general. How did you find black students over the time you were teaching?

John: Not really, on the whole, as prepared as a number of white students and remember you're talking about Rutgers Newark, so most of the black students were very much a minority. You talk Rutgers Newark, and you think of an all-black school, but that was not at all true. Most of our students were the children of white, blue-collar workers from Belleville and places like that. You got a larger student-of-color population in the evening, but these people for the most part were really geared to being taught, to learning what was really going on. They were older, but the black daytime undergraduates were not well prepared for college. It was like the grade school teachers gave up on them early on. That's why we had the academic studies foundation to drill them in basic skills. Toward the end of my time there, we got students from Asia, the Middle East, and Africa, some of whom were very good and some not so good.

Dennis: Your teaching career pretty much coincided with the last twenty-five years of affirmative action in education. How do you think that has worked?

John: It could have worked much better than it has. A lot of black faculty have in fact been staff, working in special programs. Multicultural faculty has been viewed as a threat because so many of those teachers have had to study far more than your average white teacher in order to be able to teach the various, non-European literatures. Unfortunately, many of them wind up teaching composition instead because most schools are not genuinely interested in studies that are not rooted in Europe. It has been pointed out that white women have had the most success with affirmative action, and I think this is true. Black women have been the statistically volatile "twofers," fitting neatly into two columns of the progress charts, depending on what those charts need to prove. No doubt that AA has been successful on several levels, but despite the law, it has always been challenged within the confines of academic offices. Finally, those multicultural programs AA gave rise to have rarely been fully supported.

Dennis: What do you make of the backlash to affirmative action nationwide—and the California decision?

John: I think it's all bullshit. The backlash was always right there in academia. Affirmative action as I understand it was really created to redress disadvantages African Americans had suffered throughout American history, but everybody got on this very slender raft. The main thing that began to sink it was gender. When it was opened to women—and I'm not saying they should not have, but perhaps there should have been another program to address that—they came aboard in droves. And then you got Latinos and Asians whose historical situations are quite different, and perhaps required other, distinct programs. What's happened is historically American: throw them all into the same pit and see who survives. No doubt affirmative action could use some modification, but the willingness to kill it altogether makes modification a moot point. We'll see what happens in California; that'll be the key indicator as to where and how we go with it.

Dennis: What have you been doing since you stopped teaching?

John: I've been very busy, as a matter of fact. I did that year at Bard College. I found—I may be wrong, essentially the same thing—that it was more important that I was black than being a good teacher. First semester I flunked a third of my class, and the dean wanted to know why. Students hadn't done the work, and that was it. When I signed on they wanted me to be there for quite a while, but I suggested a year. Let's see if I like you and you like me. A year was enough. Since then I've been finishing up *Colleagues*, putting together several proposals that went nowhere, and working on this opera.

Dennis: Talk about the opera.

John: Leslie Burrs is a flutist in Philadelphia. I had worked with him on an opera that Duke Ellington had not completed, and we got along pretty well. We ran into problems with Mercer [Ellington], who had asked us to do it. Later, Leslie was doing work for Opera Columbus, and they wanted this new opera. They thought I'd be interested. I was. It's on slavery in the US. Leslie and I sat down and talked over some ideas. Then I started putting together this book about a couple of characters who are part mythic and part real. Each winds up dead, but their spirits are looking for each other throughout the play on different levels. As they move through history, they encounter people like Nat Turner and Frederick Douglass, Harriet Tubman, Gabriel Prosser, and John Brown. Originally the title was *Many Thousand Gone*, but we had some problems with that because there are so many versions. At the moment it is called *Windward Passages*. It's supposed to debut in 1996.

Dennis: What was it like working on an opera?

John: The story fleshes itself out, but writing the lyrics to enhance the story is very exciting. Again, it is that kind of thing poetry does for you. What dialogue you have has to fit the poetry. You can expand whatever skills you have. The first character I did was Nat Turner, and I fell in love with the form. I'm getting into aspects not usually covered: relationships between white women who are wives of the planters and black women who are their slaves. The time frame is from the early 1700s to the start of the Civil War. Working with a musician who takes your words and transforms them into music is, for me, a stunning experience.

Dennis: Have you heard pieces with your words set to music?

John: I can't make out all the words too well. While some of it is pretty modern, there are elements that are operatic. What I can understand from the early lines on the tapes is dynamite.

Dennis: What kind of negative reactions professionally have you gotten over the years as a result of your marriage to Lori?

John: That's hard for me to pin down because few people are going to come right out with that kind of negativity. How editors and/or other literary power-brokers feel, I don't know. A friend in Europe who's known many interracial couples there and here, firmly believes such relationships are indeed professionally damaging. My opinion? Probably, but so what?

Dennis: In the sixties you did this TV program on PBS, *Omowale: The Child Returns Home*. The conclusion was that after visiting Africa you were coming back to America, which *was* coming home. How did you reach that conclusion at the time, and do you still hold that view?

John: I still hold the same view even more strongly now because I understand that black people have been here far longer than most others, except Native Americans. In fact, some old historians that no one reads anymore have written about that very obvious fact. I almost got killed twice in Africa, once in Ethiopia and once in what was then called the Congo. I didn't go there as Wright did, looking for miracles and special treatment and all that. I just didn't belong to a tribe or anything, and that made me an outsider. I've made two trips there since then and not much had changed. As bad as some of the rules are here, at least I know them. Many, many more Africans from all over are emigrating here now, so I think things have become worse there.

Dennis: What does that mean to you at this point—being more than ever convinced of your Americanness, given the fucked-up state of the country?

John: Misery. It gives me *tsouris*. It gives me ulcers. It gives me stomach spasms, back aches. There is a point at which you want to retire from the fight, but you can't; you've got to keep going to unfuck-up the country for yourself, your kids, and their kids. It means the war continues.

Dennis: I've noticed in your books these fascinating and often obscure historical details that you sprinkle through there. It's almost as if you have discovered these facts and can't wait to share them with us, the readers. How did that habit get started?

John: I'm not sure it's a habit, and I only use them when appropriate. Fiction should inform, I believe, no less than any other art.

Dennis: It's not that it's inappropriate, but it's there and noticeable. It's a form of teaching. Are you conscious of it?

John: Sometimes I'm conscious of it, and I think it's very important if you've got the right space in which to do it. Why not? Writers I admire do it all the time. It's sort of like adding stronger cement to this structure they're building.

Dennis: You read a lot of history. Are there particular areas of the world or time periods you are especially fascinated with?

John: I guess prehistorical periods and the early civilizations. But then the Renaissance, too, becomes very intriguing. This whole business of slavery began essentially during that period. The Age of Enlightenment, the American Revolution, and the French Revolution are all blatant contradictions of the humanistic thrusts of those times. That's what I like to look at and compare. A close study of pre- and ancient history puts the lie to concepts of one group being superior to another.

Dennis: Why after twenty-five years of black studies are these kinds of facts and analyses still so rare and surprising?

John: Because they don't have a platform. You take a white scholar like Martin Bernal, who's done fascinating work in this area, and you see the hatchets flying. Then you can understand why the black scholars are simply tossed aside. Feeling superior, whether you are or not, is a pernicious disease since race has become so important. It would be so much easier if we gave ourselves up to the commonality of being and living that we find in the past. But people are invested only in the present, and because white people tend to own the present, they make the erroneous assumption that that's the way it always was.

Dennis: You have also been interested in things extraterrestrial. You gaze at the stars. You think about things out there although you've never written science fiction per se. You have what I would call a science fiction mind at times. Do you have any theories?

John: I find the older I get the more difficult I find it to believe that this is the only blessed jewel in the sky. I can't believe it any longer. As for the possibility of travel between planets, I'm open to that. There are just too many damn questions that nobody wants to bother with on this earth for me to conclude that this is it, period. Certain things that have happened, certain things that have been found, certain cultures, certain technologies within certain cultures nobody wants to be bothered with, yet they are there. I think one of the problems contemporary civilizations have is that they are not interested in the past as a learning tool. They just ignore it. I've done kind of a long poem that I call "Replicata." It's about this earth and its people being out of tune with whatever fine-tunes the rest of the universe. Our problem may be that we can't, or won't, get in tune with the rest of the universe, which must be ordered or we wouldn't be here.

Dennis: What are your thoughts on the future for the country or for the planet?

John: You know, Spengler says that democracy is pretty much a weigh station, on the way to fascism, or Caesarism, as he calls it. We have to understand that democracy is still an evolving political concept and that the distance we have gained from Greece to now is relatively short. When those guys were talking democracy in Greece, and the polis, the population, the people, some of the people were slaves. And then Plato also says that Socrates said, you know, this bullshit we are telling people, well, that really ain't the way it is. What we really think is quite different. Well that continues until today. So we either realize that we're an evolving democracy and work harder to make that real or go through fascism before we can return to the problem of making democracy work at all. The media is not a help to democracy. The media, in most instances, has always been on the side of the power brokers. Now it's more concentrated, more powerful than ever, and it is not coming down on the side of the people. So here we are. Which way is it going to be, fascism or radical democracy?

Dennis: Is there still hope, speaking of the media, for emerging technologies? They have the potential, at least theoretically, to bypass some of the established media power and allow for more democratic communication. Do you see that as a possibility?

John: I don't see that as a possibility. Number one, all communities use telephone lines, which are privately owned. Two, the computer networks can be outlawed in a second, if those people using them begin to show signs of positive radicalism. Third, the computer as an instrument to make money will have its share of operators more interested in profits than in continuing the democratic evolution. So I don't see all that great big hope in the use of computers. People have to make their voices heard in public, not hidden behind some computer. Just get out in the street, and do what you've got to do.

Dennis: Is it possible for this country ever to have a multicultural democracy? We see now routine backlash against affirmative action and the whole concept of multiculturalism as if it were some subversive virus. But the country has always been ethnically diverse. That seems to be one of the great questions for this country, whether that can work. What do you think?
John: If it doesn't work we are dead, to put it simply. It's too ingrained, whether it was under the most beneficent arrangements or not. I'm speaking of slavery and immigration and of people seeking political and religious relief on these shores. This is what made the US a multicultural society. To now say to hell with it is one of those steps toward fascism, where everyone has to be, act, and think the same. If we do not have a multicultural society we will cease to exist. This society is probably more multicultural than Rome ever was, and Rome expanded over the known world. The problem with the decline of Rome was not, as some historians claim, that it was a multicultural society. It had to do with the politicians buying and selling power, betraying the trust people placed in them. Multiculturalism has got to continue to exist, or the United States as we know it is dead. Period.

Dennis: How do we get past the politicians?
John: We can't get it through political reform because Congress doesn't really want that. They want to maintain power. People are beginning to demonstrate that they are not going to go along with this for much longer; that shows in the decline of the numbers in which they vote. They're saying the political process sucks, and they're not going to bother with it. But this is a two-edged sword. One, it says you retract your voice, you have nothing to say about the process; two, it allows the people who are powerful to exert even more power because there are fewer bodies in the arena that will respond. I don't know what the answer is.

Dennis: Well that's not very helpful. [laughs] You're supposed to be wise.
John: I'm sorry.

Clifford's Blues: A Conversation with John A. Williams

Gilbert H. Muller, Michael Blaine, and Raymond C. Bowen / 2000

From *New York Stories* 1.5 (2000): 18–25. Reprinted by permission.

In the most recent of his twelve novels, John A. Williams presents the story of Clifford Pepperidge, a gay, black jazz musician placed in protective custody at Dachau in 1933. Surviving in the camp by working as a jazz pianist, bandleader, and prized household servant, Clifford for more than a decade is a witness to the unfolding horrors of the Third Reich and the Holocaust. Meticulously researched, written, and revised by the author over a twelve-year period, *Clifford's Blues* completes, along with Williams's earlier novels, *The Man Who Cried I Am* and *Captain Blackman*, a trilogy of historical fiction exploring the hidden aspects of the African American experience. Williams discussed his novel during a visit to the LaGuardia campus of the City University of New York, where he served as Distinguished Professor from 1974–77.

Muller: John, *Clifford's Blues* has a rather interesting history. How did the novel evolve? What was the original impetus?

Williams: The original impetus was Lori (Williams's wife) and I driving from Italy up to Amsterdam where we were going to spend about six months. We went through Munich, which is down the road from Dachau, and we thought we would stop there. We kept asking directions, and nobody seemed to know where the hell it was, which I thought not strange, but funny. Then we saw a young black American soldier, and we asked him where it was. He said, "Right here."

We looked around, saw one great big main building, and went in. They were just preparing it to be a museum, and they had some of the original ID patches that prisoners wore on their clothes, all dirty and wrinkled, stapled on the wall. Then there were some ID photos of some of the prisoners, and I noticed two black prisoners. And I'm saying, "How the hell did they get caught in this crap?"

We spent a couple of more hours there and drove off, and every once in a while through the years, this kept coming back to me, these two guys, these two guys. And finally I said, "Let me make some inquiries," so I wrote to the Dachau International committee. They said they had no verifiable record of there being any black prisoners at Dachau. However, they did know of a Belgian black man who had been a prisoner.

But as it turns out, this guy, if he went to Dachau, probably spent very little time there because his name is Joseph Nassy, and he spent most of the time in an internment camp, which is vastly different. That's for illegal aliens who got caught in transit; they're not criminals or adjudged to be criminals. So I got a whole history on Nassy, and I just kept getting a lot of stuff, more and more information.

After the book was out, I got a fax about twenty-four thousand Germans of mixed descent who were given a choice: die or get sterilized. They all got sterilized. This is recounted in a documentary that was run by the BBC in '97. It seems that more and more information is coming out, and that's good for me because it verifies what we've done.

Muller: The central character, Clifford, is a unique figure but also familiar. He reminds me of characters we've encountered in your previous fiction. Jazz musicians have figured prominently in your novels, starting with *Night Song*. Max Reddick, the protagonist in your best known novel, *The Man Who Cried I Am*, is, like Clifford, a repository of history. *Captain Blackman* also serves to crystallize centuries of forgotten, neglected, or abandoned history. Do you see Clifford in a similar way—as a uniquely realized character on the one hand, but as (and you use this word more than once in the novel) a witness to history?

Williams: A witness for that particular time in history. All the other characters that you mentioned sort of move back and forth, and they have a much wider range in terms of recounting history and historical experiences. Clifford's is confined to his life in the camp and some reference to his young manhood, growing up in New Orleans, then getting away to New York and being able to get this trip to Europe, which, you know, was too bad, ultimately.

Blaine: You've written a novel where the narrator is a gay, black jazz musician caught up in the Holocaust. There are, of course, several elements here. How did you come to decide that Clifford was going to be the narrator?

After all, you saw a picture of black prisoners at Dachau, but it didn't have to be a gay, black jazz musician.

Williams: I felt that I couldn't have a character in a camp who didn't have things to look forward to, and music is his thing. Actually two things keep him alive, and that is the fact that he is a musician and that he's gay. It is quite clear that gay people in those camps managed to live if they found a guard who would look after them. That was pretty common, and that's precisely what Clifford manages to do.

Also, the sense of difference is what makes him attractive not only sexually, but as somebody who might be more honest than your average prisoner. He's an unusual guy in Dieter Lange's eyes, so maybe he could work in the canteen and help rip off the system while he was there, which he does. He sees everybody else ripping it off, and finally the tables are turned and they are ripped off by their superiors.

Bowen: John, it appears that you've taken three marginal types—black, musician, and gay—and sort of amalgamated them into one, remarkably.

Blaine: Yes, this is part of my great interest in it. I think choosing Clifford's point of view has multiple, very rich and humane effects. What other effects, other than illuminating the fact that there were black people in the camps, does choosing Clifford as a narrator have for you?

Williams: I think other characters I've used in other works have been somewhat like this, too. And that is, the most raunchy of characters, of human beings, who somehow harbor a belief in a god. When I use the voodoo god and the god that everybody else is involved in, it wasn't so much to set them up as opposites, but to see if their combined forces would wind up being beneficial to Clifford. When God is not coming through, then he goes to a *loa*, and whoever can get there first and rescue him out of his mess, or his friends, that's who he goes to. And he can even talk to God while cursing Him out, you know. "These people down here killin' motherfuckers left and right and You ain't sayin' shit." Like that.

Muller: Ray mentioned that Clifford is on the margins in at least three ways—as a jazz artist, as a black man, and as a gay. There's probably a fourth element that's integral here, too: he's also on the margins as a writer. And perhaps that's the reason why you decided to create this novel as a diary framed by two letters. It's a very unusual approach in contemporary fiction.

Williams: In an earlier incarnation, I had characters, a black family, who were very active in the present. I did that essentially to give me, psychologically, some distance from that camp. It was very important to me because I felt that

I couldn't stay in that camp every day that I sat down to do it. But the reaction was that the family detracted from Clifford. I would tend to disagree, but, you know, that version is still intact. It's at the archives in Rochester.

Now, what I had to do with Clifford writing the diary was to not make him too literate a person. I had to work very hard at that. Lori said, "Well, sometimes you did; sometimes you didn't. Sometimes he sounds like a poet; sometimes he sounds like a jerk." Well, that's the best I could do. I have to deal with a man who's had very little formal education, and he's been entrapped by this diplomat who's had all this education in the world and who has betrayed him. So what I'm saying as the author in this relationship is that even if you have it, it's not going to save you. Period. So I went to the diary form, and that's it.

Blaine: You touched on something—you had to get distance, so you chose the diary form. But you also have distance because his point of view is outside the camps. He's not actually living in the camp although he sees what's going on in the camp. I thought that had very interesting consequences, specifically—this, I thought, was perhaps one of the best achievements of the novel—that you made odious characters somehow sympathetic. Dieter is so vile early on and continues to be. But somehow he becomes sympathetic. Was that in your mind, that by writing from Clifford's point of view, you would make even unsympathetic characters somehow sympathetic?
Williams: Well, maybe subconsciously, I'm not sure. I just always had to figure out how I as a person would react if I were in that situation. I mean, I would, like Clifford, reach a certain limit, get pissed off, get up, walk across the room, and kick the crap out of Dieter Lange, you know. I'd just have to. And the idea of the great escape not really winding up being anything. I could see how liberty could frighten a person in that circumstance. I could really feel that. You're working on all kinds of levels in a sort of thing like this.

Blaine: I think that Dachau is a way of looking at America, all through the book. This is a book about America. At least, let me pose that. Is that in your mind as you're writing?
Williams: I think it's larger than just America. I think it's the whole western civilization as we know it. The Germans that I know (a bunch of German scholars) had gotten some material from Coffee House about Clifford, and they wanted me to fly to Germany the next day and talk about it. I said, "Well, when I was nineteen or twenty, or maybe even forty, or maybe even fifty, I could do that, but no way that's going to happen now. No way." So I

think there's a great deal of interest in Germany. Oddly enough, a German agent had the original manuscript, and she was really angry. She said, "You know, we Germans are sick and tired of everybody talking about us, writing about us." That was at a time when two or three very important books had come out about what was going on with the Nazis, and this one just added fuel to the fire.

Muller: So you're obviously taking risks in creating Clifford as the largely unknown representative of the concentration camp experience. Starting the novel in 1933 alerts the reader to the fact that concentration camps didn't just burst on the landscape of World War II in 1939–1940. There's a whole precedent leading up to it. Correct?

Williams: Right. There was. Well, I think part of the responsibility of any thinking writer is to take risks. Sometimes it's bothersome to be attacked by people who are not talking so much about the work, but an experience that they think is theirs alone.

Now, in terms of the Holocaust, I heard a guy on NPR talking about a month ago. He said, "You know, there's no guarantee that we're talking about six million Jews." The Nazi hunter, Simon Wiesenthal, came up with—let's say—six million, and that's what stuck. Now even if it were six million Jews, fifteen million people died in those camps. What are we going to say about the other nine million? I mean, just leave it silent, all those gypsies, all those political prisoners, all those people who believed in God? On and on and on. You simply cannot do that, at least, not from my point of view.

Furthermore, if one wants to deal with the nitty gritty, some of my wife's family members are survivors of those camps, and nobody has ever written about them that I know of. I know their history better than people who are Holocaust scholars. The dedication is for "those without monument or memorial," and that's the people I'm talking about.

Blaine: But *Clifford's Blues* is a novel first, not a political tract. Maybe we could talk about the novel's nonpolitical aspects. I thought that the book was just a tremendous novel of character.

Williams: If I'm going to deal with a black musician at that period, I really have to work with basic discography to get the personnel and read as much as I can about these people in their circumstances. And that took a little while. I guess, essentially, I am still a frustrated musician. I just wanted to know as much about that time as I could, the instruments they played, what they sounded like. For me, that was fun. It certainly didn't make me into a musician, but vicariously I enjoyed doing that part. I was really kind of sad when I had to leave it at that particular time, but that's actually what happened when the war actually started. They said, "No more of these foreign prisoner jazz bands, everybody's got to be a German. And that's it." So the band went to pieces.

Bowen: Would you say that the narrative possesses, apropos of the title, a blues rhythm?

Williams: I would. I think there are some parts that are deeper blues than the others, like the kid, for example. I did find it difficult—one of my friends said that she was not entirely convinced with the kid, but I was trying to create a situation to deal not only with Clifford's humanity, but with other people's and the fall from grace of other people when you're trying to get them to exercise the same kind of humanity that you have. Like Clifford going to Werner and Werner saying, "You want this kid out of the garden? Okay, let's go in the closet." You know, that kind of stuff.

Blaine: You're touching on a deep aspect of the novel. It's a novel about varieties of love, even varieties of love that border on hate.

Williams: Well, he does say a couple of times that he's very grateful to Dieter Lange and to the Colonel because without these two guys, he was gone. He was gone.

Blaine: As great monsters as they are, they love jazz, at least to the extent that they can grasp it.

Williams: Yes.

Muller: They even try to preserve jazz. When jazz becomes unacceptable to the Reich, they relabel all of their music. Is there a historical basis for that, or did you just invent that?

Williams: Well, I got that from Mike Zwerin's book, *Jazz Under the Nazis*, which I discovered in San Francisco back in '87. And, of course, I had to give him credit for it; he's got a section in the book where he talks about all these German officers speedily having the labels ripped off their records and having new ones typed in so they won't get caught with any forbidden material.

Blaine: How did you imagine yourself into the sexual relationships? You have a gay character and, as you said, you're not gay. It's a novel that's convincing to me on a sexual level.

Williams: Well, my brother, who died earlier this month, was a gay person, not that I sat down and asked him how these things took place. I just used common sense. And he was not flamboyantly gay. As a matter of fact, he came out of the closet, he thought, sometime in the seventies, but everybody in the family knew it from the time he was like thirteen.

Then, in terms of dealing with the women in these things—haven't you ever imagined an orgy? (Silence)

Blaine: It's your interview, John, not ours. [laughs]
Williams: Imagine an orgy. That's all. No holds barred. And then, of course, I think there's always been something a little, *odd* is too mild a word, something very strange about all this death taking place on the same plane with all of this sex. I mean, it's nuts; it's just nuts. It's like I know I'm going to die, but I must somehow be involved in a ritual that's supposed to further life in a nongay union.

Muller: Would you say that Clifford's sexuality gives him a measure of security as well?
Williams: This occurs after the point when he is more certain that he is going to be safe because when he first goes in, and before Dieter Lange enters the processing room, he's really, really very nervous about what's going to happen to him.

Blaine: You glancingly talked about voice before. When you're creating the voice of Clifford you said, "Well, you thought he was an uneducated guy."
Williams: Not formally educated.

Blaine: Not formally educated but I found him incredibly articulate at the same time. How do you go about creating a voice? How do you go about sustaining the voice of Clifford, specifically?
Williams: I'm not sure. I just have to imagine not having had the knowledge of tense changes, for example. Or how to create a paragraph subdivided by semicolons and stuff like that. It's difficult for me to explain. I mean, these are things that have become pretty automatic with me.

Blaine: Do you find your own language creeping in and then you strike it out?
Williams: Yes, yes.

Muller: Aren't we hearing two voices, those of Clifford and the author?

Williams: I think that's probably most true in the long ride to the escape. I've never been in a situation like that. I've never read of a situation like that, so I'm making it up as I go along. I've got to come up with some kind of voice that's really partly mine and this guy's, who is scared shitless, and these two people who are trying to calm him down after revealing themselves as friends. I mean, talk about going into a closet and closing the door—that was a little tough to try to handle.

Blaine: I found this scene, from a technical point of view, very bracing because you have a kind of static situation in the diary. Things are evolving slowly, and, suddenly, there's this action. It's absolutely terrifying.

Williams: Some people at Coffee House were indignant. They couldn't understand how come the Germans brought him back without killing him. They killed the officer and his girl but not Clifford. I said, "Don't you understand that he is their clown; he is their music maker?" And they didn't get it.

Muller: John, why did you add a bibliography at the end of the novel?

Williams: Well, for people who had questions or complaints.

Bowen: Get everybody's fingerprints on it.

Williams: That's right.

Blaine: In other words, did you feel that you would have readers who would say, "This is completely impossible; I don't believe it"?

Williams: Absolutely. And this opinion was formed by, as I told you earlier, letters that I had gotten from various editors in this twelve-year career of being involved with this thing.

Bowen: What were some of the things they were questioning?

Williams: The fact that I was not writing that much about what was happening—the phrase always went—"in the East." That's a quote, "In the East," that is, the extermination camps, the big ones.

Blaine: But I have to say I thought, "This is great,; I know what's happening." You're referring to it without seeing it.

Williams: Well, it's referred to in the book several times.

Blaine: What sources really stand out in your mind as original—sources that gave you information that really surprised you, that our readers might be interested in looking at?

Williams: I think the Richard Plant book on gay prisoners, *The Pink Triangle: The Nazi War against Homosexuals*. Stuff in Chorover's book, *From Genesis to Genocide*, was good. Of course, Lucy Dawidowicz, right away. Terrence Des Pres. Englemann's *In Hitler's Germany*.

Muller: Where did you get information on the Jehovah's Witnesses?

Williams: *The Watchtower* people have publications about this. I had it a long while before I got to the places where I was going to use it, but that's invaluable stuff too. So all the Jehovah's Witness stuff, and Mike Zwerin's book, *La Tristesse de Saint Louis*, and Richard Rubenstein, *The Cunning of History: The Holocaust and the American Future*. I also discovered this book *The Day of the Americans*, published in 1966 by a former inmate of Dachau who was there when the Americans came in. His name is Nerin Gun. I think he was a Turk. And then Eugen Kogon's book. Invaluable.

Blaine: Do you feel that the documentary aspect of what you've done is of paramount importance or is it the imaginative act of creating this character that is in the foreground in your mind or are you balancing the two?

Williams: I think it's balancing because what's most important, however you get to it, would be the details of this man's life and the lives of people close to him. I must, of course, be able to use imagination quite fully since I'm not a musician and I'm not gay, and I can only set up these situations that he's involved in.

Muller: Clifford just kind of disappears at the end. What becomes of him?

Williams: I toyed with the idea when I had the other family, the African American family, and the daughter and her boyfriend maybe wandering into a nightclub—this is before her parents head back home—they wander into a nightclub, and they see this old black guy playing the piano there. It's Clifford, except that they don't know who he is because the parents have not shared the diary with them. But I decided to hell with that.

Muller: I think this ending is better.

Blaine: This is much better.

Williams: The German soldier is right out of something that happened to me going up to Scandinavia through northern Germany. And we did stop.

I had to go to the bathroom to take a leak in the worst way. I went into this john, and there was this wreck of a guy standing there, just barely missing pissing on me and all over. And he looks at me, and he's startled. He starts talking to me in German (which I don't understand) a few words, but he made me understand, you know, the *schwartze* and the *Amerikaner* kind of stuff. And then I just changed that. . . .

Blaine: So he managed to communicate to you that his life had been spared by a black American soldier.
Williams: Yes.

Muller: This is your twelfth novel. Are you going to start on a second dozen?
Williams: I've got two in the works now. One is actually a rewrite, and the other is brand new. It's entirely different from the rewrite.

Blaine: Why would you work on two at once? Why not be a monomaniac and finish one and then go to the next one?
Williams: Change of pace. I get bored with one thing. I used to work on fiction and nonfiction simultaneously. Change of pace because fiction could be boring at certain points or I could get stuck or vice versa. It's worked well for me. It's not anything I would recommend to a new writer, but all I can say is it's served me very well.

A Cry in the American Wilderness: John A. Williams Reflects on Life, Work, and the American Way

Vincent F. A. Golphin / 2003

From *about... time* Magazine 31.4 (June–July, 2003): pp. 20–25. Courtesy of the *about... time* Magazine archives.

The first time I set eyes on John A. Williams, a cliché burst into mind—I thought he would be taller. As a writer and journalist, I might have hoped for a more clever or perceptive thought.

Williams's novels, *The Man Who Cried I Am* and *Clifford's Blues*, although decades apart in setting and writing, seemed to come from the pen of a guy that stakes out a space on earth and refuses to budge. They are markers from an observer determined to mark a path or a herald that announces what is about to come down the road. The neatly dressed, short, thin man near the entrance of the Del Monte Lodge in Pittsford, a tony but tiny Rochester, New York, suburb, did not fit the bill.

He was in town to be honored as a literary giant. Williams is a two-time winner of the American Book Award (*!Click Song*, 1983, and *Safari West*, 1998), named distinguished writer by the Middle Atlantic Writers in 1987, chosen for the Richard Wright–Jacques Roumain Award in 1973, a 1998 National Literary Hall of Fame inductee, winner of the Syracuse University centennial medal for outstanding achievement, and the 2002 Phyllis Wheatley Award for Outstanding Contribution to African American Culture.

The description omits a slew of other honors including an honorary Doctor of Humane Letters he received from the University of Rochester during his visit. So, at age seventy-eight, the Department of Rare Books and Special Collections in the University of Rochester's Rush Rhees Library put together *Writings of Consequence: The Art of John A. Williams*, a five-month exhibition on his life and works to celebrate the gift of the author's private papers. It closes on September 30. The rest are in the vaults.

The university's website details the collection: 179 boxes and 1 folder of Williams personal papers, including 51 boxes of correspondence; 90 boxes of manuscript and printed material by Williams; 14 boxes of works by other authors; 6 boxes of printed material and ephemera; 4 boxes of financial, legal, medical, and personal documents and materials; 10 boxes of ephemera and memorabilia; and 4 boxes and 1 folder of oversize ephemera.

The majority of this collection consists of materials related to Williams's personal life and career as a writer, editor, and journalist after 1950, though some items can be found before this period, such as correspondence and photographs. That includes correspondence from well-known writers and celebrities including Chester Himes, Ishmael Reed, Gwendolyn Brooks, Chinua Achebe, Imamu Amiri Baraka (Le Roi Jones), Henry Roth, Toni Morrison, Alice Walker and William Heyen, Ruby Dee, Carl Van Vechten, and many others, as well as a significant amount of family, publisher, and fan mail correspondence; numerous original typescripts of Williams's novels, nonfiction books, edited and coedited works, plays, *Vanqui*'s libretto, articles, essays, speeches, short stories and poems; an extensive amount of research materials and ephemera from both published and unpublished works; photographs of Williams, his family, and friends, including several original Carl Van Vechten photographs; awards and honors Williams received throughout his writing career; and many personal items, including date books, a well-traveled Smith Corona typewriter, and memorabilia from his world travels and teaching career at the City University of New York and Rutgers University.

From *The Angry Ones* in 1960 to *Clifford's Blues* in 1999, the works have opened a vein that let flow the rawness in the black American experience, yet he was never as well known or read as Richard Wright and James Baldwin. Those authors ran off to Paris to tell the world what it was like to live in pre–civil rights America. John Alfred Williams raised his testaments from New York.

He earned a bachelor's degree in English and journalism from Syracuse University in 1950, when there were few jobs for nonwhite males in major newspapers. Williams hustled to find chances to write, even doing some broadcast work in radio and television, but the opportunities were slim. That is why in 1955 he ended up downstate in New York City as a public relations person for a vanity house, Comet Press Books.

The job gave him steady money, a base to write his first novel, and a chance to marry his boss, the former Lorraine Isaac, a Hungarian-Jewish immigrant. *The Angry Ones* takes readers into Rocket Press, a publishing house where Steve Hill, a black man with big dreams and an interracial love life finds the Big Apple to be rotten. Hill is continually denied a chance for better jobs, housing, and opportunity, as were most African Americans who filled the North's urban centers after World War II.

If not transparently autobiographical, the reality was pushed home in 1961 when critical attention to Williams's second novel, *Night Song*, earned him a grant to the American Academy in Rome. The award was revoked, literary experts say, because of his race and growing relationship with Lorraine, whom he married in 1965. Two years later, with the publication of *The Man Who Cried I Am*, he gained a permanent berth among controversial US literary icons and international triumph.

The novel's main character, Max Reddick, taps into King Alfred, an American plot to wipe out blacks. Most whites might find the suggestion extremely paranoiac, but the author dared to shed light on a fear that haunted most African American minds and intracultural conversations. Even today, there is a staunch but small group of African Americans who believe Acquired Immune Deficiency Syndrome (AIDS) was invented in a white-run laboratory to kill blacks.

"In one sense blacks have been systematically killed off in the United States since their first introduction to its shores," the author explained to Robert E. Fleming in *Contemporary Literature*. "Malnutrition, disease, poverty, psychological conditioning, and spiritual starvation have been the tools, rather than military operations and gas chambers, but the result has often been the same." That was the voice I hoped to hear.

Ishmael Reed calls Williams, "the best pure African American novelist of the last hundred years." In the *Dictionary of Literary Biography*, contributor James L. de Jongh hails Williams as "arguably the finest Afro-American novelist of his generation . . . denied the full degree of support and acceptance some critics think his work deserves."

Both of those quotes bounced around my memory as I prepared to speak with Williams for *about . . . time* Magazine. That is why the brief mental note about his stature was quickly cast aside. I pushed myself to hold no expectation about Williams because that was where others made the mistake. I understood from his prose and poetry—the main thing he tries to tell the world—African Americans are almost never what they seem.

As he and Lorraine stood in the Del Monte lobby to shake my hand, I wondered whether the rather slight, but obviously devoted husband-wife team held the thoughts that ran through Williams's stories and poetry. I suggested we move to a more private sitting area off the lobby because his voice could barely be heard above the pedestrian traffic.

As we talked, comments about his career and legacy seemed diffident. He made it clear that John A. Williams does not see himself as some sort of icon. He is a writer like a slew of others he has known for more than forty years. At times, Lorraine stirred his memory. Her comments sometimes prodded him to be a little more open. That is why at certain points in this interview her remarks are included. They are a team.

Williams's most passionate responses were on African Americans and the nation—subjects that haunt him. Here is the interview.

about . . . time: I have read your books and have read about how others see you. What do you think about your legacy?
Williams: I don't think that way at all in terms of a legacy, or whatever. I just think about getting over it, taking care of my family, and doing my work . . . the work that I select. That's the great thing about being a writer. Only editors tell you what they would like to do after the fact, and you can say, "Okay" or "I don't want to do that." Period. I think it's very important to be your own boss to the extent that one is capable of doing that these days. There is always somebody down the line who will have something to say about something that you do.

about . . . time: So you didn't start out trying to write the great American novel?
Williams: No, I was just enamored about reading about things, and I finally got to the point where I said, "Let's see if I can do this kind of stuff." That's how I got started.

about . . . time: When were you convinced that you were really a writer?
Williams: When I made some money at it, I guess. . . . No. It wasn't actually the money. The first thing was just getting published.

about . . . time: You were with the between-the-war group of black writers, a little bit ahead of the Black Arts Movement. *The Man Who Cried I Am*, an international favorite, became one of the big novels in that period between the Harlem Renaissance and the Black Arts Movement, but your works are not as well known in the popular sector as some others. How do you explain that?

Williams: I don't know what it is. I would like to think it's always there. It's sort of like a section of the Rocky Mountains. It's going to be there, period, whatever people say.

about . . . time: You don't evaluate it at all?

Williams: I'm too old for that. Believe me, I can't sit around brooding about what other people think my writing is like. I just have to get my work done.

about . . . time: Why did you decide to donate your papers to the University of Rochester versus Syracuse University or some other institution? Or even some place in Mississippi?

Williams: I would never leave anything in Mississippi. I will never forgive them for what they did to my mother's family. Never, ever! I have been asked to publish with the University of Mississippi. I simply said, "No." My family grew up at a time when things were really bad for black folks. The family goes at least three or four generations back in slave times. They just had a bad time, and a lot of them were running out of Mississippi as soon as they got the chance. In those days the family was a bit closer because my uncle Ulysses, who got out and went up north to Syracuse . . . Actually, my mother was the first one, then everybody followed where the first one went. She would help the next one, and together they would help the third one. The three would help the fourth one, and eventually everybody left Mississippi and came up to Syracuse or either Washington, DC.

about . . . time: Do you think you will write about that in a future novel although it has come out in several of your works?

Williams: I am working on a memoir as well, called *Over My Shoulder*, and I think I have already begun that section.

about . . . time: This is a gradual project that is not slated for a particular deadline?

Williams: No, I have projects that are always like that.

about . . . time: How much time do you spend writing now?

Williams: If I'm not off somewhere or just sitting there brooding, most of the time, about six hours a day. When I'm off, I like to fix up the house and take care of the grounds.

about . . . time: What's your favorite television program?

Williams: I like what they produce on Channel 13, PBS, and I have done work for PBS. I think commercial TV sucks, and it's getting worse, all of it. It's just terrible, but they don't give you too many alternatives.

about . . . time: What do you think about the representation of African Americans on TV today?

Williams: Not enough African Americans in a serious vein. You get some like Ed Bradley, and I'm not even sure he's there now. I would like to see more black commentators on the screen. I think there are a lot of things that people are not getting into. I don't know if you know the book, *Rich Media, Poor Democracy*. It came out in 1998, and you never hear about it. But everything that guy says about the media, from live weekly and daily papers to radio and TV is true—it's just stuck away in some big corporation or conglomerate where they don't want you to make any noise, like about Bush . . . I hope you are not a Republican, but if you are, it's too bad. I can't imagine a guy who steals an election—and everybody agrees that he stole the damn election—and they let him become the president. The guys who are in the Congress just sit there and do nothing.

about . . . time: What about the latest thing with his weapons of mass destruction?

Williams: Well, he can't even find them, can he?

Lorraine: But we will be in this war for the foreseeable future.

about . . . time: Now we're liberating them, yet today they announced the US and Britain decided that they are not going to turn the government over to local rule in Iraq. So now we are going to be an occupier.

Lorraine: I knew that was going to happen as soon as the religious leaders said they wanted to rule the country.

When you ask how much time he spends writing, he used to literally spend all day writing. The last few years he has had some serious health problems that have really slowed him down, his energy level is not what it used to be, and he has to take a break in the afternoon and nap and go back to work for a few hours. We were busy getting stuff together for this show and picking up papers. He has papers everywhere and we keep discovering things, so it's been a distraction.

Williams: That means I will have to put a steel plate on my kicking.

about . . . time: I don't know, *Clifford's Blues* doesn't look like you've lost your game!
Williams: Thank you. Thank you very much, but you know it's getting harder and harder to publish that kind of stuff.

about . . . time: How long did it take to find a publisher for that?
Lorraine: Years, and the last two publishers he's had have been from small presses.

about . . . time: Let's go back to what you mean by "that kind of stuff." Break that down.
Williams: The kind of stuff that deals with issues of historical interest that we ought to know about in order to perform today. "We" means everyone. From my point of view, we've got a bunch of editors who don't have a sense of history, and they don't have a handle on the reality of what has happened here. Other writers may not agree. They are just out for the buck! That's a part of that *Rich Media, Poor Democracy* thing.

about . . . time: Do you think that's because the audience has changed, and shows like *Donahue* and others have gone away because people say they aren't interested in thinking anymore.
Williams: Well, I don't believe that. I think if you put it out there, people will reach for it. Media owners just are not interested in putting it out there, and they are not doing that because they know they won't get advertisers to support it.

about . . . time: Some ultraconservative commentaries are calling for a new House on Un-American Activities–type committee. Do you think we are going back to an age of repression where people are monitoring what other people write?
Williams: It looks like it. I don't think it has ever really left. I think it has been sort of muted. Let me give you an example. This business down in Maryland with the father and son—in the beginning when the search was going on for the sniper, I got two calls in the middle of the night. One was a man's voice asking me if I was John Muhammad Williams and a woman called (obviously another police officer) asking if I was John Muhammad Williams. Now where does this begin? In 1946, I came out of the Navy and me and my buddy were walking down the street and got into a fight with

a couple of white guys. I hate to take you back this far, but this is how far back it goes.

In 1946, some drunken white boys and me and Freddie—two drunken black guys in Syracuse, my hometown—were walking down the street. Freddie hadn't been in the service, and he was always feeling apologetic for it. If I had said, "Freddie, jump off the top of that building for me," Freddie would have done it. Now here come these guys, and they want to fight. They are in our part of town going to our drinking places and wanted to get bad about it. So we started fighting, and, man, we were whipping up some asses. Somebody called the cops, and a car comes and takes us down to jail overnight. We spent the weekend in jail, and my mother and father, who were divorced at that point and still in the same town, got together and came down and bailed us out. Now we paid the fine, and I assumed that was it.

I used to go hunting up in the Catskills with my uncle Fred Page before he died. Then when I moved to New Jersey, I wanted to go hunting with him, and I had to get a license for a long gun. In New York State you don't need it. So I went down to the police station, talked to the chief, and applied for a license, and it seemed to take him a long time to get it approved. I called him, and he said, "Come into the office. I want to talk to you." He said, "We've got you down here for a felony." I said, "What felony?" He asked if I remembered anything about 1946. I said, "I was in a street fight, a misdemeanor, and paid a fine, and I'm down for a felony!" Obviously that information went to the FBI, and it's still there! I know because of that Muhammad call, so that's a way of saying that the s--- never left, it's still here.

Lorraine: I think in the beginning in Maryland they referred to the sniper suspect as John Williams Muhammad. I believe that's when he got those calls. After that they dropped the Williams and just referred to him as John Muhammad. But it was really, really strange because the calls literally were in the middle of the night, like around two o'clock in the morning, and the calls were like thirty minutes apart. It was strange. There was no way to tell who was calling. All he said was no and hung up. There was another time when a man came out when we lived in a big apartment building, and we heard clicks on the phone. He went downstairs to the basement where the phone connections were, and there was a guy fiddling with the phone lines.

about . . . time: But what does that do to a society?

Williams: Well, if society lets it happen, they are no better for it, and that's exactly what's happening. I don't see anybody jumping up and down denouncing the corporations. Every week they run this list where so many corporations have been indicted, and nobody has gone to jail. They want to disobey, alter, and twist the law, and people just lay back and let that happen.

about . . . time: Why do you think that is? Is it just the nature of the American people?
Williams: I would not have thought so.

about . . . time: You have seen this country grow over a large part of this century. So has this part of the cycle been repeated before, and where does it go from here?
Williams: Yes. I can't help but think that it goes from bad to worse because of the bad economic situation. People don't dare take risks anymore because "I need this job. I have to feed my family. I have to accept this program."

about . . . time: Well, where is the heroic side? Where are the people with moral vision? Maybe I misunderstood that in the 1960s and early 1970s people got involved because they had some sense of moral vision . . .
Williams: Well, at that time they could get some media coverage as well. These days that ain't happening. In the 1960s you could have all the marches and get coverage in the papers and on television, and reporters were dogging the parades and bothering people. That's not happening now.

about . . . time: Let's switch tracks. Have you seen yourself evolve into becoming a kind of global person, an average American citizen, or citizen of the world?
Williams: No. [laughs] I don't think I'm an average American, and I'm pretty sure I'm not a citizen of the world. I haven't done that much traveling, but I know something about what's going on in the world and certainly here at home. My primary concern is looking after my family and their family's families because that's where it all begins, with the family. I think all of us are pretty much that way. We can't just walk out on the limb and forget what's back home and how to put food on the table and help raise the kids.

about . . . time: Among the things Ishmael Reed said about you in the introduction to the exhibit catalog is that you were a person who explored the underside of the American experience. Have you given that up with some of your later writings?

Williams: With *Clifford's Blues*, a lot of people just do not believe what those gentlemen did, and it's not only Jews and politicians and gypsies in New York. It was these old black people, too, you know.

about . . . time: How did you get turned on by that? Was it that photograph that they had of the black guy in the concentration camp at the Holocaust Museum?

Williams: I forget, do you remember?

Lorraine: Yes, we were living in Europe when we first got married in 1965 and stayed six months outside Barcelona and six months outside Amsterdam. We met in New York on the job. I'm an editor. He was hired to do PR (public relations), and I was doing editing and PR because they had nobody else. Then I needed someone who really knew what he was doing, so I hired him. We were working for a vanity house, Comet Press Books.

Anyway, we were living in Europe and going up to Scandinavia and had to go through Germany, which I really didn't want to do because I lost most of my family in the Holocaust. I was born in Hungary. We came here before the war, but we lost a lot of family. My maiden name was Isaac, but in Hungarian it is Ishack.

So I always had a thing about Germany and Germans, and it seemed like everybody was still acting like the Gestapo. They wanted the passport and this and that, but, anyway, we had to get through Germany to go where we wanted to go. We saw that Munich was pretty much on the way, so we decided to stop there because it was just outside Dachau. So that's what we did. When we started to ask where Dachau was, nobody had ever heard about it. As we were driving around we finally saw this black American soldier outside, and when we asked him where it was, he said, "Right here, madam."

They had preserved one of the buildings as a temporary museum, but it had not been set up properly yet. We went in there and saw artifacts and uniforms and other things, including a crematorium that was still intact. Then there were photographs, and several of them really caught John's eye—two actually. One was a line of inmates/prisoners and among them was a black man who looked very much like John. And we said, "Wow, where did he come from?" Then in another picture was a whole column of blacks, so the genesis of this really goes back to 1965–66. And it kept coming back to him.

He wanted to find out just who were these people and why they were there. So over the years he started to read stuff and talk to people, and he got in touch with the Holocaust Museum. He found out they were Afro-Germans— part German, part African. So there were a lot of people who were caught up in this thing, and nobody was aware of it at all. Over the years he read, researched, and gathered notes, then he was ready to start the book.

about . . . time: How long did it take you to write the book?
Williams: I've forgotten, maybe five to six years, and it took just about as long to sell the book.

about . . . time: What was the most acerbic comment you got from some-one you tried to get to buy/publish the book?
Williams: Nobody would be interested in anything like this.
Lorraine: I remember specifically somebody saying, "You know, the Holocaust is a Jewish thing. You can't have a black man in a concentration camp because the only people interested in Holocaust stories are Jews," which was ridiculous. And then he was gay and who do you appeal to—people who were in concentration camps, people who are black, people who are in the music business.

about . . . time: That was part of the beauty of the character because he was this very round character in the sense that if he had been just black, then that would have been okay, or if he had been just a white gay guy, that would have been okay, or even if he had been just a German guy, that would have been okay. But here was this complex person in chaotic circumstances.
Lorraine: And there were a lot of black musicians who went to Europe in the 1930s and did very well and established their lives there.

about . . . time: And the whole thing of jazz, blues, and the whole swing movement was a particular target of the Nazis. What was the most person-ally moving comment you heard about the book?
Williams: I don't remember. I guess I just became immune to antagonistic comments, and I just closed my mind to everything.

about . . . time: Have you gone for a reading in Germany and have you been asked to talk about the whole experience of blacks in the Holocaust?
Williams: Not in Germany, but I was asked very, very briefly when the book first came out.

about . . . time: Do you think you would write another novel about what's happening to African Americans in society today?
Williams: Yes, actually I think I'm always doing that.

about . . . time: Do you agree with Belafonte's statement about Powell?

Williams: He [Colin Powell] should have resigned when they didn't let him go to the racism conference in South Africa. I wrote about that, and I've been expecting someone to knock on my door since then. . . . Here's a man who is the first black man to run the whole Army and chairman of the Joint Chiefs of Staff who had kicked butts. He should have said, "I quit." Period! He didn't have to take that stuff. He could have quit and left clean!

Lorraine: Plus, he is the only US government official in the world who is respected to some extent and who people will talk to. They need him desperately.

Williams: I think he and Rumsfeld get along like water and oil.

about . . . time: You said you continue to write about today's African American experience . . . how would you characterize what is happening now? Are we in the promise land?

Williams: No. I really don't know what to say. Let me give you an example. When September 11 happened, that same day Ford Motor Company was forced to pay back 2.5 million dollars it had held back from its black employees in a shop in New Jersey. Now here these foreigners are blowing the s--- out of the World Trade Center. Everybody is running around talking about democracy this and democracy that, and here is Ford cheating workers out of their money. It seems like you can never get out of it. There's always some corner where somebody is holding you back, cheating you, stomping you, killing you, and what have you. I don't see that changing. I see it getting worse, particularly with the downturn in the economy.

about . . . time: Do you think that an even worse sign is that we are doing more to ourselves with the divergence of the middle class and black-on-black violence?

Williams: I don't see that. Look man, the black-on-black violence has been around for a long time. It has been written about by the black press. Now look at the world and see how these white people have been killing each other for thousands of years. This is nothing! Don't get me upset.

about . . . time: Do you see a bright future?

Williams: No, not particularly because I think the hump is too big to get over. Americans have to wake up. It's not only black people in trouble; white people will never believe they are in trouble, too. Yet, you have people walking off with all the money and not going to jail, but if I stole $25 they would put my ass under the jail! It's incredible, a two-way justice and law.

about . . . time: It's like I was telling someone that on September 10 George Bush couldn't even get elected as a dog catcher, but on September 12, all of a sudden he's giving away $40 million over here, $40 billion promised to wage war. And now there's a promise of more than $100 billion to rebuild Iraq in ways that they aren't even rebuilding American cities.

Williams: That's right; they aren't rebuilding American cities because American cities don't have any oil, man!

about . . . time: This stuff is going on, but almost no one ever questions anything or asks, "Where is this money coming from?" On top of it, Bush promised money to Africa and all over the Middle East, then says we are going to cut taxes. Is there a cure?

Williams: Yes, vote the man out of office! Hopefully we will find somebody who is much different. It has to happen. You want me to run for office? [laughs] I'm too old.

about . . . time: Who do you read today?

Williams: I really don't have much time to read other than history and politics. The book I'm reading now is one about the *Rich Media, Poor Democracy*. That's something else. I like that—it's from 1998—and it ties in with a lot of the stuff coming from the Left. The deals are the same thing, but it's bringing it a bit more up to date. It's like a slow-moving play that's covering this country. See no evil, and there is no evil—and that's what these suckers in DC are doing! We're the greatest. We're going to cut your taxes, baby. Don't worry about it. We'll look out for you . . . like this!

about . . . time: Do you think the country can survive? Is it on a collision course with itself with massive tax cuts and tremendous deficit spending and no additional sources of revenue?

Williams: I don't see people hitting the streets, and I think that's what they need to do—nothing violent, just parades and protests and silent marches and stuff like that with placards like they used to do. And people out on street corners on their soap boxes saying, "This is wrong, and this is right."

about . . . time: In African American writing, there is another renaissance now where you have so many more people writing and publishing in mainstream, big time publishers and that type of thing. But is the quality still there? Are writers producing the kind of purposeful writing that was going on back between the war period and the period of the Black Arts Movement?

Williams: I think it's a different kind of writing. I think it's less intrusive, less demanding. I don't want to talk about vision, but I think there's a certain kind of writing that produces its own kind of vision without saying this is what I want . . . it's just right there in the text. And I think that may be missing in some of the newer, younger works.

about . . . time: Thank you, Mr. Williams.

Hard Truths: John A. Williams Illuminates the Black Experience

Ron Netsky / 2003

From *City* (July 16 and 23). Web. Reproduced courtesy of Ron Netsky and *City* Newspaper/ WMT Publications Inc., Rochester, New York.

Part One

Visitors to the Rare Books Library at the University of Rochester this summer may feel like they have entered a parallel world. Filling nineteen large display cases are books, articles, manuscripts, journals, letters, and photographs by, or related to, the man writer Ishmael Reed has called the greatest American novelist of the twentieth century. So why is it so many people have never heard of John A. Williams?

"Right now he's under the radar," says Richard Peek, the director of the Rare Books and Special Collections Library at the UR's Rush Rhees Library. "But he will be rediscovered."

Peek isn't waiting for the world to wake up to Williams. The UR's Rare Book Library is the repository for Williams's papers. Peek decided to give them the prominence they deserve. It's an astute decision. Williams is a singular figure in American literature, one well worth getting to know through his complex novels and riveting nonfiction.

In his introduction to the show's catalog, Reed explains why Williams is not as well-known as he should be. "Nobody can accuse John A. Williams of shying away from the truth, and sometimes the truth hurts."

Over his five-decade career, Williams has often been too radical for the literary establishment and too uncompromising for popular taste. In the early 1960s he traveled across America in a new white car, recounting the hostility he encountered in a book, *This Is My Country Too*. (Williams jokes that the book, written in the tradition of John Steinbeck's *Travels with*

Charlie, could have been called *Travels with Mr. Charlie*.) Barely two years after the death of Reverend Martin Luther King Jr., he published *The King God Didn't Save*, a critical look at the life and work of King that won him no shortage of disdain from King's many admirers.

Williams's fiction initially drew praise from the literary world. In 1962 a panel of jurors consisting of John Hersey, S. J. Perelman, John Cheever, and others unanimously awarded him the American Academy of Arts and Letters' prestigious Prix de Rome, a traveling and writing fellowship. But, after an interview with the director of the American Academy in Rome, the fellowship was revoked. Something about Williams was threatening to the system.

Over the decades, Williams's achievements have occasionally been recognized. He has won a National Endowment for the Arts grant (1977), the American Book Award (1983), and the Phyllis Wheatley Award for Outstanding Contribution to African American Culture (2002).

But none of this means he can get his latest novel published. While the bookstore shelves and bestseller lists are filled with ghost-written celebrity biographies and fiction hardly worth the pulp it's printed on, Williams's 1999 novel, *Clifford's Blues* (an excellent book about a black, gay musician imprisoned in the Dachau concentration camp during World War II) was published only in paperback by an obscure press. His latest work has not found a publisher.

But thirteen of his novels, eight nonfiction books, and two books of poetry have been published and are available in libraries across the country.

We spoke to Williams recently by phone. The following is an edited version of our conversation.

City: While a teenager in Syracuse you were working on sanitation department trucks. Later you held many other nonwriting jobs. Did you know then that, even though this may have been the expectation of white society, it was not your fate?

Williams: I wasn't all that concerned about what society expected of me. I knew that my mother worked for a number of white families as a maid and my father worked for the city as a trash collector and a number of other things.

City: When you enlisted in the Navy after Pearl Harbor, you were fighting for your country, which wasn't exactly looking out for you. Were you still holding on to some idea of the American Dream?

Williams: I don't think I ever had any concept of the American Dream. When I was growing up, what I hoped to achieve was to become a super athlete. I loved playing football, basketball, and baseball, and running track. I hoped to be good enough at those things to get a scholarship somewhere for college. The war gave me that opportunity, making it possible for me to go to college on the GI Bill.

City: You had a close call in the military, and it wasn't the enemy but your fellow sailors who threatened you.
Williams: They were really pure crackers; there's no other term for it. I just didn't fit into the mold. This was an outfit in transition; it was picking up more men. And we—maybe there were five or six black guys—were also waiting for shipment ostensibly to a black outfit, which is exactly what happened. But, in the meantime, you had a lot of people transferring in and out, and an awful lot of them were southerners. I never knew there were so damn many southerners in America. These guys did not know what to do with some of us who did not come from the South. We just were not taking that shit. One night we got into it, and one cracker put a .45 to my head. The other crackers really got scared because they knew that something bad would happen to them even if something worse happened to me, so they backed off. But that was one time that I almost got killed by our own troops.

City: After a tough start, you began publishing, and your novel *Night Song* was noticed enough to make you the unanimous choice of the American Academy of Arts and Letters for the Prix de Rome in 1962. But after an interview with the director of the American Academy in Rome, the prize was revoked. What do you believe happened?
Williams: The director didn't want me there. They'd had Ralph Ellison there, and Ralph was always a compliant guy. I'm not taking anything from his writing skills, although I would have thought that he would have produced in his life a hell of a lot more than he did. I'm not saying this because he's dead. I said this when he was alive.

City: You're right. *Invisible Man* was great, but where are the others?
Williams: I think he did one more, *Shadow and Act*. Ralph was the kind of guy who would not help younger black writers. He was very, very selfish and very, very pompous. I never got close to him, and I never wanted to.

City: But, in terms of the Prix de Rome, there was some speculation that you may have been turned down because you were going with a white woman at the time, and this was in the early 1960s.

Williams: Yes, I was, and I married her, too. It's worked out really well.

City: Later on, while in Rome, you wrote the director a note saying, "How does it feel to have almost finished my career?"

Williams: Yes, I did. [laughs] But I never heard from him.

City: This real episode in your life became a central plot element in one of your most acclaimed novels, *The Man Who Cried I Am*. In the book you blend fact and fiction in terms of your personal life and the life of the protagonist and also in your use of fictionalized historical figures. Is that a delicate thing to balance?

Williams: No, not at all, because I've always loved history, and I can't see writing a book that doesn't contain some level of the parameters of history.

City: In the same book you wrote of the King Alfred plot, a plan to round up minority populations at a time of national emergency. Ishmael Reed has written that, while this may have seemed far-fetched in 1967, government documents have since shown that it wasn't too far from the truth. Were you on to something?

Williams: I don't know what got me started. I guess I have not been a very trusting person concerning our government and the way it's dealt with various people, beginning with the Indians. My father was part Indian. It's just been a mess.

City: Ishmael Reed also says that you are the greatest author of the twentieth century, but because of your radical point of view you were unpalatable to the literary establishment.

Williams: I think that's been true. Even other writers who I've admired and who have appeared to like my work have just sort of gone off on different tracks. When it all began in the late 1950s and early 1960s, we were after something, even if we didn't know precisely what it was. We wanted to correct something bad that we sensed, knew, or had experienced. I don't find that anymore.

City: There is also the idea that the literary establishment only has room for one black writer at a time, whether it's Richard Wright, James Baldwin, or Ellison.

Williams: I don't think they would deny that too much.

City: I just finished *Clifford's Blues*, and it's a wonderful book. But I noticed it's published by an obscure, small press. Is that the way things are going?

Williams: That has been the case. Nobody wanted to touch that book, and one of the senses that I got was that black people are not supposed to have been involved in the Holocaust. This is pure crap. You know, I made two trips to Dachau to do that book, and I did an awful lot of research around the country and in Germany and Europe, too. So I knew whereof I wrote. People didn't believe me, but I've seen the pictures there in the camp. I've seen an entire column of black prisoners walking down one side of the camp, and I've seen pictures of single black inmates or small groups of black inmates.

City: In the last two decades more attention has been paid to female black writers like Toni Morrison and Alice Walker. Have you observed that?

Williams: I've observed it and so has [Ishmael] Reed, and we've laughed about it and joked about it.

City: Do you think people find it less threatening?

Williams: Yes.

City: There was another irony with *The Man Who Cried I Am*. It came out in the same year, 1967, as William Styron's *The Confessions of Nat Turner*. While this book on the black experience by a white author cleaned up in terms of awards, your book got comparatively little attention. You wrote an essay questioning Styron's assertion that this was the only slave rebellion. He clearly was not aware that there were many.

Williams: Yes, that was idiotic. How can a writer make a statement like that without checking?

City: When you were sent across the country in 1964 to write the articles that resulted in *This Is My Country Too*, did you take it on as a personal challenge against the whole system? There are parts of the book when you are traveling in the South and you have some pretty close calls, but you remain defiant.

Williams: I was a grown man with kids, and I was not about to take any crap, certainly not any more than when I was a kid and overseas in the service. I wasn't always so bold; sometimes I was just very clever. If I picked up a cop following me, I would very soon pull over and rush out of the car and open the trunk and get some tools like I was having car trouble. Sometimes they would speed up and go by. Sometimes they would stop and just make sure I was doing what I was supposed to be doing and leave me alone. Sometimes I would simply tell the cop I was having car trouble and could he direct me to a station, and I could see the chagrin on their faces. I'd drive into a garage, hang around for ten minutes and get out, make it to the quickest highway I could, and then leave town.

City: How much do you think things have changed in forty years? There were incidents in the Senate in the last few years that reminded me of your book. I think it was Fritz Hollings who slipped and used the term *Nigra*. And, of course, the Trent Lott affair.
Williams: I think for some people things will never change. My editor at *Holiday*, a guy whom I loved, Harry Sions—he was a correspondent in the Italian Campaign during World War II. Twice, in the time I knew Harry, he slipped, and he said, "nigger."

City: What do you think when you hear rappers use the word?
Williams: I'd like to slap them in the mouth. I really would.

Part Two

When the revered novelist Chester Himes read *The Man Who Cried I Am* by relative newcomer John A. Williams in 1969, he could not contain himself. In a letter to Williams dated June 13, he wrote, "But for my money, *The Man Who Cried I Am* is the book . . . a blockbuster, a hydrogen bomb. It is by far the greatest book, the most compelling book, ever written about THE SCENE . . . It is a milestone in American literature, the only milestone produced since *Native Son*. . . ."

Williams is indeed a powerful writer. His novels encompass the scope of history and the personal struggles of individuals tangled within it. Williams has a gift for language that drives the narrative forward while making the reader want to linger over his wonderfully descriptive prose.

At the age of seventy-seven, Williams is the author of thirteen published novels, including *Captain Blackman* and *!Click Song*, eight nonfiction books, and numerous articles and essays.

But, when it comes to his frank descriptions of the black experience, Williams may be too powerful for popular taste. Despite praise from writers like Himes and Ishmael Reed, he has clearly not received the recognition his work deserves.

This may be changing. *The Man Who Cried I Am* is included among the QBR (*Black Book Review Online*) Sacred 100. Williams's career is the subject of a fascinating exhibition at the Rare Books and Special Collections Library at the University of Rochester's Rush Rhees Library. Richard Peek, the library's director, believes Williams will eventually be viewed as one of the most important American writers of the second half of the twentieth century. The Rare Book Library is the repository for Williams's papers.

In last week's *City Newspaper*, Williams discussed his early years, his literary career, and his encounters with prejudice. In the second part of our interview, we began by asking Williams about covering the civil rights movement as a black journalist.

City: In the 1960s you were covering the civil rights movement for *Newsweek* and other magazines. Obviously you had strong feelings about this. Did you have any trouble with the blurring of the line between journalism and participation?
Williams: No, I didn't, and I probably overstepped my bounds when I got on King's case.

City: You've written more critically than most about Martin Luther King, and very early on. What did you see as his major short-coming?
Williams: Women, primarily. Even as a kid that always upset me, when I would hear parents talking about Reverend So-and-so and Miss So-and-so, and the preacher's married and he's got a family of his own. I would ask myself, "What is this?" I decided I would never, ever be a preacher because I would never be able to screw around—literally.

City: Still, King has been elevated to a saint.
Williams: That's alright with me. I've had my say-so. As it happened, one of my major informants was a woman I was going with at the time. She had been going with Martin Luther King. He was even double-crossing her and everybody else he went with, let alone his wife. He was not a very trustworthy man in that area.

City: You met Malcolm X in Africa. You seem to have had a higher opinion of him.
Williams: We all knew where he came from and what he was doing. He was a man of very few words, but they were very powerful words. I was very much attracted to him. I would put Malcolm in a separate category from

the Black Muslims who were going to just run out and shoot people. I think Malcolm was much too wise for that. Though he sounded at times like he was very willing to do it, we never saw him pick up the gun.

City: Do you think he would disapprove of the kinds of things Louis Farrakhan has said in recent years?
Williams: Probably not now, if he were alive and Farrakhan's age.

City: In *The Man Who Cried I Am* you contrast characters that closely resemble King and Malcolm X, and the Malcolm X character—Minister Q— plays a role in the book's climactic scene. He gets a phone call, disclosing a government plot, and then he gets murdered by government agents. In real life wasn't he murdered by rival Black Muslims?
Williams: My information is they were paid to kill him by other forces.

City: What do you think of the state of black leadership today?
Williams: Where is it? Who is it? I think there is a vacuum. I just don't see conditions changing soon enough or well enough for us to ever produce the kind of person who would be acceptable to the rest of America, and I think what we have now are poor selections. The people who could be leaders— Ralph Bunche for example—they're just not around, and if they are they're just drinking their mint juleps and laying back saying, "The hell with it."

City: Of course, if you asked me about white leadership, I'd have some trouble. [laughs] I have some general questions dealing with issues you've written about or touched on. Do you believe in any form of reparations for blacks in America?
Williams: Yes, I think that would be a big help. When I think of the Jewish situation in Germany and I think of a comparable and perhaps even longer situation for black people here, it would be a big help. Historically, we are not even given the true figures of what happened here. I just keep stumbling across a lot of stuff. When I was up in Rochester I mentioned this work that was done in 1870 by a guy named Weston, I believe. And it was used in a book published in 1909 in which the figures given were upward of forty million Africans. We're not talking ten million; we're talking forty million all brought from Africa by the French, the Spanish, the British, anybody who had a ship. Nobody ever deals with that figure. People don't even bother to check out the figures that are going around.

City: I think the prevailing attitude is that the statute of limitations has run out on that crime.
Williams: Ah, but it hasn't.

City: Would you be in favor of monetary reparations?
Williams: Well, if you could give me a better one, I might think about it. [laughs]

City: Some people say policies like affirmative action are a way of dealing with this.
Williams: But it's the same old thing. Look what they're doing with affirmative action. They're jawboning it to death.

City: Do you think the *New York Times* abused affirmative action by putting Jayson Blair in a position way over his head to create a black star reporter instead of giving him time to learn the ropes?
Williams: Yes, I do, and you're the first person who's asked me that. [Former *New York Times* executive editor Howell] Raines is a southerner. He's probably trying to do a good thing, but you can't do that. If you've got somebody young you've got to guide him. You've got to watch him. You can't forgive and forgive and forgive. In a way I feel sorry for Raines. I can't imagine copy editors letting that stuff get by in the first place. You're not talking about one or two guys; you're talking about something like a board of directors.

City: Getting back to books, you use flashbacks extensively in your novels. Is this to create a more dream-like feeling? Did you consciously work out this technique?
Williams: No, it just seemed to come naturally. You reach a certain point where you feel you are now able to go back or perhaps even forward without losing the reader or yourself at that point.

City: Some of the passages in your books seem to be written in a stream-of-consciousness sort of flow. In the course of your writing are these passages the toughest, or do they simply flow?
Williams: Sometimes you want the stuff not only to flow, but to flow very well, and somehow differently from other sections where things seem to be so smooth. You do this to get yourself out of that rut and brighten up your writing and lead the reader onward to expect even more.

City: In *Clifford's Blues* there is a wonderful passage where jazz players use musical quotes from songs to communicate to each other. How important a role has jazz played in your work?

Williams: I've always loved it, and I've always been a frustrated musician. When I was a kid I was a very good bugler in a drum and bugle core. I went to Boy Scout camp outside of Syracuse, and I was the camp bugler there. I would do morning calls and evening calls, tattoos. When I went into the Navy, I became the regimental bugler in my boot training camp, but I couldn't afford trumpet lessons, which, in a way, may have been for the best. My third son, Adam, is a musician. He's a guitarist and a producer.

City: In *!Click Song* the protagonist goes to see Bud Powell and George Shearing at a club, and Powell ends up punching Shearing. In another scene he goes to see Charles Mingus, and when he talks too loud, Mingus tells him to shut up. These scenes seem very real. Are they?

Williams: Yes, they were. [laughs] I remember a session where Charlie Mingus was playing at a club called the Five Spot on Third Avenue, kind of a smallish club. I went there with a couple of buddies of mine, and we were chatting. Mingus was trying to play, and finally he said, "You niggers, shut up down there!" The Bud Powell story was told over and over again, and everybody thought it was both funny and sad.

City: Looking back, who are the twentieth-century writers you most admire?

Williams: I try not to do that, but one writer I've never gotten out of my head or my gut is Malcolm Lowry—*Under the Volcano*. It's been a long time since I've read it, but it's still there.

City: What is your view of the current state of book publishing and the lack of solid literature? Are we losing a generation of real writers?

Williams: It stinks. If they are depending on writing to earn money we're going to lose some talent, I think. It's very easy to fall into a groove where you don't have to think, scheme, dream, or anything else, you just write out the copy. These books that are selling for $24 and $29 and $32, that is ridiculous. There's nothing there.

City: One thing that turns up again and again in your books is the relationship between blacks and Jews. How important has that been in your life and work?

Williams: I grew up in a community that was essentially black and Jewish in Syracuse. Neighbors and people who ran stores and guys I played ball with and went to school with were Jewish, and my mother worked for a Jewish family, the Rubinsteins for, God, it seemed like five hundred years. She was a maid. It was like two families together. They had two children. The boy was crippled; he couldn't talk too well or see too well. There were actually two families looking out for him. Our neighborhood in Syracuse was essentially Jewish and was called Jewtown as opposed to another section of town which was primarily black and that was called Bloodsfield. [laughs]

City: In your early work you talk about the tension between blacks and the Jews who owned stores in ghetto areas. By the time you get to *Clifford's Blues* there seems to be more of an empathy.
Williams: It's called survival. I've been to Israel three times, and it was an extraordinary experience. I made a lot of friends there.

City: One of the things I like about your books of a few decades ago is that you are not inhibited by political correctness. Does political correctness ever get in the way of your writing today?
Williams: [laughs] No.

City: What does it mean to you to have your life's work in a university archive?
Williams: It's very special. I'm always disappointed that my own university—Syracuse—was not terribly interested, but Rochester's close enough to Syracuse.

City: Are you working on any current books?
Williams: I'm working on a novel which is big and fat, and I've got one called *Colleagues* which, believe it or not, has been running around for eight or nine years. It's a big sucker. It's about college professors and all the politics.

City: You have no shortage of ironies in your books, so I have to ask you about this unintentional irony. In *!Click Song* one of the themes deals with black culture going unrecognized at museums. Discussing one exhibition, you write that King Tut looks like Michael Jackson. What does it say, culturally, that since your 1982 publication Michael Jackson has had himself carved into a different statue?

Williams: I never liked Michael Jackson. As a matter of fact, I can't deal with artists who give in to this whole public thing. That makes me quite uneasy.

City: The Prix de Rome incident may have hurt your career. If you'd gone to Rome, you'd have had more opportunities, but you talked about Ellison and how he didn't write too much afterwards. One thing that's never happened to you—you've never lost your edge. I'm not saying it's good that they took away the award, but sometimes it's the struggle that makes the work great.

Williams: I think I've gotten over it, so I'm always a bit surprised when people bring it up these days. I think I've gone way past it. I've survived. I don't harbor that many grudges. What the hell, if you're going to ride the train of life, sometimes you have to stand up. The seats are all filled.

Vanqui: Original Opera that Blends African and Classical Themes

Tavis Smiley / 2004

TAVIS SMILEY (host): From NPR in Los Angeles, I'm Tavis Smiley. Opera and African drumming make an unlikely pair to some, but Leslie Burrs didn't find that an obstacle when he created the compellingly original opera *Vanqui*. Leslie, a composer and flautist, blended African rhythms with classical elegance to develop the unusual piece. Leslie partnered with the renowned author John A. Williams, who wrote the libretto for *Vanqui*, both a touching love story and polemic about slavery in the 1700s and 1800s. Leslie and John join us now from our bureau in New York City. Nice to have you both on the program.

JOHN A. WILLIAMS (writer): Good to be here.

LESLIE BURRS (composer): It's a pleasure.

SMILEY: John, let me talk to you first about the story told in this opera, *Vanqui*. It's the tale of two Africans enslaved in America. After they are murdered, their spirits seek each other in the afterlife. This is—it seems to me—both an American story and a spiritual African tale. How did you come up with this thematic blend, if you will?

WILLIAMS: AME Zion Church. [laughs]

SMILEY: There's a nice, easy, direct, and understandable answer for those who know anything about the AME Zion Church, but I digress. Tell me more.

WILLIAMS: Well, there was that, and, of course, I had my own soup to stir in this whole historical business of slavery and how much America developed because of it. I wanted us to come out on top as some of the characters do, and pretty much that's it.

SMILEY: Leslie, you composed the opera. As I said a moment ago, your signature sound is very unusual in its blend of jazz and classical and those wonderful African sounds. Explain this "urban classical sound" and how you used it in this opera format.

BURRS: First and foremost, I feel as though the opera and the style of my writing are really representing the exposure to all the eclectic styles that we encounter here in the United States, so it just becomes second nature for me as an artist to try to incorporate those varying aspects of music and culture. The urban classical concept comes because I spent a long time in my career being viewed from the classical standpoint as a jazz artist and being viewed from a jazz artist standpoint as a classical musician. I thought I better take the responsibility of defining the music that I'm doing and that's where I came up with the title "urban classical." I'm a native of South Philadelphia, and I feel as though the exposure of living in a city life like that has impacted heavily on me. I spent a lot of time at my grandmother's Baptist church as well as growing up in the Episcopalian church, making a living at it and having that church put me through college. I had the best of both worlds in that respect, and it impacted heavily on me as a musician.

SMILEY: How do you make the blend of all those sounds actually work, though? I mean, it could very well have come off sounding like a bunch of noise.

BURRS: The libretto helped to dictate a great deal of how I was going to approach any particular work. There's a beautiful lullaby that John has written based on the goddess Moremi and the story of Miss Garner, who is compelled to kill her baby to avoid having the baby be subjected to slavery. Moremi was responsible for killing her children in order to save a whole village of people, so I knew that that work needed the most tender approach in my writing. I tried to make sure that it was represented in that manner in the melodic line and trying to create this beauty even though ultimately she does kill her child, more to save the child than to harm the child for what they would be exposed to as time goes on.

And then with a work like "There's a Land," where under the guise of a prayer meeting arrangements are being made for the slaves to escape from their plantation, I knew I had to have a down-home-church kind of feel in the beginning and letting it convert itself into something that was more of a very contemporary and hip sound because they're going from being afraid of escaping to the joy of knowing that they're going to a land of freedom. So we needed to have this traditional sound, then transferring itself into a very contemporary and hip, jazzlike quality.

SMILEY: This is a question, I guess, for both of you. When you're writing an opera, which comes first, the music or the story, or was it more of a back-and-forth throughout this creative process?

WILLIAMS: Well, Les got me involved in it, and then he ran away. He said, "You do the story!" Then he ran away and left me to do the story. Then he came back and stacked it full of more character with the sounds, tones, shadings, all of the rest of that, so it was a pretty good mix, I believe.

SMILEY: Leslie, why'd you do that to John?

BURRS: Well, we had no choice. I knew that I wanted to respond to the rhythm and the pulse of whatever John was going to write, and John was very considerate in that way, writing in varying meters and writing in a way that made it pretty easy for me to envision how I could treat it musically. The one frightening part was originally—since writers are so accustomed to doing drafts, John would send me what I thought was a final version, and then, unfortunately, I would write a complete work. This happened on the very first piece, and then John said, "Oh, you know, that's wonderful, but I made a new draft now." So I was in a panic. We decided at that moment that the best thing to do is John would finish whatever final draft he would have before he would submit it. Then I would know that I could safely go and write the music to exactly the text, and it worked out perfectly for us.

SMILEY: Leslie, to your personal history, you have a new album out, *Blue Harlem, Black Knight*. I think it's fair to say it's far more contemporary than classical. How is your musical style evolving these days?

BURRS: I've always—I started out primarily in the jazz world, but I always wanted to do large works. *Blue Harlem, Black Knight* represents my efforts solely as a jazz artist, incorporating some of the finest players, which includes Gerald Veasley, the Heads Up bass player, and Doc Gibbs, who's music director on the *Emeril Live* program, and people of that nature. So these works are inspired specifically by African American artists, including Sterling A. Brown, the poet, and Roy DeCarava, the photographer, and Selma Burke, the sculptor. It's an interesting, once again, juxtaposition of a way of involving music and art but having a contemporary jazz quality about it.

SMILEY: John, my time is up. Let me give you the last word. *Vanqui*—What do you like most about this piece of work?

WILLIAMS: The combination of word and music in which I am involved, and I hope it lives forever.

SMILEY: John Williams is the author of a dozen novels and several works of nonfiction as well as two plays and a poetry collection, *Safari West*. Leslie Burrs is an award-winning composer. His new CD is called *Blue Harlem, Black Knight,* and you can hear some sounds from it on our website at npr. org. Congratulations, Leslie and John, all the best to you, and thanks for coming on.

WILLIAMS: Thanks a lot.

BURRS: Thank you.

On *Safari West*

Jeffrey Allen Tucker / 2005

Interview conducted October 6, 2005. Courtesy of the Department of Rare Books, Special Collections and Preservation, University of Rochester River Campus Libraries.

Jeffrey Allen Tucker: We're back with John and Lori, October 6. We're discussing *Safari West* now, which is a collection of poems spanning most of your career, John, from 1953 to 1997. Many of these poems were published previously. Before they were published in this volume, they were published in volumes such as the *New Black Poetry* and in journals and periodicals such as *New Letters* and *Callaloo*. This collection, *Safari West*, was published by a press in Montreal. I'm going to try the name. Is it . . . ?
John A. Williams & Lori Williams: Hochelaga.

JAT: Hochelaga. How did you come to publish with Hochelaga? It is a press in Montreal.
LW: My niece lives in Montreal. She's a writer and teacher as well, and she is married to a writer and journalist. He's an editor at the *Montreal Gazette* and a publisher, a small publisher. He had published one or two other things, I think, before this. He is an admirer of John and thought it was a pity that he never had a volume of poetry under one roof, in one volume. That was the theme for this, for doing this.

JAT: Was *Safari West* distributed mainly in Canada? Was it distributed in the United States widely?
LW: Well, I think he used a distributor in the States who didn't do much with it, really, unfortunately, and he didn't have the financial wherewithal to do a real advertising-and-PR kind of thing with it.
JAW: And I didn't have the energy to push it any more than I did or could at that time.
LW: Old Ish gave it another award, Ishmael Reed.

JAW: Right. Yes. I had done another volume of poetry, which I had typed up myself and copied and sold. It was just called *Poems*. I'm sure there's an old raggedyass copy around here somewhere. I've been writing poems for as long as I've been writing. Period.

JAT: It's interesting that you say that because one of the blurbs on the cover says that poetry is your first love. Is that true?

JAW: Well, yes, because I first learned the magic of poetry as a Sunday school kid. When Easter comes, you get all these little pageants and things, and Thanksgiving, you get these little pageants and things, and Christmas . . . oh, boy.

JAT: You'd be reciting Bible verses and popular songs about the holidays and so on.

JAW: Yes.

JAT: That's really interesting. You're saying, though, that you've written poetry as long as you've written anything?

JAW: Yes.

JAT: Now, this other poetry volume that's just entitled *Poems*, when was that put together?

JAW: I think that was in the fifties and sixties, and it was—

LW: I think earlier. Not sixties, certainly; it was before I met you.

JAT: Would we have a copy of that in Rochester, you think?

JAW: I don't know.

LW: There was something in the booklet about it, so it must be.

JAW: It's a mimeograph work, and a gray cover sheet with a big P on the front saying "Poems."

JAT: Is anything from that in *Safari West*?

JAW: I doubt it very much. That was another life practically.

JAT: You've written poetry throughout your career. Any sense as to why poetry doesn't figure more prominently?

JAW: Because I'm always torn between fiction and poetry. There are periods that I have when I do write poetry, and I'm sure I have a bundle of stuff that

I haven't collated or gone over again to see if I really want to use it. But I've got at least one ankle in poetry and will always have one.

JAT: A saying about books and their covers comes to mind, but I do have to ask about the artwork on the cover of *Safari West*. It's a sculpture, and it's described in the book's front matter as a "lifesize head of John A. Williams by James Earl Reid, 1998." Who's James Earl Reid?
LW: As I recall, he had done a bust of Billie Holiday that was in the town square. Where was she born? Do you know? Because I have a feeling that the statue he did of her is in the town square of where she is from.[1]
JAW: I don't remember anything about that, honey. I can't help you.
LW: He'd heard John and said he would like to do this bust of him. He started coming up that summer and spent . . . I forgot how many sessions. He came with that other friend, remember, who used to drive. Anyway, he would sit out there in the backyard, and he was sculpting.

JAT: Did he make a number of trips up here?
LW: Several. We assumed that he would fire it and make several and that we would get one, but apparently, he never was able to raise the money in order to do it. He was sort of a strange guy. We took some pictures of it when it was finished, but as far as we knew, he never did have it cast. It probably disappeared.

JAT: So we don't know where this—
LW: No, if it's even still in existence.

JAT: Was this picture taken here?
LW: Yes.

JAT: It's fuzzy. Lori; you took the picture?
LW: I guess so.

JAT: It says you took the picture.
LW: If it says that, I guess I did.

JAT: "Cover photograph by Lori Williams."
LW: My second cover photograph.
JAW: You're getting there. [laughs]

JAT: Is photography a hobby for you?

LW: No. [laughs]

JAW: Point and shoot.

JAT: Because it's a really good picture.

LW: It is.

JAW: No shade, point and shoot.

LW: I also took the picture of John and Dennis that's used on the back of the Pryor book. That was up in the country.

JAT: I was surprised. I thought, "Wow, I didn't know Lori was a photographer."

LW: Just a fluke.

JAT: I'd like to ask you brief questions about some specific poems in the collection. It looks like I have questions about a lot of the poems, more than I thought I had. Let's start with "Safari West" the poem, starting on page 14, from 1969. The speaker of this poem describes being in coastal Nigeria near Popo Channel and the Barracoons in which Africans who were shipped to the New World were held. I assume that the poem is based on your own visit to this location.

JAW: Yes.

JAT: What had brought you to Nigeria?

JAW: I forget now what it was. Was I doing something for *Newsweek* at that time?

LW: Possibly. I think Nigeria specifically—it was where Wendell was at that time.

JAW: That's true.

JAT: Wendell?

JAW: Wendell Roye was an old buddy of mine. He was with the USIS.

LW: Some governmental agency based in Lagos.

JAW: How do I want to say this? It's a cockeyed title because a safari west obviously was not a safari for Africans, and I hope people understood that.

LW: The irony.

JAW: The irony.

JAT: I appreciate and I take you at your word when you say it's a cockeyed title, although I think it's an apt title in some ways. I like Nikki Giovanni's take on it. There's a blurb from her at the beginning of the book where she says, "Yes, this is not my home, only my safari west." Speaking not only about herself, but African Americans in general. The word *safari*, I think—I'm not completely sure about this, but I think it translates to *journey* or *expedition*. Certainly, the expedition of enslaved Africans into the New World was a forced one. It was an imposed one.

JAW: It's tongue-in-cheek; it's ironic or should be looked at that way.

LW: Because we think of safaris as being enjoyable and pleasurable.

JAT: A vacation and fun trip looking at lions and elephants and that sort of thing. It's cockeyed in the sense that it causes the reader—prompts the reader to rethink what a safari is.

LW: Yes.

JAT: There's some great poetry in just the words that you select: *barracoon* and *barracuda* get repeated. I love the line describing barracudas' noses "like secret smells of red lightning."

JAW: You ever seen a barracuda?

JAT: I've never seen a barracuda.

JAW: They are frightening. They are absolutely frightening.

JAT: Are they big?

JAW: They're not as big as a shark, no.

JAT: Are they long?

JAW: They're long, and they've got this thing—

LW: Where did you see one that close up?

JAW: You go to the beach, and they tell you, "Don't go past a certain place."

LW: Did you ever actually see one up close?

JAW: I saw one in a tank in a zoo over there in Nigeria somewhere.

JAT: There are lines from the poem that read as follows:

> Chains for the slow, the strong, the quick;
> chains for the mothers, the young,
> chains for the nations of westbound blacks.
> Crouching, I reach out of it, out of the heat;
> the instruments were only metal, rusted now and

hot with the silent sun that had not screamed.
I fit them to my neck, my wrists, my legs,
feeling for what I could never feel, but
knowing that feeling hides in time, I waited.
Waited to feel, wishing for pain. Waited. Wished.
Nigerians drifted through the heat, the awful heat,
their voices like music played on the smiles
and they called: Hello, America, unhinging my
place, and wondered at the black man clothed in
the West, grasping irons, eyes swinging over the island,
to the quiet, green, sea-swirled westward wake
of the Passage, eyes thundering wet missiles.

There's more, but that "eyes thundering wet missiles" is brilliant. It's really quite effective. These are lines that I think are powerfully understated and powerfully poetic. Did you actually do this? Did you actually put—lift irons, put them to your body?
JAW: Yes, I did. Yes, I did.

JAT: This is how you felt doing it?
JAW: I think they left them loose for travelers to see what they felt like, to feel what they felt like. They were rusted and specks of black paint but still strong as hell, and they still clinked and clanked and clunked. Boy, it was something.

JAT: It was quite an emotional experience for you?
JAW: Yes.

JAT: Africa, the middle passage, the history of slavery, and their meanings for modern African Americans are themes and topics that other poems in this volume take up. I wanted to jump to page 76, the poem "Facing Jura: 50 Years After." This is a poem that I might expect John A. Williams to write—the type of poem I might expect from you, John, in the sense that it recognizes connections between a modern personal experience and history or, again, how history shapes personal experience because there's a link made between—there's this white captain ordering a black detail around and ordering the destruction of their ballots. This is in France in 1944. There's a connection between that scene and Toussaint

L'Ouverture and his betrayal, capture, and imprisonment. The poem says that L'Ouverture was buried in Jura?
JAW: Yes.

JAT: This is in the mountains in France, like between France and Switzerland?
JAW: That would be the place.

JAT: This was a location that you had seen yourself, or is this a completely imagined?
JAW: No, no. I think I did see it. I think we went to an area where it was.
LW: We have been in that area. I can't remember.
JAW: Yes, I think that's where, France.

JAT: Now, the situation with the black detail and the white captain, that—is that imagined?
JAW: That's coming out of World War II for black guys who—the early black outfits, as history, American Army history, had always had white officers. It wasn't until about the middle of World War II where you got sufficient black officers. There were a few in World War II—World War I, but not that many.

JAT: This is not something—because you were in the—
JAW: I was in the Navy. The Navy was even poorer.
LW: Wendell was in the Army.
JAW: Wendell was in the Army. Yes, that's why. And Bill Robinson.

JAT: Bill Robinson?
JAW: He was a friend of mine, and Wendell is, too.

JAT: Friends from Syracuse?
JAW: From New York.

JAT: These are black men that you associated with.
JAW: Yes.

JAT: I want to jump back to the beginning of the book. On page 23, there's a poem entitled "John Brown" from 1995. A lot to say about this poem, but I'll limit myself to the final lines, which I think are quite eloquent

Old John Brown.
A common name with simple stops, Captain,
like freedom unadorned, a rock, just there,
nicked with age, too deep to move, embedded.
So men gather guns and guts to free you,
and in the doing, know they free themselves.

That's good. What is the legacy, or what are the legacy and the lesson left by John Brown, especially for twenty-first-century Americans?
JAW: Like so much of American history, it's one of those pieces that's dropped or obliterated completely. That's really sad because we do have a sense of forgetting where we came from, what we've done, how much good we've done, and how many terrible things we've done. We just don't remember that stuff. You get guys like John Brown and others, and my sense is that you always remember them.
LW: You should. This is from—this is one of the pieces from the opera.

JAT: From *Vanqui*?
JAW: *Vanqui*. Yes.

JAT: There are other poems from *Vanqui* as well; "Moremi," for example. Was there any particular reason you selected those poems to appear in *Safari West* or those verses from the libretto to appear in *Safari West*?
JAW: I thought the interchange between them would extend life for both. I think the book has done better than—
LW: I'm trying to remember now. Was it your choice, or did Ray select these particular four poems from the opera?
JAW: I think Ray did. I may have—
LW: Or you worked on it together?
JAW: Yes. Yes.

JAT: "Many Thousand Gone: Version 95"; "Nat Turner's Profession"; "John Brown"; and "Moremi"—I'm jumping around a little bit, but starting on page 26, we have "Journey without Name" from 1980. I take it that this poem is a verse narrative about migration north and south and back north again. It's about your parents?
JAW: My family. Yes. Grandparents too.

JAT: And your birth?
JAW: Yes.

JAT: Your parents are described as "These shoots of Tony and Sarah Jones, / of Gorman Williams and Margaret Smallwood," correct?
JAW: Yes. The latter is my dad.

JAT: Can you say more about your grandparents? We've talked about your parents a great deal.
JAW: I only knew my grandfather on my mother's side and her brothers and sisters. On my father's side, yes, there were older relatives. His sisters and cousins. Aunt Vi, Aunt Edna. I think there was one other aunt. We knew them all as kids.

JAT: You saw them?
JAW: My grandfather came up from Mississippi two or three times every year. I remember the starched collar with the curve at the edge.
LW: How old were you?
JAW: I guess I was about nine or ten or something like that.
LW: Your parents were still together?
JAW: Yes. My mother's sisters and brothers began coming up from Mississippi. She was the rest stop. Uncle Bud, Uncle Ulysses, Aunt Florence, Aunt Julie, Aunt Elizabeth. My favorite, Aunt Betty. They all came up. My mother was the first up, so she was where everybody stopped.
LW: Was she the oldest?
JAW: Yes. My father, this first line, "Journey without Name", he went down there—I don't know why the hell he went down there, but—
LW: Wasn't that when she went down to give birth?
JAW: Yes. That must have been it. Right.

JAT: The question isn't necessarily why your father went down there. It's why your mother went down there when she was pregnant with you.
LW: That was the tradition, to have your first child in your—I guess where you're from.
JAW: That's right.
LW: In your home with your parents.
JAW: And to be birthed by your parent, your mother.

JAT: That's interesting. I've never heard of that, although it makes a kind of sense. Certainly, the poem says, "She was, / simply said, homesick and swelling / with glory."

JAW: You know what wound up happening? Ola and John were the base for very nearly every relative that Ola had in Mississippi to arrive at when they left there. They all came to Syracuse.

JAT: That's interesting. That's a pattern that you see very frequently with migration. Somebody comes, and they became a home base for family and friends who follow in the new environment. Then the poem goes on to talk about your father coming south.
JAW: Yes.

JAT: Following on page 29, there's a line,

> Father'd worked his way south with
> the circus: eighteen hundred miles
> of shoveling horse shit, elephant
> excrescence, tiger turds, gorilla
> glops, and other jungle dumplings.
> In his starched white shirt of good
> cotton.

That's a motif that repeats throughout the poem, the "starched white shirt of good cotton." Your father came south with the circus?
JAW: That's right. About the only way he could get there.
LW: He couldn't afford it.
JAW: Because when he got there, he'd have to pay two fares back to Syracuse. "At Grampa's said they in / that soft Southern way: 'Folks down here / don't wear white shirts during the week.'" [laughter]

JAT: What does that mean? What does that signify, wearing a white shirt in the South, or for black folks in the South?
JAW: That you're not working that week or something like that. You're on a holiday.
LW: Or that you think you're better than the other black people who are laborers.
JAW: No, no. He was never like that.
LW: No, no. Not that he was like that, but is that the interpreted—
JAW: No. It just means he wasn't working. He wasn't wearing his work clothes.
LW: You only dressed like that for church?

JAW: Not necessarily. If you're going traveling, if you're going to a party, something special, you'd wear a white shirt.

JAT: He's wearing a white shirt before he goes back south in a variety of contexts. Within the poem, it becomes a symbol for your father—
JAW: *Starched* white shirt.
LW: He didn't dress like that up in Syracuse every day, did he?
JAW: Obviously not every day, but he did.
LW: I guess that's what we were trying to get at.

JAT: Yes, the starched white shirt is a kind of—it represents—
JAW: A special event.

JAT: There's that wonderful, although also disturbing, image of—the language is wonderful; the image is disturbing—of the blood flowering on his shoulder from a pitchfork tine when he's forced to go back north.
JAW: I think I mentioned I used to play in that wound in the book. Where is that line? I remember he was shorter even than I, but he was very, very bulky, very muscular. He had this wound in his shoulder, and it healed, and it went into a—
LW: Keloid.
JAW:—not a keloid. The skin pulled together, and it made a pit in his skin. I used to play in that when I was a kid. I'd ask him what it was and so on. He'd say, "I'm just a tough guy. That's a bullet," [laughs] and stuff like that. I remember very well.

JAT: Toward the bottom of page 29, a formulation that you use in this poem and in "Before Electricity, 1927," "The sun in Sagittarius saw me / in, slid me smoothly into the / midwife's mellowed hands." John is born. Because this is a formulation that you use both in this poem and in the next poem, "Before Electricity," suggested to me that your birthday is in either late November or early December.
JAW: Early December.

JAT: Then "Before Electricity" on page 31, from 1984. Again, the conclusion of the poem. Lines speak of "to moor the sun in Sagittarius." The poem recounts a childhood memory of your father lighting a stove, basically, right?
JAW: Yes.

JAT: "Out of a quieting chaos, / a dominating dusk, there danced, delicate / as a firefly, a firespot." Lots of asonance.[2]
JAW: Yes.

JAT: A few lines later, "More golden warm than a silver cold star / this firespot moved to meet a sibilance— / a soft and magical pop!"
JAW: Those old houses used to have gas pipes coming out of the wall. You could move them to the left and right, and you lit them.

JAT: You lit the pipe coming out of the wall?
JAW: Yes. It was a decorated kind of fancy pipe. All the houses had them.

JAT: It would light up.
JAW: Yes.

JAT: There'd be light fixtures attached to them. This is a very vivid childhood memory from 1927.
JAW: Yes. I can even tell you the address. It would be 503 East Washington Street, down the block from Rescue Mission.

JAT: Now, this is from 1927.
JAW: Yes.

JAT: You were two years old?
JAW: Something like that.

JAT: That's amazing.
JAW: It may be that my parents were always talking about the place and describing it, and then I remembered it. Don't worry. [laughter]

JAT: I can't remember what I was doing yesterday. [laughter]
LW: I have the same—I don't really remember much about my life at all, my childhood the way he does, but there are a few incidents that are very, very vivid. And I realize I can picture it all. Two incidences that I'm thinking of were both very traumatic. I think it's because they were stories that were told so many times about how I almost drowned and how I was run over and all this stuff that after a while, the stories I heard became—because those were the only things I really remember that well from my childhood.

JAT: Sometimes, those are the sorts of things that you can't forget, no matter how much you want to, right?

JAW: I did something stupid like that. Maybe yours wasn't stupid, but mine was. When I first began swimming, my dad would take me to Wilson Park where there were two ponds, two pools. Both were over my head, but I went to the smaller one. My dad was a great swimmer, and he was doing something. I'd seen him swim. At this point, I just jumped into the pond and knew that how to swim would come to me instantly.

LW: And it didn't. [laughter]

JAW: Then people were like, "Oh, he's coming up. I can see him." And I wasn't coming up. People started diving in the water and calling my dad, and they hauled me out. That made me learn how to swim in a hurry. [laughter]

LW: That was not my drowning experience.

JAT: A similar poem follows, "My Father and Ring Bologna" on page 32. Another poem about you and your father.

JAW: He loved ring bologna.

JAT: I guess like "Before Electricity" and some of the other poems in this collection, this poem paints the portrait of domestic life, but also a relationship between a father and son. I think perhaps for me, the most important lines are the last three lines. "We shared the meat bread tea / (milk in mine) and we were happy. / There were such times." It seems to me that the poem asserts that there were such times not only in your life, but in the lives of African American families in general. The black domestic space was more than, say, like the pathology identified in the Moynihan Report, for example.

JAW: That's true. That's true. I think the presence, or could even say the dominance, of the church helped that immensely. Immensely. You had Baptists. What are all the other denominations? Methodists. We were Methodist. Every Sunday, people would—you'd see they'd dress up and go to church. Of course, there'd be these special church things. Then we had established the Dunbar Center that provided space for all kinds of affairs and things of that sort. Then there were the card games. Women played cards like they were going out of business. They were as bad as the men. My mother was a chief dealer. [laughter]

JAT: Playing bid whist?

JAW: Yes, and just about everything else, too.

LW: She taught Adam how to play cards.

JAT: We were talking about this when we were discussing *The Junior Bachelor Society*, how there were figures like the coach and social institutions that looked after kids and were places where people could come together, provided opportunities for people to come together.

JAW: Very, very important, and it worked most times.

JAT: "The Cool One" on page 35. I have to admit, there are a number of poems that I just don't get, [laughs] and this might be one of them because I'm unsure as to the subject of the poem's portrait.

JAW: In 1953, there was this thing going around called cool, the essence of cool.

LW: Hip.

JAW: It's hip, but it's also cool. Being cool is part of being hip. You don't lose your cool. You're always together.

JAT: The birth of cool?

JAW: Yes. This is 1953, and that was very big at that time, being cool. The musicians were always talking about it. Of course, that wore off on those of us who were wearing zoot suits and wanting to be cool, too, and so I came up with this, "The Cool One."

JAT: This is just a cool dude?

JAW: That's right. [laughs] Just about "The Age of Bop" and Charlie Parker, huh?

JAT: Yes. It's right next to the next poem.

JAW: Being cool.

JAT: Exactly. It makes sense. Right. After "The Age of Bop," there's a poem entitled "P."

JAW: Yes.

JAT: As with "The Cool One," the identity of the individual described escapes me. The speaker in the poem addresses P and compares her to Astarte, the Phoenician deity, the goddess of love and beauty. The speaker tells P, "You graduated me, gowned me in rhythms / by moonlight," and then at the end of the poem says, "back you came cloaked in / lime and mint, to race the nights again, to / taunt the dawns once more, to raise a boy to man." The poem seems like an ode to a former lover or first love.

JAW: You got it.

JAT: Okay. [laughter]
JAW: What's the big deal?

JAT: The question: is this a fictional situation, fictional people?
JAW: Where do you think most literary work comes from?

JAT: Most poems are about—or most poems that men write, that hetero-sexual men write, are about women that they're in love with. Most of the poems that I wrote when I was a kid were about that.
JAW: I was a bad young man. This was a married woman.

JAT: There is that line about the husband, the husband stalking the aching streets.
JAW: She wouldn't let go. I was scared shitless. [laughter]

JAT: Are we naming names here?
JAW: No, we are not.
LW: Anybody I know?
JAW: No. No one you know.
LW: This was a long time ago.

JAT: All we have is P.
JAW: All we have is P.

JAT: I can't get anything more from you on that?
LW: Peggy? Patricia? [laughs]

JAT: We could play that game, but I won't.
LW: You won't go there. [laughs]

JAT: Not going to go there. On page 40, the poem "Corion Jones." Hearing you read this poem on Tyrone Brown's CD, *Suite for John A. Williams*, it's easy to understand why you selected this poem to be among the poems that you read on that CD because there's a real musicality to this poem, the rhythms and the rhymes. It's a very entertaining poem to hear read. It's a celebratory poem. There's a Corion Jones in *!Click Song*.
JAW: I love this name.

JAT: It is a great name.

LW: I think Tyrone picked the poems. He picked a few, and then he said he'd like a few more, whatever you chose, but I think this may have been one that he picked.

JAT: It makes sense—

JAW: Yes, he's got good taste. [laughter]

JAT: Yes, because this really has—it's a song. It's very much a song.

JAW: I've always liked it. I've been to Carriacou, and I know all his business about Anansi and Shango.

JAT: Was there an actual Corion Jones whom you met?

JAW: No. It was something like—about a historical figure.

JAT: Corion Jones is a historical figure?

JAW: Yes.

JAT: (In *!Click Song*) Cato Douglas meets a Corion Jones.

JAW: I do lots of things with lots of people.

LW: And names.

JAW: I like "Tinabu" because it's sparse and to the point.

JAT: "Tinabu Square" might be my favorite poem in this collection.

LW: Yes, I like it too.

JAT: And it's another poem that's on the Tyrone Brown CD. I think in the hands of a less skillful writer, its theme could come across—it would be conveyed in a heavy-handed manner, but this is very subtle. "Tinabu Square" is not a square, and its namesake became a rich person, but not really, or only in terms of material wealth.[3]

JAW: I saw a number of markets in Africa, and some of them were just very, very splendid.

LW: Were they named after slave traders?

JAW: I don't remember their being named after slave traders. And I don't know what they were always called, but this one, I knew, was Tinabu Square because the market was right there.

LW: You knew something about the person?

JAW: Right.

JAT: I really like this poem quite a bit. I like the way you read it on the recording. It's very brief and to the point and eloquent and makes a statement without—
LW: Bludgeoning you.

JAT: Exactly. Let's see. I want to jump to page 46, "Alejo's Poem." Alejo is another character in *!Click Song*, Cato Douglas's son.
JAW: Cato *Caldwell* Douglas.

JAT: Cato *Caldwell* Douglas's—
JAW: You are forgiven. [laughs]

JAT:—Spanish son by Monica. A poet who meets—who's likely killed as an adult by fascists in Spain. Why attribute this brief haiku-like poem to Alejo? "I crept up behind the sun / resting on a blue hill, / laughing down in time." What makes this Alejo's poem?
JAW: Because he's young, and he can laugh in time or at time, which is not to say that he doesn't cry, too, but for me, it's always marvelous to hear kids laugh or see them laugh. He found the sun resting on a blue hill. That would make me smile.

JAT: I appreciate what you just said. That actually adds an awful lot to my appreciation of the poem. Does that experience that Alejo has of seeing the sun and laughing, does that mean that this is a poem that he writes, or is it a poem about Alejo?
JAW: It's a poem about Alejo's reaction to the time and place where he is.

JAT: It's not necessarily a situation in which you have created this character, Alejo, a poet, and this is a poem that Alejo has written. Because I was then going to ask, because you've written about so many writers, I was wondering, does John actually imagine what these people have actually written? Do you actually write out plays?
JAW: There's something else about Alejo that I think you might have missed.

JAT: What's that?
JAW: What do you think he is?

JAT: What do I think Alejo is?
JAW: Yes. Is he a boy? Is he an adult? Is he midrange? Alejo can be any of those.

JAT: Sure. In the novel, he doesn't make contact with Cato *Caldwell* Douglas until he's an adult.

JAW: He's all right. [laughs] Yes, it is everybody's son.

JAT: The poem "Brother" a few pages before that, another pithy poem reads as follows: "Don't 'brother' me / unless you be / superior / to history." which also has a kind of rhythm to it that makes it special. What does it mean to be "superior to history"? I think I know, but I want to hear it.

JAW: To people who call themselves "brothers," but turn out not to be.

JAT: Like knuckleheads?

JAW: Doesn't even have to do with what they've got up there. It's the way they perform with other people, essentially. That's all it is.

LW: What's the line about history?

JAT: "Don't 'brother' me unless you be—"

JAW: "Superior to history."

JAT: "Superior to history."

JAW: Which is filled with cats who will come up and slap you on the back and hug you and embrace you and this, that, and the other, and turn out not to be brothers at all. That's all. You don't have to write a tome about it. [laughs]

LW: The phrase "superior to history"—

JAT: That's just an interesting way to put it. Here's another question. I have a question—I wasn't actually going to ask about this poem. Then I reread it, and I'm like, "What's John up to here?" On page 45. It seems like chapter and verse. It's "1:2.8 At F 30: Diana in Chelsea".

JAW: It's a camera focus, isn't it?

JAT: You tell me. It's an F stop?

LW: Mmhmm.

JAW: Yes.

JAT: I should be asking the photographer.

LW: I guess you want to know who Diana is.

JAW: She will be happy to tell you. She was a photographer.

LW: Yes, Diane Arbus.

JAT: We've spoken about her before, but if you could—

LW: She was a well-known photographer and has become bigger since her death, I think. There have been special shows of her stuff. She took pictures of a lot of circus performers, kind of freaky people.

JAT: Your initial title for *!Click Song* was "Photo"—

LW: No. "Photo by Jill Krementz." She just photographed a lot of well-known writers at the time. Diane Arbus was a totally different kind of photographer. John knew her. She lived in the—I guess it was a carriage house of a private home. His friends had the house, and then he got to meet Diane through that. They had a brief fling. She was a strange woman, but very, very talented.

JAW: How many flings am I going to have to go through in the rest of this book? [laughter]

LW: I don't know. I still don't know who P is.

JAT: Actually, it's all up to you, John. You wrote the poems. Let's see. On page 50, I have "Omowale X," which is another snapshot, if you will, of an individual. This is Malcolm. You met Malcolm in person?

JAW: Yes.

JAT: Again, when was that?

LW: In Nigeria, right?

JAW: Yes.

JAT: Yes, in Nigeria. There's much to admire formally in this poem, particularly the comparison of Malcolm's cameras to albatrosses, suggesting both a burden and a fate. That bird imagery is connected to his fate in the sense that he was assassinated in the Audubon Ballroom. His eyes are described as "heirlooms of a devil," alluding to the name he bore in prison.

JAW: What was that?

JAT: Satan.

JAW: I was thinking about his blue eyes.

JAT: Malcolm had blue eyes?

JAW: Yes.

JAT: I didn't know that.

LW: Me neither.

JAW: He had blue eyes.

JAT: There appears to be a contradiction in the poem I wanted to ask you about. The third stanza, the first two lines of the third stanza. "We worried Lagos; he lovingly murmured Mecca / But our travels bent—"

JAW: The fourth stanza, right?

JAT: I'm sorry. Fourth stanza. You're right. "We worried Lagos; he lovingly murmured Mecca / But our travels bent home for this was not." Then at the end of the final stanza, the fifth stanza, the last three lines. "He had said, 'Here they call me Omowale / Al Haj Malcolm X. That means, brother, / 'The child returns home.'" Where is home? Because the fourth stanza says—

LW: That this is not home.

JAT: "Our travels bent home, for this was not."

JAW: What Malcolm says, or when he said it to me, "Here, they call me," et cetera, et cetera, the child returns home, he was in Africa, and he was home.

JAT: Africa was home?

JAW: Yes.

JAT: In the fourth stanza, home—Africa is not home.

JAW: Mmhmm.

JAT: Because our travels—"We worried Lagos; he lovingly murmured Mecca / But our travels bent home for this was not."

JAW: I see what you mean, but I know that he would have been pleased to be buried in Africa. I know that. You're right. We were in Lagos. "He murmured Mecca, but our travels bent home, for this was not." Where is the continent that Mecca is in?

LW: Africa.

JAW: Africa.

JAT: Africa. I guess—

LW: It seems to be a contradiction.

JAT: It also seems to be not only a contradiction, but it's also—it's an inescapable contradiction. It's the contradiction that African Americans have—live with. It's the double consciousness that Du Bois writes of. This is our home. Then again, it's not our home. Africa is our home, but then again, it's not our home.

LW: My sense was that when you were in Africa, you never felt this was your home.

JAW: I never did. No.

LW: I think Malcolm did.

JAW: I am not quite so sure about that.

LW: Oh, really?

JAW: No. My sense was that behind all the love and everything else, he was not so sure because Malcolm was a lightcolored African American. I could see people gazing at him with some caution, and I'm sure he was aware of it.

LW: When you said before that you thought he would have wanted to be buried there, wouldn't that indicate that he did think of it as his home?

JAW: He did, but what I'm saying is that not everybody—

JAT: You said he got strange looks from Africans?

JAW: Mmhmm.

JAT: That he was conspicuously American or conspicuously—

JAW: A different color, pretty much.

LW: I always wondered, your show *Omowale*—the TV thing. Did that come before or after your meeting?

JAW: I don't remember.

LW: Because it seems to me that you may not have known the word *Omowale* had it not been for this conversation where he explains that it means the child returns home because that was the name of your show, *Omowale: The Child Returns Home.*

JAW: I didn't get it from—oh, yes, I guess I did. I was thinking the name came from the TV. No, you're right.

JAT: This poem does bring to mind a poem by Robert Hayden, "El-Hajj Malik El-Shabazz" about Malcolm, but Hayden uses Malcolm's Islamic— the Arabic name, the Islamic name in the title of the poem to suggest Malcolm's embrace of a race-transcendent philosophy represented by "Allah, the raceless." The poem says that Malcolm embraces, ultimately, a raceless God as opposed to, say, the race-fixated philosophy of the Nation of Islam. In fact, Hayden calls it "racist"—a racist God and a racist philosophy. Any thoughts about those ideas that Hayden writes about in his poem about Malcolm X?

JAW: I don't remember the poem, so I can't really discuss it. But he, like me, is entitled to his opinion. [laughs]

JAT: That goes without saying. [laughs]
JAW: He's a fantastic writer, and he writes things that make sense. He's just good.

JAT: That brings me to another question just about Hayden in general. It sounds like you hold him in high regard.
JAW: Yes, but I haven't read him in quite a while now. I think I've done too much reading too early, and now I've become lazy and my eyeballs are falling out.

JAT: The front cover material to *Safari West* says that the poems in this volume are "reminiscent at times of Langston Hughes or Robert Hayden." I was wondering what you thought about that, whether there's some truth value to that, or is that pure salesmanship?
JAW: I will gladly accept that without hesitation. [laughs]

JAT: Is it racial pigeonholing?
JAW: You're going to get racial pigeonholing even today. Right now, we laugh about it, but there were times when you could get really, really pissed off about it. And I was, and we were. I think there's a different kind of pigeonholing these days, more subtle and less harsh, if I can use that term.

JAT: You're generally comfortable with comparisons to Hayden and/or Hughes?
JAW: I can live with it. Sure.
LW: Did Ray write this copy? I guess so.
JAW: Yes.

JAT: Ray being the—?
JAW: The editor.
LW: Ray Beauchemin.

JAT: Let's see. "The Caretaker" on page 55 appears to be about your land in Worcester.
LW: Mmhmm.
JAW: I think it would apply to almost any land that anyone cares for.

JAT: Questioning the notion of owning land.

JAW: Caring for it.

JAT: Caring for it. Then the following poem is "South Worcester Mission House," which is really interesting. I was wondering if you could elaborate on the story behind this mission house. It's the remains of a mission house from the late eighteenth century?

JAW: Yes, it was. Somebody told us about it up there. Do you remember?

LW: This is the church in the meeting house across the street.

JAW: Right.

LW: What we had heard was that it was this small church, and one of the people—one of the members of the congregation had a black servant. Of course, she couldn't attend church with them, so they built this other edifice across the road, directly across the road.

JAW: It's still there.

LW: It's just as big as the church is, if not bigger. I don't know if she had a family, but that's where she went on Sundays to pray. A friend now owns both structures, and he's redoing them. It's funny to think of that.

JAT: They built her her own church?

LW: It doesn't quite look like a church. The other one, you could see was a church. This one looks like a building, but it's large.

JAT: That is really quite a—I don't know what to say about it, the lengths to which some people will go. [laughs]

LW: This must have been a pretty wealthy community that they were able to do that. You would think they'd just build her a little shack or something. [laughs]

JAT: It's quite remarkable. On page 64, "A Stone for Marty Scheiner," which reads as follows: "The stone was cast into the sea / Only the Ancient beheld the hole it made / Silt and slugs embraced it * Sun caressed it * Life arose / Around it." There are a number of—there's at least one other poem in *Safari West* that refers to "the Ancient."

JAW: The old ones, the wise ones, like you and I are going to be. No? [laughs] You don't want to join me?

LW: You're already there, John. You're going to be eighty.

JAT: I took "the Ancient" to be something even more than that, the Ancient. Because actually, the first poem in *Safari West*, "Genesis": " . . .

the Ancient woke and looked about / Its waking yawn a seeming shout / In all that vast and silent space / Then sadly made the human race." The Ancient is—

JAW: The Lord.

JAT: Right. A deity. A supreme being.

LW: You're a creationist. [laughs]

JAT: Lori's performed an exaggeration of my own response to this poem, which is that it's written from the perspective of someone who believes in a supreme being.

JAW: Like me maybe?

JAT: Like you. I guess that's my question.

JAW: Some days, it could be. Some days, I'm not so sure. In other words, I'm pretty much like everybody else, I think.

LW: He's not what you would call a religious person.

JAT: That was not my sense, no, but it was—and so any degree of spirituality articulated is—I'm not going to say a surprise, but—it's not spirituality, but a description of a higher being.

JAW: Open to the possibility that the higher being exists.

LW: I frankly have never understood this poem.

JAW: No?

LW: No.

JAW: Marty's?

LW: Yes, Marty Scheiner was a dear friend of ours.

JAW: Yes. We never talked about religion at all, but Marty is the one person in my life who always struck me as being filled with religion.

LW: Really?

JAW: It was incredible.

LW: Really?

JAW: Yes.

LW: I never knew that.

JAT: Would you say more about Marty and his importance in your lives?

LW: He married a very old friend of ours, of John's, who he met at Breadloaf, who became Adam's godmother. She's a children's—storybook writer of children's books.

JAT: What's her name?
LW: Ann McGovern.

JAT: She writes children's books?
LW: Right. She no longer does, but she did. We had known her many, many years. There have been several men in her life during the—she was married at a very young age—she was still in college—and divorced soon after she had her child. It didn't work. Anyway, so over the years, we knew her. There had been men in her life, and nothing ever came of anything, really. Then she met Marty, and he was a widower, and just a wonderful, wonderful person. They had a very good life together. As it happened, he was—in addition to being a wonderful person, he was very bright, and he had invented some medical devices that made him a very wealthy man. He was an engineer.
JAW: And improved the quality of medicine.
LW: He invented the, I think, heart lung machine or something like that. They did a lot of traveling. He was very interested in scuba driving. He invented underwater cameras and things. Anyway, they had a place in West Hampton, and we used to go out there every summer to spend some time with them. They were always going off scuba diving. We would sometimes be in Grenada at the same time. Anyway, he got lymphoma and was sick for a while, and then he died. I know it has something to do with his own being, going back to—he was a man of the sea. He sailed and he did all these things, so that's the connection with the sea. I was not aware of the spirituality part.

JAT: A similar poem in a way on page 69, "A June in L.A." It's an excruciating poem to read. There's a great deal of affect packed into the poem. The pain of impending loss dominates the poem. I assume that this is a reminiscence of your mother's passing.
JAW: Yes.

JAT: It's from 1987.
JAW: Yes. Do you want me to read it?

JAT: Sure.

[Williams reads "A June in L.A."]

JAT: It's a remarkable poem. Tremendously affecting.
LW: She was not buried in LA. She's buried in Worcester, her ashes.

JAT: That's right. There are a number of poems about people passing away and your feelings around them. Page 70 is "Willis Passing."

JAW: Yes. He was a great guy. He was my first wife's cousin.

JAT: There is a stanza that I wanted to ask you about in this poem. "Who runs the rhymes of William Blake / For victims of the State's mistakes? / Resist we do, this view not ours / With no embalming, no sad flowers." I guess two questions. Why Blake? There's "State's mistakes"; State's capitalized, meaning the United States' mistakes?

JAW: I knew I was going to need something to rhyme with "mistake," so I went with Billy Blake.

JAT: Are there any particular mistakes in—that you have in mind that you're referring to?

JAW: Oh, lots and lots. It would take me half a night to speak about them. America is still developing, and a lot of old mistakes are just being discovered. I don't think we ought to take the time to run those down. Too damn many of them.

JAT: What's the purpose behind giving reflections about death a conspicuously songlike structure?

JAW: To make it easier to digest.

JAT: I want to ask you about another poem that I had a question about, or I found particularly perplexing. It's "Miami Red" on page 60.

JAW: 60. 60.

JAT: Perplexing for a number of reasons. You said you're torn sometimes between writing fiction and writing poetry.

JAW: Mmhmm.

JAT: "Miami Red" seems to me a poem that could have been a short story or could have been something from a longer work of fiction.

JAW: This came out of a newspaper story, something I read.

JAT: It also seems to be—it seems very different from—just—not only the setting, Miami. I don't know if we've ever been to Miami in anything you've ever written before.

LW: Have you been to Miami?

JAT: It's not a locale I associate with John A. Williams.

JAW: I don't think so.

JAT: Also just what happens, although I'm not completely clear on what happens. It seems someone takes out a gun and shoots someone.

JAW: This is something I got from an old newspaper, but I don't quite remember the overall story.

LW: Must have impressed you one way or the other to have written a poem.

JAW: Yes.

LW: When was this written?

JAT: 1989.

JAW: There aren't too many gunmen who run around with a nine millimeter piece. I think this came from some newspaper or magazine. "Miami Red." Then of course, I wanted to get in the Super Bowl. "The red roar snatches his hum, / pierces his Mambo." Not bad. Not bad. [laughs]

JAT: I think I'm going to have to puzzle over this poem a little bit more. Then similarly, on page 68, "Walking the Wire" from 1993 is actually a fun poem to read. It's enjoyable. I like the words.

JAW: It's the way a lot of us live, walking the wire. If you're a writer, that is certainly true. Essentially, that's really what it's all about, keeping your balance so you can make it from one end to the other.

JAT: I really like the last lines of the poem, the last three lines. "We must see ourselves arrived there and safe, / the one like the tick before midnight, / the other like the tick at, symmetried beside." That really conveys the kind of narrow margin of error that one finds oneself in the middle of as a writer or as a person.

JAW: In the middle of boo-boo. [laughs]

JAT: Also, your gloss on it reminds me of Ferlinghetti's "Constantly Risking Absurdity."

JAW: Right.

JAT: Again, that narrow margin of error that one has when you're trying to achieve or acquire meaning.

You know what? I skipped a poem that I wanted to ask you about, actually. That's "Nat Turner's Profession."

JAW: What page is that?

JAT: It's early in the book; it starts on page 18.
LW: Is this from *Vanqui*?

JAT: I think so.
JAW: Yes.

JAT: It's a longer poem. What's interesting about it is that it involves different voices speaking to Nat—Nat Turner speaking and voices speaking to Nat and about him. There's an awful lot to say about the poem. On page 21, the second stanza is one that I quite like: "Who visions see and think them God's / turn upsidedown the laws of State, / make what is fixed seem wrong and odd, / what's firm, what's right, a thing of hate?" The way in which Nat Turner destabilized the dominant ideology.
JAW: The community.

JAT: The community, but just the way of thinking about everything, right? The things that early nineteenth century America took for granted were, at least momentarily, questioned, destabilized. All those certainties were— James Baldwin writes about blacks moving from their fixed place and threatening to change the way in which whites see the world, the universe, and their place in it. That's what Nat Turner did.
JAW: To a large extent, that has happened. The way one dances. When I was a kid, white kids were just getting into the Lindy. Then all of that happened. Then you got the different ways of playing football. Black schools in the South, white schools in the North. Black schools in the South tearing up football, and when those cats started getting—what do you call them? Free passes. You know what I mean.

JAT: Scholarships?
JAW: Scholarships. Then these brutes would come in and start kicking ass all over the place, just changed the whole thing. Not to mention what it did to boxing. It practically destroyed boxing.

JAT: That's a whole other thing, right, the way in which African Americans have—what is quintessentially American culture is also black culture when you're talking about sports and music. It's a very Ellisonian sort of argument. There's also this sense that whiteness defines itself against and in opposition to a constructed notion of blackness, and when a Nat Turner operates outside of that definition—
JAW: That's it. [laughs]

JAT: That's all she wrote, at least for a moment, for white identity and everything else that's constructed around it. Just a couple of questions then to wrap up. We were talking about Nat Turner. I guess I have William Styron on the brain lately. *The Confessions of Nat Turner* won the Pulitzer Prize but was quite a controversial novel, and it still continues to be a very controversial novel. I was just wondering if you had any thoughts about the novel.

JAW: I liked it, and I was waiting for somebody else to do a novel on Turner that was better than his, and I haven't seen it. I haven't seen it at all.[4] [laughs]

JAT: Then really quickly, let me just ask you about, again, about poetry and writing poetry. You talked about how your interest—your familiarity with verse and pageants when you were a child and being in church and your familiarity with the Bible and all of that . . . when you were older, when you were a teenager, when you were reading or when you were in college, were there poets that you were reading that had an impact on your development as a writer, poets who you admired, or even contemporaries of yours throughout your career that you admired?

JAW: It's got to be poets you usually study in college, starting with Eliot and going all the way down through the alphabet. I found that to be fascinating. The thing that probably led me in that direction was that, as I may have mentioned, as a kid in the church during Christmas, Easter, and so on and so forth, I would always wind up with the longest thing to study and blab out, so it came almost natural. My mother would bring home old books from the people she worked for, and some of them would be poetry books. I would read those and notice how they rhymed out the chime and rhyme and go and know. Things like that. It always sounded so very pretty to me. More perfect than pretty. The two sounds coming together at the end of passages just seemed like a marriage, a wedding, the way things should be. I'm still enamored of poetry, though I haven't read a great deal of it lately. I think it would be good if every student who's taking English takes a bit more poetry than they're now taking, studied a bit more poetry. Poetry has a virtue of being concise, and yet doing the job a novel sometimes doesn't manage to do. That's why I love it. I'm all for it. Yay, yay, poetry! [laughs]

JAT: On that note, then, I think we can stop. Thank you very much.
JAW: Thank you very much.

Notes

1. Reid was born in Princeton, North Carolina, and created a statue of Billie Holiday unveiled in Baltimore, Maryland, in 1985.

2. And, perhaps more accurately, alliteration.

3. In Lagos, Nigeria.

4. Williams made more extensive and critical comments about Styron's novel in "The Manipulation of History and Fact: An Ex-Southerner's Apologist Tract for Slavery and the Life of Nat Turner; or, William Styron's Faked Confessions," the essay he contributed to *William Styron's Nat Turner: Ten Black Writers Respond* (1968), edited by John Henrik Clarke.

Index

CPSIA information can be obtained
at www.ICGtesting.com
Printed in the USA
BVOW08s1055270118
506367BV00001B/1/P